The Origins of France
From Clovis to the Capetians, 500–1000

NEW STUDIES IN MEDIEVAL HISTORY
General Editor: Maurice Keen

Chris Wickham, *Early Medieval Italy: Central Power and Local Society 400-1000*

J. K. Hyde, *Society and Politics in Medieval Italy: The Evolution of the Civil Life 1000-1350*

Roger Collins, *Early Medieval Spain: Unity in Diversity 400-1000*

Angus McKay, *Spain in the Middle Ages: From Frontier to Empire 1000-1500*

Eric Christiansen, *The Northern Crusades: The Baltic and the Catholic Frontier 1100-1525*

Edward James, *The Origins of France: From Clovis to the Capetians 500-1000*

Henrietta Leyser, *Hermits and the New Monasticism: A Study of Religious Communities in Western Europe 1000-1150*

Michael Haren, *Medieval Thought: The Western Intellectual Tradition from Antiquity to the Thirteenth Century*

Lynette R. Muir, *Literature and Society in Medieval France: The Mirror and the Image 1100-1500*

Felipe Fernández-Armesto, *Before Columbus: Exploration and Colonisation from the Mediterran to the Atlantic, 1229-1492*

Other titles are in preparation

The Origins of France

From Clovis to the Capetians, 500–1000

EDWARD JAMES

New Studies in Medieval History

MAURICE KEEN

To the Memory of Denis Bethell,
15 January 1934 – 15 February 1981

MACMILLAN

First published 1982 by
THE MACMILLAN PRESS LTD
Houndmills, Basingstoke, Hampshire RG21 2XS
and London
Companies and representatives
throughout the world

ISBN 0-333-27052-5

Printed in Hong Kong

Reprinted 1985, 1987, 1989, 1992

Contents

List of Maps

List Of Plates

Acknowledgements

This book is dedicated to the man to whom it owes the most, Denis Bethell, the founder of the series 'New Studies in Medieval History'. He invited me to write it, spent very many hours discussing it with me, and, before his tragically early death, had read and commented on the first half, in his capacity as General Editor. His contribution was more than that, however. In the eight years during which he was my colleague in the Department of Medieval History at University College Dublin, I learnt from him more about my subject, and about the art of teaching, than I have from anyone else. He will always be missed by those who knew his wit, humanity and great erudition.

I am also most grateful to Michael Richter, from whom I learnt much when we lectured together on the Merovingians and Carolingians at UCD; to Clare Hall, Cambridge, for making me an associate in 1977, when I was beginning work on the book, and to UCD for helping to finance that stay in Cambridge; to Helen Humphreys, of the York Archaeological Trust, for drawing the maps; to Maurice Keen, and above all to those kind friends who have read through the final draft with great care and perception, and whose advice I have not always followed: Richard Fletcher, Rosamond McKitterick, Patricia McNulty, Ian Wood, and my wife Columba. In a happier year this book would have been dedicated to her, for without her support and assistance it would have been impossible.

York
October 1981

Chronological Table

406	The 'Great Invasion' of Vandals, Alans, Sueves and Burgundians across the Rhine
418	Visigoths settled in Aquitaine
443	Burgundians settled in Sapaudia
466–84	Euric king of the Visigoths
475	Auvergne ceded to Euric
476	Last Roman Emperor in the West deposed
481?–511?	Clovis king of the Franks
486	Clovis defeats Syagrius, 'king of the Romans'
507	Clovis defeats Visigoths at Vouillé
507–11	Pactus Legis Salicae drawn up
516	Death of King Gundobad of the Burgundians
534	Frankish conquest of Burgundy
536	Provence ceded to Franks by Ostrogoths
542	Death of Caesarius of Arles. Bubonic plague reaches Gaul
558	Chlothar I sole king of the Franks
561	Partition of kingdom among Chlothar's four sons
575	Sigibert assassinated
584	Chilperic assassinated
587	Treaty of Andelot between Guntram, Brunhild and Childebert II
591	End of Gregory of Tours' *History*
599	Defeat of Chilperic's son Chlothar II by Childebert's sons
613	Chlothar II sole king of the Franks; death of Brunhild; Edict of Paris
615	Death of St Columbanus
623	Chlothar makes son Dagobert king in Austrasia
629–38	Dagobert I sole king of the Franks
641	Pippin I's son Grimoald becomes mayor of the Austrasian palace
642	End of Fredegar's *Chronicle*
657664/5	Regency of Balthild in Neustria
660?	Grimoald exiles King Dagobert II to Ireland
673–5	Childeric II sole king of the Franks
676	Dagobert II recalled from Ireland

677	Ebroin, mayor, has St Leger killed
680	Ebroin defeats Austrasians under Pippin II; Ebroin assassinated
687	Pippin defeats Neustrians at Tertry; establishes Theuderic III as sole Frankish king
714	Death of Pippin II
717	Charles Martel chooses own king
721	Eudo defeats Al-Samh ibn Malik outside Toulouse
732	Charles Martel defeats 'Abd ar-Rahman near Poitiers
735	Death of Eudo; Charles Martel campaigns in Aquitaine
741	Charles Martel succeeded by Carloman and Pippin
746	Carloman becomes monk in Rome
751	Pippin king of the Franks
754	St Boniface martyred in Frisia
768	Waifar defeated in Aquitaine; Pippin succeeded by Charlemagne and Carloman
771	Death of Carloman
774	Charlemagne crowned king of the Lombards
778	Charlemagne's army defeated by Basques at Roncesvalles; death of Roland
781	Louis King in Aquitaine; Pippin in Italy
789	Admonitio Generalis
792	Revolt of Pippin against Charlemagne
800	Charlemagne crowned Emperor in Rome
804	Death of Alcuin
814	Louis the Pious succeeds Charlemagne
817	Ordinatio Imperii
818	Death of Bernard of Italy
821	Death of Benedict of Aniane
822	Penance of Louis at Attigny
823	Birth of Charles the Bald
829	Lothar revolts against father Louis
833	Lothar declares self sole master of Empire
834	Restoration of Louis
838	Pippin I of Aquitaine dies
840	Death of Louis the Pious

843	Treaty of Verdun
844	Vikings raid up Garonne as far as Toulouse
848	Charles the Bald crowned at Orleans
855	Partition of Lothar I's Middle Kingdom
858	Louis the German invades West Francia
864	Pippin II of Aquitaine forced into monastery
869	Charles the Bald crowned at Metz
875	Charles crowned Emperor in Rome
877	Louis II succeeds Charles the Bald
879	Boso declared king at Mantaille
882	Hincmar of Rheims flees from Vikings; dies
884	Charles III 'the Fat' elected king of West Francia
885–6	Siege of Paris by the Vikings
888	Odo king in West Francia; Rudolf in Burgundy
890	Louis, son of Boso, king in Provence
898	Charles III 'the Simple' succeeds Odo
901	Louis of Provence Emperor
905	Louis blinded by Berengar of Friuli
910	Foundation of Cluny by William of Aquitaine
911	Treaty between Charles III and Rollo of Normandy
919	Much of Brittany falls to Vikings
922	Revolt against Charles III: Robert crowned king
923	Robert's son-in-law Ralph succeeds; Charles III imprisoned by Herbert of Vermandois
929	Death of Charles III
936	Death of Ralph; Charles III's son Louis brought from England and crowned
942	William Longsword of Normandy assassinated
943	Death of Herbert of Vermandois
954	Louis IV succeeded by Lothar
956	Death of Hugh 'the Great'
960	Hugh Capet made 'duke of the Franks'; his brother Odo duke of Burgundy
962	The Saxon Otto I crowned Emperor in Rome
978	Lothar's invasion of Lotharingia
986	Louis V succeeds Lothar
987	Death of Louis V; Hugh Capet crowned
992	Death of Charles of Lorraine
993	Rudolf III 'the Sluggard' succeeds Conrad 'the

	Peaceful' (937–993) as king in Burgundy
996	Robert II 'the Pious' succeeds Hugh Capet
999	Gerbert of Aurillac becomes Pope Sylvester II

The Civitates of Gaul, *c.* 600 (Key to Maps 2 and 3)

The civitates are grouped into the ecclesiastical provinces of the late sixth century; but the provincial names, the form of the city names, and the order in which they are listed are taken from the fifth-century list of cities, the *Notitia Galliarum*. The Latin name for the town is followed by the modern town name and, where appropriate, the name of the modern province which corresponds to the old civitas. As in the rest of the book, the modern spellings are followed except in the cases of Köln , Lyon, Marseille and Reims, where the traditional English forms are used. If there are two modern town names, this normally indicates a shift of the civitas-capital.

A. Lugdunensis Prima

1. Metropolis civitas Lugdunensium: Lyons
2. Civitas Aeduorum (Augustodunum): Autun
3. Civitas Lingonum: Langres
4. Castrum Cabillonense: Chalon-sur-Saône
5. Castrum Matisconense: Mâcon

B. Lugdunensis Secunda

1. Metropolis civitas Rotomagensium: Rouen
2. Civitas Baiocassium: Bayeux (Bessin)
3. Civitas Abrincatum: Avranches
4. Civitas Ebroicorum: Evreux
5. Civitas Saiorum: Séez
6. Civitas Lexoviorum: Lisieux
7. Civitas Constantia: Coutances (Cotentin)

C. Lugdunensis Tertia

1. Metropolis civitas Turonorum: Tours (Touraine)
2. Civitas Cenomannorum: Le Mans (Maine)
3. Civitas Redonum: Rennes
4. Civitas Andecavorum: Angers (Anjou)
5. Civitas Namnetum: Nantes
6. Civitas Curiosolitum: Corseul

7. Civitas Venetum: Vannes
8. Civitas Dolensium: Dol

D. Lugdunensis Senonia

1. Metropolis civitas Senonum: Sens
2. Civitas Carnotum: Chartres
3. Civitas Autisioderum: Auxerre
4. Civitas Tricassium: Troyes
5. Civitas Aurelianorum: Orleans
6. Civitas Parisiorum: Paris
7. Civitas Melduorum: Meaux
8. Civitas Nivernensium: Nevers

E. Belgica Prima

1. Metropolis civitas Treverorum: Trier
2. Civitas Mediomatricum: Metz
3. Civitas Leucorum: Toul
4. Civitas Verodunensium: Verdun

F. Belgica Secunda

1. Metropolis civitas Remorum: Rheims
2. Civitas Suessionum: Soissons
3. Civitas Catalaunorum: Châlons-sur-Marne
4. Civitas Veromandorum: Vermand
5. Civitas Atrebatum: Arras (Artois)
6. Civitas Camaracensium: Cambrai
7. Civitas Turnacensium: Tournai
8. Civitas Silvanectum: Senlis
9. Civitas Bellovacorum: Beauvais
10. Civitas Ambianensium: Amiens
11. Civitas Morinarum: Thérouanne
12. Civitas Bononiensium: Boulogne
13. Civitas Lugduni Clavati: Laon

G. Germania Prima

1. Metropolis civitas Magontiacensium: Mainz
2. Civitas Argentoratensium (Stratoburgensis): Strasbourg
3. Civitas Nemetum (Spirensis): Speyer
4. Civitas Vangionum (Vuormiacensis): Worms

H. Germania Secunda

1. Metropolis civitas Agrippinensium, Colonia: Cologne
2. Civitas Tungrorum: Tongres

I. Maxima Sequanorum

1. Metropolis civitas Vesontiensium: Besançon
2. Civitas Belisensium: Belley
3. Civitas Elvitiorum, Aventicus: Avenches
4. Civitas Basiliensium: Basel

J. Viennensis

1. Metropolis civitas Viennensium: Vienne
2. Civitas Genavensium: Geneva
3. Civitas Gratianopolitana: Grenoble
4. Civitas Albensium/Vivarium: Aps/Viviers
5. Civitas Deensium: Die
6. Civitas Valentinorum: Valence
7. Civitas Valensium/Sedunensis: Wallis/Sitten
8. Civitas Tarantensium: Tarantaise
9. Civitas Mauriennensis: Maurienne
10. Civitas Augusta: Aosta

K. Aquitanica Prima

1. Metropolis civitas Biturigum: Bourges (Berry)
2. Civitas Arvernorum: Clermont (-Ferrand) (Auvergne)
3. Civitas Rutenorum: Rodez (Rouergue)
4. Civitas Albigensium: Albi
5. Civitas Cadurcorum: Cahors (Quercy)

6. Civitas Lemovicum: Limoges (Limousin)
7. Civitas Gabalum: Javols/Mende
8. Civitas Vellavorum: St-Paulien/Le Puy (Velay)
9. Civitas Tolosatium: Toulouse

L. Aquitanica Secunda

1. Metropolis civitas Burdigalensium: Bordeaux
2. Civitas Agennensium: Agen
3. Civitas Ecolisnensium: Angoulême (Angoumois)
4. Civitas Santonum: Saintes (Saintonge)
5. Civitas Pictavum: Poitiers (Poitou)
6. Civitas Petrocoriorum: Périgueux (Périgord)

M. Novempopulana

1. Metropolis civitas Elusatium: Eauze
2. Civitas Ausciorum: Auch
3. Civitas Aquensium: Dax
4. Civitas Lactoratium: Lectoure
5. Civitas Convenarum: St-Bertrand-de-Comminges
6. Civitas Consorannorum: St-Lizier (Couserans)
7. Civitas Benarnensium: Lescar (Béarn)
8. Civitas Aturensium: Aire
9. Civitas Vasatica: Bazas
10. Civitas Turba ubi castrum Bigorra: Cieutat (Bigorre)
11. Civitas Illoronensium: Oloron

N. Narbonensis Prima

1. Metropolis civitas Narbonensium: Narbonne
2. Civitas Biterrensium: Béziers
3. Civitas Agatensium: Agde
4. Civitas Magalonensium: Maguelonne
5. Civitas Nemausensium: Nîmes
6. Civitas Lotevensium: Lodève
7. Civitas Elnensium: Elne
8. Civitas Carcassonensium: Carcassonne

O. Narbonensis Secunda, Alpes Maritimarum, parts of Viennensis

1. Civitas Arelatensium: Arles
2. Civitas Aquensium: Aix-en-Provence
3. Civitas Aptensium: Apt
4. Civitas Reiensium: Riez
5. Civitas Foroiuliensis: Fréjus
6. Civitas Vappincensium: Gap
7. Civitas Segesteriorum: Sisteron
8. Civitas Antipolitana: Antibes
9. Civitas Ebrodunensium: Embrun
10. Civitas Diniensium: Digne
11. Civitas Telonensium: Toulon
12. Civitas Saniensium: Sénez
13. Civitas Glannativa: Glandève
14. Civitas Cemelensium/Nicea: Cimiez/Nice
15. Civitas Vencensis: Vence
16. Civitas Tricastinorum: St-Paul-Trois-Châteaux
17. Civitas Vasiensium: Vaison
18. Civitas Arausicorum: Orange
19. Civitas Carpentoratensium/Vindascensis: Carpentras/ Vénasque
20. Civitas Cabellicorum: Cavaillon
21. Civitas Avennicorum: Avignon
22. Civitas Massiliensium: Marseilles
23. Civitas Uticensium: Uzès

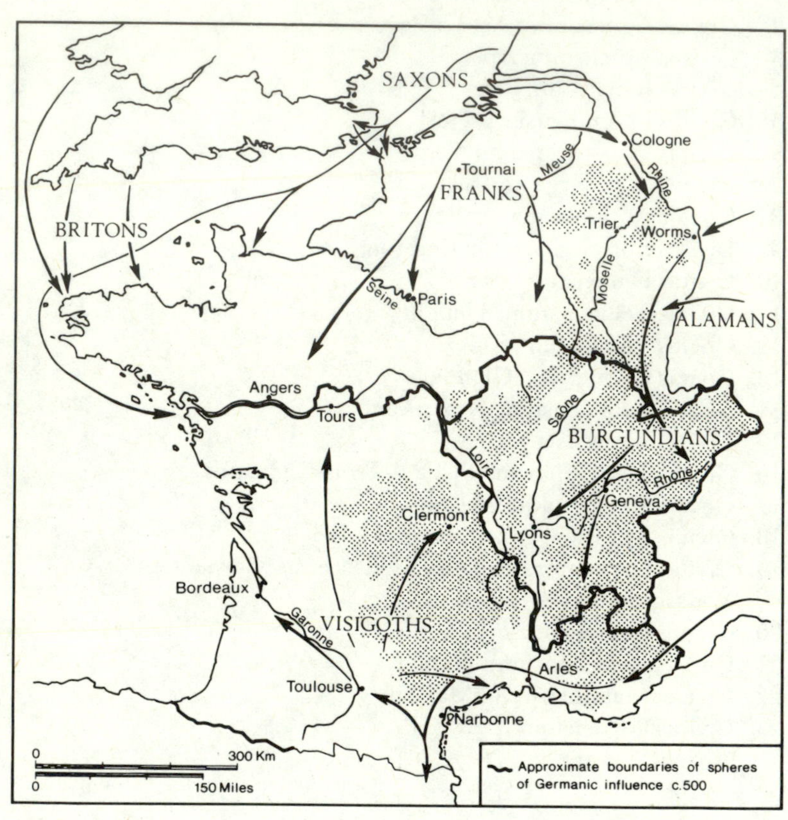

Map 1
Gaul in the Fifth Century

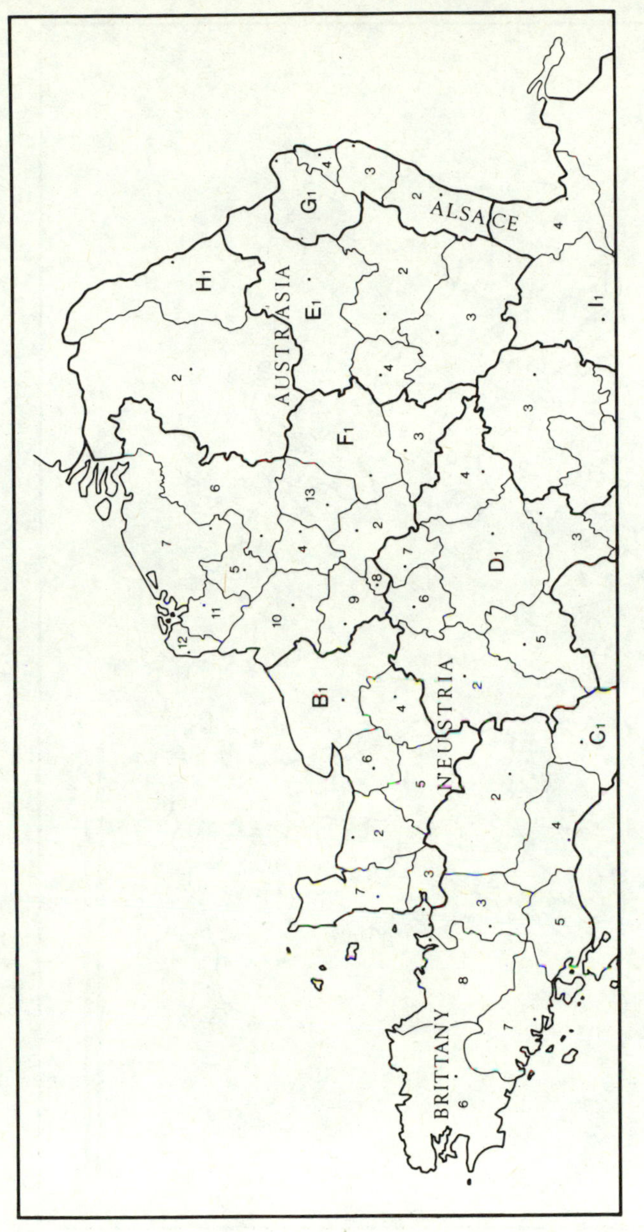

Map 2
The Civitates of Gaul, *c.* 600

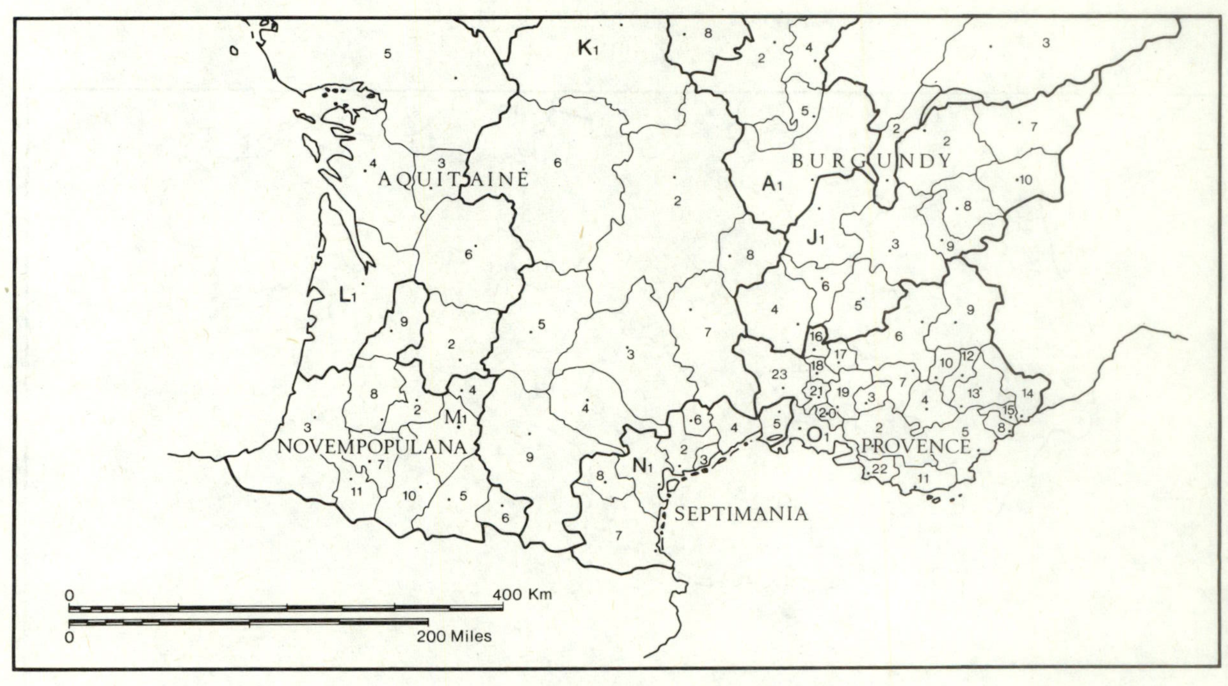

Map 3
The Civitates of Gaul, *c.* 600

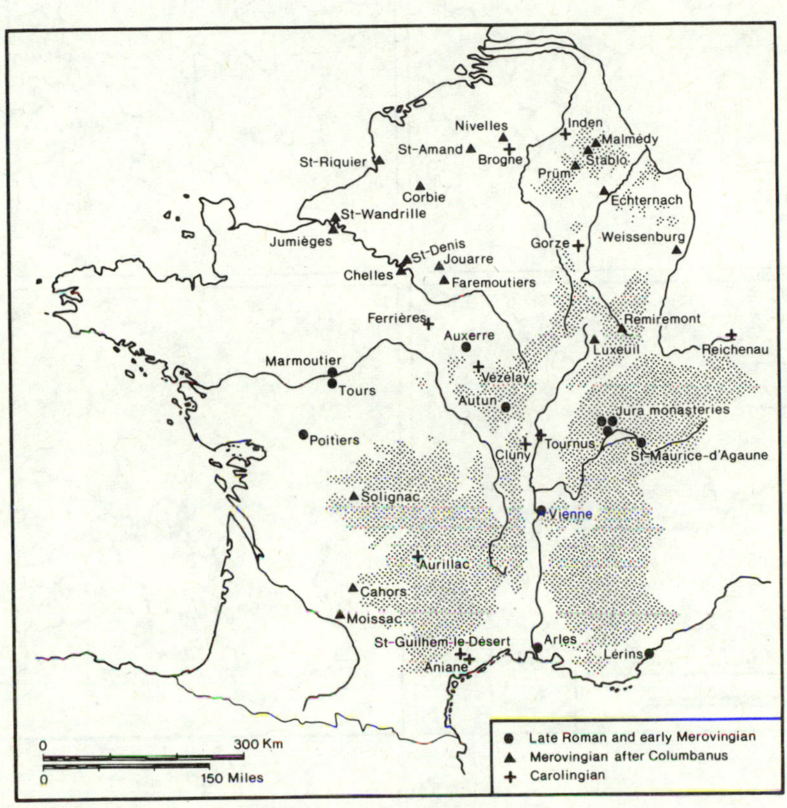

Map 4
The Monasteries of Frankish Gaul

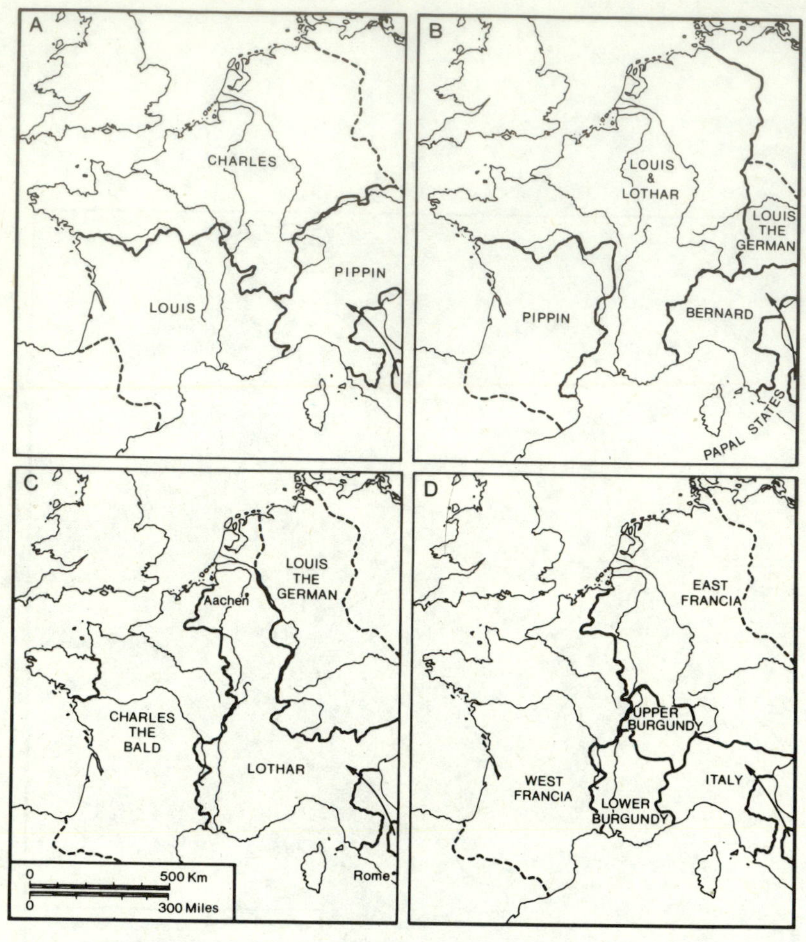

Map 5
The Partitions of the Ninth Century.
A. The proposed partition of 806.
B. The divisions of the Ordinatio Imperii, 817.
C. The partition of the Treaty of Verdun, 843.
D. The kingdoms after 888.

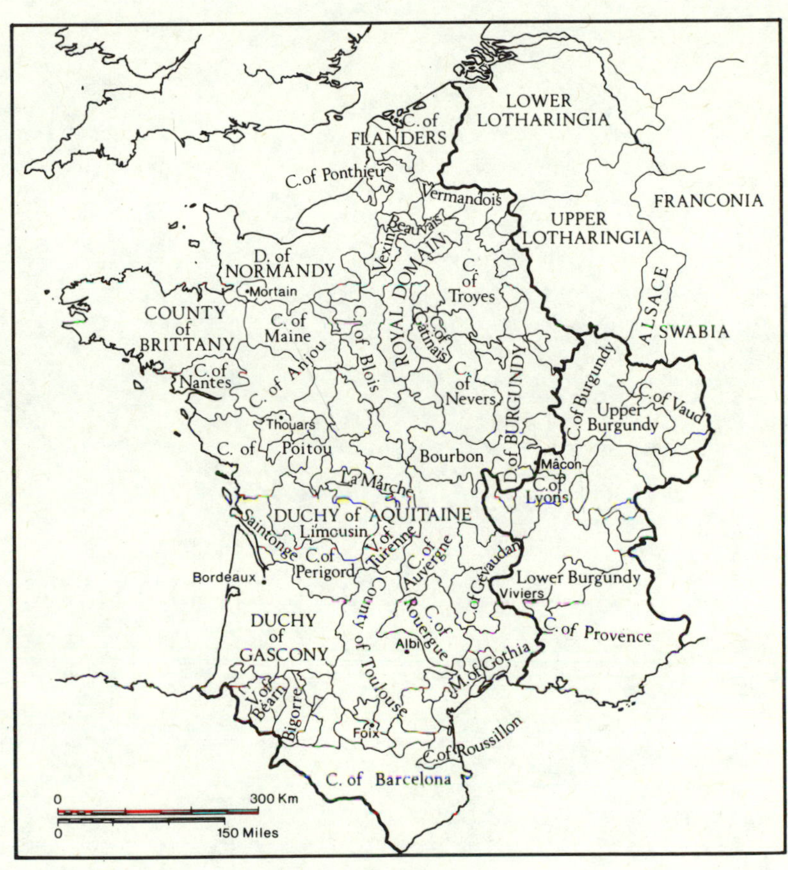

Map 6
Gaul around the year 1000

Introduction

IT has been said of France that governing a country with three hundred and twenty-five varieties of cheese is an impossibility: so, arguably, is writing its history. With the disappearance of Roman rule, the history of Gaul fragments into the histories of scores of different regions and political authorities: a realistic narrative history would be the sum of these innumerable local histories, formless, unwieldy, unreadable. This is no doubt one reason why so much historical attention has been given to those figures who, briefly, welded most or all of Gaul into one political unit: Clovis and, above all, Charlemagne. And those who have written narrative histories of longer periods have seen that the best way to deal with the mass of disparate material was to concentrate upon the history of the monarchy. Thus we can find histories of France under the Merovingians and Carolingians whose geographical scope shrinks as the political power of each dynasty wanes; histories whose focus of attention is in the north, where the Frankish monarchy had its roots.

The traditional histories of early France have some shape and consistency. They begin with the invasions of the Germanic barbarians in the fifth century: the Franks, Burgundians and Visigoths between them parcelled out the former Roman province of Gaul, and persuaded or forced the Romans to work with them. The Frankish king Clovis, at the very end of the fifth century, converted to Catholicism, thus predisposing the Catholic Romans to prefer the Franks to the other Germanic peoples, who were all Arian heretics. Under Clovis and his four sons, among whom the kingdom was partitioned upon Clovis's death, most of Gaul was conquered by the Franks, and Frankish power was extended beyond the Rhine into Germany and even into Italy. Clovis's descendants, the Merovingians, kings distinguished by their long hair, retained the kingship for two hundred and fifty years. The first century and a half of their rule is illuminated by the histories written by Gregory, Bishop of Tours, and Fredegar; the Merovingian kings emerge as typical barbarians, violent, deceitful, bellicose, and yet at the same time energetic, lusty and effective rulers. Gregory's story is of the civil wars between the different members of the royal family, each of whom held a portion of the Frankish kingdoms, and of the efforts of Roman churchmen to alleviate the resultant suffering and present an alternative model of charity and peace. Gregory's story ended in 591; it is taken up by Fredegar, who related the end of the civil wars and the establishment of Frankish unity once more under Chlothar II, and told of the rise of powerful aristocratic dynasties within the Frankish kingdom. The most important of these was the dynasty later known as the Carolingians, who managed in the course of the seventh century to establish themselves as Mayors of the Palace – prime ministers – of first a part and then the whole of the Frankish kingdom. But by the time they achieved dominance over the whole kingdom, in 687, that kingdom had lost a good deal of its power. All over Gaul, but above all in the south and west, aristocrats had set up their own independent states, sometimes achieving their political position by the wholesale pillage of the lands of the church. Laymen held bishoprics; the revenues of monastic estates were used to finance secular ambitions.

The saviours of Gaul – or so the traditional story runs – were the Carolingians. In a series of vigorous and, indeed, very bloody campaigns, Charles Martel and his son Pippin 'liberated' most of Gaul, and set about the restoration of the Church. In 751 Pippin abandoned the fiction of being merely the 'prime minister' of the Merovingian kings: King Childeric III was deposed and Pippin became the first Carolingian king. His son Charles, Karolus Magnus, or Charlemagne, completed the reunification of Gaul and began the conquest of the rest of western Europe. By the time of his death in 814 he had established an Empire which included not only Gaul but also north-east Spain, much of Italy and the whole of Germany, right across to the plains of Hungary. Charlemagne's collection of kingdoms, dignified by the title of Empire on his coronation as Emperor in 800, was greater in extent than that of any west European ruler between the time of Roman Emperors in the fifth century and the French Emperor Napoleon in the nineteenth. As well as being an indefatigable warrior, Charlemagne was also a patron of learning; he assembled scholars from all over Europe at his court at Aachen, and the revival of Latin learning, of art and of architecture which he initiated is known to historians as the 'Carolingian Renaissance'.

Charlemagne's Empire was hastily assembled and imperfectly united, and did not long remain a political unit. His son Louis the Pious inherited the Empire intact, but it was divided among his sons upon his death. The western portion, West Francia, or France, was ruled by Charles the Bald, under whom the weaknesses of the Carolingian system began to make themselves apparent. He could win the loyalty of the aristocracy only by granting them royal estates; the more he did so, the weaker the monarchy became. There was little that he could do to defend the shores of France, or even its interior, from the attacks of the Vikings from Norway and Denmark, and the more successful the Vikings were, the lower was the prestige of the monarchy in the eyes of its subjects. The greater aristocrats became stronger and more independent; in 888, only eleven years after Charles the Bald's death, one of them, Odo, became king of West Francia. The Carolingians recovered the crown again, but little of their original power. The history of the tenth century is the history of the humiliation of the French monarchy. The feudal system, by which the kings had bound their greater subjects to them by oaths of loyalty and service, in return for donations of royal land, destroyed the unity of the kingdom; the kings lost the obedience of their subjects, and the aristocrats built up their own independent states with the help of formerly royal land and revenues. Outside the estates which still remained theirs, in the Ile-de-France, around Paris, the French kings had little influence. Eventually, in 987, the Carolingian dynasty was extinguished, and Hugh Capet, the grandson of Odo's brother Robert, became the first king of the Capetian dynasty, which was in the twelfth and thirteenth centuries to lead France once more to unity and glory.

Such a brief résumé of the traditional shape of early French history is inevitably a distortion and a parody. Yet it gives an idea of the framework within which many historians still work. They may disagree with some of its details. Few historians would now blame 'feudalism' for the break-up of the Carolingian state: the greater aristocrats built up their independent power not because of the estates given to them as feudal vassals, but because of the political power granted to them as official agents of royal power, as dukes, counts or viscounts. But the structure of French history imposed by the concentration upon the monarchy has survived. It has the merit of providing narrative simplicity, of ensuring that there is a thread which may lead the would-be Theseus through the labyrinthine corridors of Frankish history. Its origins lie back in the history of nationalism, whose prejudices have had such profound effects on the way in which early medieval history has been written. German historians have traditionally seen the history of the kingdoms set up in the former Roman provinces after the Germanic invasions as part of their own,

German, history. The major sources of Gallic history in our period have been edited and published as the *Monumenta Germaniae Historica* – the Historical Monuments of Germany; the creative role of the Germanic invaders has been consistently exaggerated. French historians in the nineteenth century were in disagreement as to what perspective they should take. Some saw the French as the descendants of the Gallic race, and belittled the Germanic invaders; others saw the French monarchy and the French aristocracy, and hence all that was best of French civilisation, as being founded by the Germanic Franks, and thus were forced to share in the Germanic perspective. On the whole the Germanic view was predominant. Feeling that it was the monarchy which gave France its mystical identity, and that it was the manifest destiny of France to be ruled from Paris, French historians were able to impose a pattern on post-Roman history which was no doubt very satisfying but which gave rise to some strange value judgements, which can still be found in the history books. Periods are to be judged in terms of the degree of centralisation and of loyalty to central government. The political fragmentation of the late seventh or the late ninth and tenth centuries is to be viewed with considerable distaste. A relatively stable coexistence of numerous regional governments is anarchy, and the crushing of such governments by the monarchy or its agents is progress. The centre or potential centre of power always drew the historian's attention. 'The real France is northern France' wrote the Parisian and historian Michelet. The geographer Vidal de la Blache, in his introduction to Lavisse's history of France, devoted 180 pages to the Paris region (although only 15 for the Mediterranean south), since that was where 'national history essentially took place'.[1] Indeed, that region was the home of the French language, and of the French monarchy, and in so far as a French nation exists today it is because of the relentless policies of centralisation pursued by one Paris-based government after another. But the true history of modern France obviously has to be more than a history of its centralisation. France is still, and was before the twentieth century even more so, a collection of regions with very diverse climates, landscapes, institutions, traditions and languages. As late as 1863 a quarter of the population of France did not speak French, and perhaps another quarter used it as their second language.[2] In 1864 a school inspector visited a school in Lozère in which not one child could correctly answer such questions as 'Are you English or Russian?' or 'In what country is the département of Lozère?'[3] *Pays* and *patrie* – country and fatherland – were one and the same: the province, and not France.

Regional diversity could only with difficulty be incorporated into a history of France as conceived in the last century: regional histories were usually left to fiercely partisan local patriots. In recent years the tide has changed. It has become increasingly clear that 'the origins of France' are to be found not just in the origins of its monarchy, but also in the origins of its various provincial traditions. Diversity can be valued for its own sake – now that it has almost disappeared. And the origins of these provincial traditions can be seen above all in the centuries under consideration in this book. The invasions or migrations of Bretons, Basques, Franks, Alamans and Normans brought into being some of the most obvious of the distinct traditions; other regions developed their own identities thanks to their isolation and independence. The geographical limits of this book are in most cases the regions of modern France: the traditional history of France which only dealt with those areas over which the French kings had some influence would for some periods ignore much of the area of modern France, and thus avoid having to explain that the traditions of those regions are in fact not 'French', but German, or Breton, or Basque. But clearly in this book it would have been anachronistic to stay within frontiers established only in the twentieth century after innumerable historical accidents. Instead I have drawn all my examples from within the boundaries of Roman Gaul, north of the Pyrenees and west of the Rhine and the Alps, and I speak more often of Gaul than of France. The word *Francia* was commonly used in the early Middle Ages, but to mean very different things, and none of them can be translated as 'France'. Some authors used it of the whole area controlled by the Franks, which would under Charlemagne include most of Catalonia and modern West Germany, while others restrict it to northern Gaul, the homeland of the Franks, or even to a small portion of it. The origins of France for our purposes are to be found in the history of Gaul after the collape of the Roman Empire.

The chronological limits of this book are, roughly, AD 500 to 1000, a period often called the 'Dark Ages' by British historians. For some, indeed, the Middle Ages begin only when those 'Dark Ages' are over; a strangely parochial attitude, which ignores not only the normal conventions of continental historians but also the very meaning of the term 'Middle Ages', that period between the fall of the Roman Empire in the West and the age of the printing press and the discovery of

America, of Renaissance and Reformation. Even historians have to overcome an unconscious feeling that there are such things as typically 'medieval' institutions, such as knights, castles or crusades, and a typically 'medieval' way of life, and that the 'Dark Ages' does not fit into this picture. The term 'Dark Ages' is misleading in at least two ways. They are 'dark' in the sense of being mysterious and unknown only in relation to later periods: Gaul and Britain in the sixth century or the ninth are far better known to us than at any time during the Roman period. The first Gallic writers whose works survive lived in the very last century of Roman rule: the first Romano-British writer whose works illuminate British history is St Patrick, who died in the 490s. With the early Middle Ages, in fact, north-western Europe is emerging for the first time from its 'Dark Ages'. But the post-Roman period is also regarded as 'dark' because it was a primitive, violent and superstitious age during which nothing of note happened, a lacuna in the history of civilisation. There are some elements of truth in that picture, particularly if the history of civilisation is primarily thought of as the history of a small élite of learned and enlightened men. But it embodies a very simplistic view of the Roman period, seeing it (as Sellars and Yeatman would have done) as a Good Thing, and it fails to appreciate the very real achievements of the early medieval period; it fails to sympathise with and hence to try to understand those who lived at the time, or even to define and explain the primitiveness, violence and superstition. The idea of Dark-Ages-as-lacuna reaches its apotheosis in the statement of a distinguished historian of early medieval Gaul, Ferdinand Lot: 'The tenth century is truly sterile. It is one of those periods of which one can say that it would have been better if it had never existed'.[4] There have been all too many historians who have approached the early Middle Ages with that negative attitude.

Why study early medieval Gaul? Of what interest or importance is it for people in the 1980s? There is a standard answer to that question: that learning about the emergence of a west European nation, about the roots of its culture and its regional diversity, help us to understand a country which has been an important European or even world power for a very long time. It could be argued that there is an inherent interest in the study of a political and cultural system in collapse, of the mechanisms by which a society attempts to preserve the political and social fabric together with the collected wisdom of the past, and of the pressures and circumstances leading to a radical transformation of that society. The contemplation of the efforts of people living amidst the ruins of a great civilisation may have a gloomy fascination for an age conditioned by its pundits and its popular literature to imagine the unimaginable. But from the point of view of a teaching historian there are other reasons for studying the origins of France. It is a country of central importance in European history because of its geographical position and its disproportionate influence upon the cultural and intellectual life of Europe. It is a country whose history has been much studied by historians writing in English, and is thus more accessible to the student and to the general reader. And the history of early medieval France is one of the few areas in which a student can hope to master most of the important historical sources (increasing numbers of which are available in translation) which relate to a specific period or problem, and hence to experience at first hand the problems of the professional historian. The techniques of textual criticism which are so essential for the study of history as a whole have been refined and exploited to a high degree for this period, as have other disciplines which the historian has to attempt to master: the study of placenames, of inscriptions and of archaeology. The student and the proverbial general reader for whom this book is intended will learn something of the problems of the Frankish historian who, in Lynn White's apt Uncle Tom metaphor' 'too often recalls to the wearied mind Eliza in the ice: hypothesis clutched to bosom, he leaps from suspect charter to ambiguous capitulary, the critics baying at his heels'.[5]

This is then an introduction to the origins of France for those who know little or nothing about the subject. It is also a guide for those who read French and German with difficulty, or not at all, to the kind of work which has been done in recent years. I have tried to tell a coherent story, but I have also tried not to cover the same ground as has already been covered in English by such scholars as F.-L. Ganshof, R. Latouche, P. Riché or J. M. Wallace-Hadrill. To reconcile these objectives has not been entirely possible. Much that has been dealt with in excellent books in English has not been touched upon in any detail here – such as intellectual and economic history, and the reign of Charlemagne – and this has diminished the coherence of the story (although in the case of Charlemagne it may also reduce his general importance for the history of France to more realistic proportions). Less excusably, I have betrayed the fact that I know the earlier part of the period rather better than the later, although the emphasis on the earlier period also results from my choice of subject.

I have concentrated on two fundamental areas in which great changes can be discerned in these five hundred years, changes which help to define the new 'medieval' society that had emerged in France by the year 1000: changes in *community,* in the ways in which people relate to each other, and in *authority,* in the ways in which people impose their will upon others. In the first chapter I discuss the new ethnic identities which were established within Gaul, not only by the settlement of newcomers such as Franks or Britons but also among the native Gallo-Roman populace. This chapter will also introduce the reader to those great movements of peoples which give shape not only to the early medieval period as a whole, but also to the subsequent ethnic map of Europe. In the second chapter we focus upon a smaller community, the *civitas* or city-community, the fundamental political unit of Roman times which encompassed most people's political and social lives, and enquire into the disappearance of this Roman institution and the emergence of a very different and more limited concept, the medieval town. In the third chapter the focus narrows still further, and we examine the family and the kin, whose existence and whose sense of identity and of honour were so fundamental to the workings of the early medieval legal system. The final type of social relationship we look at is very different in nature, and much more recent in its origins: the Christian community, both in its broadest possible sense as the community of all believers, defined above all by its relations with outsiders such as pagans and Jews, and also in its more concrete sense of a group of people living a communal life together, as monks and nuns, in order to follow Christian ideals. In the second part of the book we look at the nature of power and authority, and examine the ways in which kings and aristocrats have imposed their political will upon each other and upon their subordinates, from the beginning of the Merovingian dynasty, whose kings took over the mantle of the Roman Emperors, to the end of the Carolingian dynasty, when the Roman concept of the state had virtually vanished. The second section ends, as the first, with a discussion of the role of the Church in the introduction of new concepts and attitudes, this time in relation to the role of the Church as a wielder of authority.

The reconstruction by a historian of an age as remote as that of early medieval France is fraught with academic dangers. The historian does not have the freedom or the daring – or the imagination – of a first-rate historical novelist, who would be in a position to speculate what it would have been like to live in a land much of which was covered by forest, mountain and marsh inhabited only by wolves, bears and hermits, a land littered with the relics of a Roman past, to whose inhabitants martyrs and demons might seem as real and as awesome as bishops and counts. But I hope the reader may get tantalising glimpses of such a world, which may lead him or her to investigate further, and I have tried to avoid approaching the subject in terms of kings-and-battles or institutions-and-constitutions, and instead to introduce the reader to what should be the prime concern of the historian: living people.

PART I

Community

1. The Peoples of Gaul

GAUL had since prehistoric times become the home of successive waves of invaders or immigrants from the East. The Roman armies brought a brief interlude of stability, but Roman rule ended with another wave of invasions, the Germanic invasions of the fifth century. Towards the end of the period covered by this book come the very last of the invasions, those of the ninth and early tenth centuries. Genetically, therefore, the population of Gaul was very mixed. Five hundred years of Roman rule had not entirely obliterated earlier ethnic differences, and the Germanic invasions introduced a new set of ethnic traditions. By the year 1000 there were at least eight distinct peoples, with their own more or less well defined territory and their own sense of community: Franks, Aquitanians, Burgundians, Goths, Gascons, Bretons, Normans and Alamans. 'Gallia' might still be used as a geographical term, to distinguish the land west of the Rhine and Alps from 'Germania' and 'Italia', but only by those of a scholarly disposition. Certainly no one in 1000 would have thought of themselves as 'Galli', as they might well have done five hundred years earlier. How did these new patriotisms come into being?

When Julius Caesar arrived in Gaul, it was divided into four parts, each clearly distinguished from the others, as he put it, by language, custom and law. There was the Mediterranean littoral, south of the Alps and the Cévennes, only thinly settled by Celtic peoples and early under the influence of Greeks and Romans. In Caesar's day it was administered by Rome, so that he did not even think of it as part of Gaul; as Pliny said, it was more like Italy than Gaul. To the west of this Roman base was Aquitania, mouth of the river Garonne, with a population closely related to the Iberians of Spain, speaking probably the non-Indo-European language from which modern Basque derives. Most of Gaul was populated by Galli (Latin) or Keltoi (Greek), that is, by a people or peoples whose language and traditions had derived from, or been imposed by, a warrior aristocracy coming originally from central Europe some five hundred years earlier, the Celts. Finally, to the north and east of the Seine and Marne rivers were the Belgae, who were, said Caesar, of German origin and had crossed the Rhine into Gaul long before. By 'German' Caesar meant 'from beyond the Rhine', which in the first century BC included many Celts as well as Germanic-speaking immigrants from the north: the Belgae themselves were certainly Celtic and not Germanic in our sense.

At first, probably deliberately, the Roman administrative divisions took no notice of these ethnic differences, but the late third century reorganisation of the provinces, which laid down the pattern for the last years of Roman rule in Gaul, to some extent reversed that policy. An inscription survives in which the Nine Peoples, the tribes descended from the Aquitanians of Caesar's day, thank the Emperor for having joined them into a province separate from Gaul (Novempopulana). By the last century of the Empire all inhabitants of Gaul were Roman citizens, and many by then spoke Latin rather than a Celtic dialect; to them the old distinctions must have been overlaid by the general designation of 'Romans'. But there is a hint in a fifth-century dialogue written in Gaul that memories could be tenacious. One of the participants, called Gallus, claimed that his Belgic friends scoffed at the gluttony of the Gauls. He apologised for his own speech: 'When I remember that I am a Gaul and am going to hold forth in front of Aquitanians, I am much afraid that my rather rustic speech may offend your over-civilised ears.'[1] Perhaps the Latin of northerners sounded uncouth because, as linguists tell us, it was already exhibiting features which were to result in the emergence of a Romance language distinct from that spoken in the south: Langue d'Oïl (French) as opposed to Langue d'Oc (Occitan). The linguistic frontier in 500 is thought to have run due east from the mouth of the Loire, roughly following the Roman administrative division for several hundred miles. But the uncouthness of the Gaul's speech and his need to apologise for it may also have reflected a cultural distinction. The south was more heavily Romanised and long after 500 remained the home of a more cosmopolitan and consciously Roman population. In the sixth century a northern cleric begged the Frankish king not to appoint him to a southern bishopric, 'not to submit him, a simple man, to the boredom of having to listen to sophisticated arguments by old senatorial families, or to counts who spend all their time discussing philosophical problems'.[1] For Gallus 'Aquitanian' almost certainly meant an inhabitant of south-west Gaul, south of the Loire; it had nothing to do with the Iberian Aquitanians who lived south of the Garonne, but derived from the late Roman provincial name. The Roman structure of Gaul, together with the climatic, cultural and historic factors which have helped to make southerners and northerners in France seem foreign to each other right down to modern times, was shaping new feelings of community as well as preserving some of the old.

Within Roman Gaul there were other ethnic groups. There were Jews and Greek-speaking Christians from the East, mostly in the towns. In the countryside were small communities of prisoners-of-war, settled forcibly and carefully controlled by the authorities to serve as a pool of recruits for the army and at the same time to cultivate deserted lands. Place-names have preserved the memory of the settlement in Gaul of such Germanic peoples as the Suevi and the Alamanni, and Asiatic nomads such as Sarmatians and Taifals. The Taifals of the Tiffauges in Poitou (Theifalia) lived as a separate group probably from the third century right down to the sixth, when they are mentioned as having rebelled and assassinated a Frankish duke. Some territories formerly held by the Romans had been abandoned to Germanic settlement before the end of Roman rule: the area at the angle made by the Rhine and the Danube as they flow from the Alps (now known as Swabia) was given up to the Suevi or Alamanni in the third century, and the lands to the west of the mouths of the Rhine to the Franks in the mid-fourth century. But the great influx of Germans into the west did not occur until the early years of the fifth century. In the year 400 a praetorian prefect governed the Gauls (which included Spain and Britain in late Roman administrative terminology) from his palace in Trier. By 420 he had been forced to flee to the comparative safety of Arles; Vandals, Burgundians, Sueves and the Asiatic Alans had been forced across the Rhine into Gaul by the arrival of the Huns in central Europe – the so-called 'Great Invasion' of 406–7; peasant rebellions had broken out in the west; and the Visigoths, arriving from the east via Italy after a similar forced 'invasion' in 376, had been irrevocably settled on Gallic soil. By 500 Gaul had been largely parcelled out among three Germanic peoples, the Visigoths, Burgundians and Franks, and Roman political power had vanished, as it had from the rest of the Western Empire.

The South-West

OF the three Germanic peoples who controlled Gaul in 500, the Visigoths might well have been seen as the most powerful. They had arrived in southern Gaul in 413, looking for land on which to make a permanent settlement. The Romans forced them into Spain and, after starving them into submission by a naval blockade of Barcelona, brought them back into Gaul in 418, settling them in the Garonne valley. The Romans seem to have been in a position to rid themselves of this potential or actual enemy; instead they chose to enrol them as allies. As with the Burgundians, the Roman authorities decided to combine the two well-tried expedients, recruiting the fighting force of a whole foreign or barbarian people as *foederati* (federates), and settling these foreigners within the Empire. Precisely how they were settled is still a matter of dispute. Many believe that in 418 the Visigoths were given portions of the estates of the great landowners of the area, in a system (known as *hospitalitas*) which was an extension of compulsory billeting. In theory the fixed proportion of the individual's estates given to the *hospes*, or 'guest', was only on loan. But it could be that the Visigoths were assigned a portion of the Imperial taxation from the region in which they were settled, thus costing the landowners nothing. Whatever the mechanism, the policy was a considerable success. The Visigoths brought a measure of peace, stability and perhaps even prosperity to southern Aquitaine. They remained, by and large, faithful allies of the Romans; the final break with Rome did not come until the virtual breakdown of imperial power in the west, with a succession of puppet-Emperors whose power barely extended beyond Italy and whose legitimacy was frequently in doubt. Then the Visigothic king Euric (466–84) extended the power of his independent kingdom to the Mediterranean, to the Loire, south into Spain and east into the Auvergne.

Our best insight into the circumstances of the fifth century is provided by the 24 poems and 146 letters of Sidonius Apollinaris, son-in-law of the ill-fated Emperor Avitus, one-time Prefect of the City of Rome, bishop of Clermont from around 470 until his death in *c.* 483, and defender of the Auvergne against Euric. Although modern commentators have found little to admire in his over-elaborate prose or his imitative verse, it was as stylistic models that his works were collected and edited during his own lifetime. But they were probably preserved because of his reputation as 'a Catholic father and a distinguished doctor'.[2] A century after his death, Gregory of Tours remembered him for his eloquence, for the Masses he composed (and knew by heart), and for the way in which he used to annoy his wife by giving the family silver away to the poor. (It was quite possibly his wife's family silver, for she came from the most aristocratic dynasty in Gaul.) For the last ten years of his life, Sidonius was a conscientious bishop. As a bishop, he opposed Euric, who like almost all German

Christians in the fifth century was an Arian, holding that in the Trinity the Son was subordinate to the Father. In his letters Sidonius paints a lurid picture of the ruin into which the Catholic Church in south-west Gaul was falling under Euric's rule. Even as a bishop he preserved a considerable pride in his membership of the Roman Senate, and his letters tell us a good deal about its reactions to the Germanic invasions. Some senators continued, or feigned to continue, the traditional life-style, living in luxurious villas on their country estates, reading, writing, playing backgammon or a somewhat elementary ball-game: 'As you know, ball no less than book is my constant companion.'[3] But others seem to have made a determined effort to exploit the new conditions, like Syagrius, who very sensibly (but to Sidonius' open amusement and incomprehension) acquired a fluent grasp of Burgundian. Some aristocrats obviously welcomed the extension of Germanic power in Gaul. They preserved their estates (or the most profitable parts of them), and their social status, and in all probability they increased their political influence. Under Euric, Romans acted as advisers and ministers; one of Sidonius' friends commanded Euric's navy. For how many senators was Arvandus, the praetorian prefect of Gaul, speaking when he wrote to Euric suggesting that he make war on the 'Greek' Emperor (Anthemius, appointed in Constantinople), and divide Gaul up between the Visigoths and the Burgundians, 'according to the law of nations'?[4] Other sections of the populace may have viewed the disappearance of Roman rule with still less regret. The strange Christian moralist Salvian of Marseilles, one of the founders of the long-lived historical myth of the clash between late Roman decadence and Germanic virtue, pointed out around 440 how heavy the burden of Roman taxation was (a fact confirmed by modern research) and concluded that 'it is the unanimous prayer of the Roman people in that district that they may be permitted to continue to lead their present life among the barbarians'.[5] Even the loyal Sidonius, exiled by Euric for his opposition, in the end comes to feel that the important conflict was between Christian and non-Christian, and not between Roman and German, and that the future lay with the barbarian and not with a distant and powerless Emperor. 'It is your troops, Euric, that are called for, so that the Garonne, strong in its warlike settlers, may defend the dwindled Tiber.'[6] The Garonne remained the heartland of Visigothic power; Toulouse and Bordeaux were both royal residences, but the royal treasure seems to have been kept at Toulouse. From this area comes the only possible archaeological witness to a Visigothic presence in south-west Gaul in the fifth century: a belt-buckle similar in type to those found among the Goths of the Crimea, discovered in a grave near a Roman villa, belonging, perhaps, to a Visigothic 'guest'. The Goths did not stay long enough to make their presence felt archaeologically; it was in the sixth century that the custom of burying the dead with their personal apparel spread widely, and by then the Visigoths had been driven from the kingdom of Toulouse.

When Gregory of Tours wrote his *History* later in the sixth century, he portrayed the Frankish invasion of Visigothic Aquitaine as a Catholic crusade against the Arians – almost certainly an anachronism. The Visigothic campaign was merely one phase of Clovis's ambitions. He was lucky to be up against the weak Alaric II rather than his father Euric. Alaric was in financial difficulties; he had been forced to devalue his coinage. Many of his Gothic followers, the backbone of his army, had gone south during the late fifth century to settle in the newly won province of Spain. The senators in his kingdom seem to have supported him; others, with less to lose, may have been less loyal. Even so, the kingdom did not immediately collapse in 507 with the death of Alaric at the battle of Vouillé (near Poitiers); prolonged fighting continued in the south, and a part of Visigothic Gaul, the strip of coastline between the Rhône and the Pyrenees called Septimania, remained in Visigothic hands. For the next two hundred years the province (often called 'Gothia' by those in Gaul, and 'Gallia' by those in Spain) was ruled from Toledo. It acquired close cultural links with Spain (expressed in archaeological terms by its dress fashions and sculpture), and yet at the same time probably acquired in addition a feeling of its own individual identity, manifested in a number of revolts against the Toledan kings. When the Arabs invaded Spain in 711, the last Visigothic kings retreated northwards to Septimania; after Septimania, too, was conquered, it served as a base for Arab raids on Gaul for thirty years, before becoming the first part of Arab Europe to be 'liberated' by Christendom. From then on Gothia was part of the Frankish kingdom, or, as it was often expressed, it was one of the *regna* or kingdoms ruled by Frankish kings, and its inhabitants, Goti, were one of the eight peoples of Gaul. The Goti remained distinct from the Hispani, Spanish refugees who flocked into Gothia. Here we meet for the first time the phenomenon of a people taking on the ethnic identity of its ruling élite. In the sixth or seventh century Visigoths themselves had probably formed only a small, but powerful, proportion of the population. Yet the Gallo-Romans came to think of themselves as Goths, and could distinguish themselves from their neighbours in Gaul by their use of the Lex Gotorum. This was not just local custom, whether Gothic or Roman in origin; W. Kienast (B.I) has shown that many charters of the ninth or tenth centuries contain direct references to clauses of the known seventh-century text of the Visigothic law-code. In the eleventh century the Goths have their own duke: a sign that they were recognised as a separate people.

The destruction of the Visigothic kingdom of Toulouse by the Franks in 507 did not lead to any great changes in Roman society south of the Loire. Few Franks settled in the area, and Roman landowners continued to dominate through their social position and their control of the Church. The Merovingian kings were, for the most part, content to exploit Aquitaine from a distance. Thanks to its own cultural and historical traditions, and those of its social élite, Aquitanians too preserved, or more probably found, some kind of ethnic identity during the Merovingian period. In the early eighth century, Franks called them, significantly, 'Romani'; by the end of that century, after the Franks had begun to have close relations with the real Romani of Central Italy, they began to call the inhabitants of south-west Gaul 'Aquitani'. In 768 the first Carolingian king, Pippin I, guaranteed the Aquitanians their own law, the Breviary of Alaric, the compendium of Roman law which the last Visigothic king in Aquitaine had compiled for his Roman subjects. Aquitanians thus had an ethnic name and their own law, and clearly they had also some desire for political autonomy. In the late seventh century, as the power of the Merovingians waned, we find an Aquitanian aristocrat, Lupus, called *dux* or duke in northern sources. One of the few Aquitanian sources, however, calls him *princeps,* and claims that he wished to make himself king. In the early eighth century there is Eudo, *dux et princeps,* acting as the unchallenged ruler of Aquitaine, and after him Hunald and Waifar, who lead the long and bitter struggle of the Aquitanians to preserve their independence from the Franks, a struggle against three generations of Carolingians that ends only in the early years of Charlemagne's reign. It must have been to appease Aquitanian feelings that Charlemagne had his youngest son Louis made king of the Aquitanians in 781, and had him dressed in the fashion of the Aquitanian aristocracy even as a young boy, 'with the round mantle, the sleeves of the shirt long and flowing, full trousers, spurs attached to the little boots'.[7] Louis's son Pippin succeeded him as king of the Aquitanians, and after him came Pippin II, Charles the Bald and Louis the Stammerer. The lengthy history of Aquitaine as a sub-kingdom within the Carolingian Empire, brought about not so much because of the desire of the Carolingians themselves but rather as a result of pressure from the Aquitanians, indicates the strong particularism of the Aquitanian aristocracy and the feeling of community within the Aquitanian people. The evidence suggests that this was fuelled by a strong dislike for rule from the Frankish north. The traditions of independence continue into the tenth and eleventh centuries, when they were ruled by a duke, not a king. The title *dux Aquitanorum* is one of the earliest of the regional ducal titles to appear, and has an almost continuous history thereafter, right down to when the Angevin kings of England took the title for themselves.

Within the old Merovingian territory of Aquitaine a new people with its own very distinct traditions emerged in the late sixth and seventh centuries. The invasion of the land of the Nine Peoples, Novempopulana, south of the Garonne, by the Vascones is perhaps the least known of all the barbarian migrations of the early Middle Ages. The Vascones, or Basques, were not barbarian in a technical sense: they did not come from outside the Roman Empire. But they were among the few peoples in the Empire who seem stubbornly and successfully to have resisted Romanisation. They had retained their own pre-Indo-European language, Euskara, and, presumably, their own pre-Christian religion. Although the Aquitanian churchman Amandus is said to have attempted some missionary work among them before becoming the Apostle of Belgium, it was not until the tenth century or later that they became even nominally part of Christendom. Towards the end of the sixth century they forced themselves on to the attention of the kings of both Gaul and Spain, raiding north and south of their homes in the Cantabrian mountains and the western Pyrenees. Expeditions against them appear to have been quite ineffective, and by the middle of the seventh century 'Vasconia', which once referred to their mountain homes, had replaced 'Novempopulana' as the name for the territory between the Garonne and the Pyrenees. Vasconia or Guasconia (Gascony) is even used in a seventh-century Italian text to refer to the whole of Aquitaine, a confusion probably brought about by the use the Aquitanian dukes of the late seventh and early eighth centuries made of Basque or Gascon troops, who seem to have been crucial in the long wars fought against the Franks. After the final conquest of Aquitaine in 769 Charlemagne allowed the Gascons to have their own native dukes, and from the mid-ninth century they seem to have had virtual autonomy, under the nominal sovereignty of the Frankish kings. Almost nothing is known about the internal development of Gascony at this time, about its administration, its law or its culture. But linguistically at least it became increasingly distinct; whether because of its prehistoric Aquitanian or Iberian substratum or through Basque influence, the Latin dialect of the area was much closer to Spanish than the other dialects of southern Gaul. To northerners, Gascony seemed a strange, foreign country. When Abbo of Fleury crossed into Gascony he turned laughing to his companions and said, 'Here I am more powerful than our Lord the Frankish king, for no one in these parts fears his lordship.'[8] Nor, of course, was the king able to provide any protection. In 1004 Abbo was killed in the course of a fight between his men and the Gascon monks whose monastery he was trying to reform.

The South-East

IN 500, when Alaric II was ruling the Visigoths, Gundobad was king of the Burgundians, in south-east Gaul. Unlike the colourless Alaric, Gundobad was a man around whom legends quickly clustered. Eldest son of Gundioc of the Burgundians and the sister of the Emperor-maker Ricimer (himself grandson of the Visigothic king who had led his people to Gaul in 418), he started his career as an influential figure in Italian, and hence imperial, politics. According to John of Antioch he killed the Emperor Anthemius with his own hands, before becoming Emperor-maker himself and gaining the title *patricius*. When he returned to Gaul he began to call himself *patricius Galliae*, patrician of Gaul, and eventually inherited the royal title. According to Gregory of Tours, to further his ambitions he killed one of his brothers, drowned the wife and drove the two daughters into humiliating exile; one of them, Chrotechildis or Clotild, was spotted by the envoys of Clovis and brought to Francia as his queen. Gundobad's other brother Godigisil was more cautious; he survived one war against Gundobad by allying himself with Clovis, but succumbed in the second, and was killed. By the end of the year 500 Gundobad was sole king of the Burgundians.

Like the Visigoths, the Burgundians had been settled in Gaul as part of deliberate Roman policy. They had invaded in the 'Great Invasion' of 406–7, and, after supporting an unsuccessful Roman usurper, were settled as a defeated people within the Empire, possibly just west of the Rhine near Worms. In 436 they were again defeated, by the Huns acting as allies of Rome, and a few years later the remnants of the people were settled in Sapaudia. The precise location of late Roman Sapaudia is unknown, but archaeologically speaking the main area of Burgundian settlement in the sixth century appears to have been between Lakes Neuchâtel and Geneva. If this was the area of primary settlement it made good military sense, for the Romans thus placed an obstacle in the way of another and much more dangerous Germanic people: the Alamans. These were settled just to the north of the Rhine, and were in a position to launch raids on the prosperous towns of the Rhône valley through the gap between the Alps and the Jura. The Burgundian presence in this gap may have been crucial in the defence of southern Gaul against the Alamans. Baulked of easy conquest, the Alamans instead trickled slowly across the former Roman frontier from the seventh century onwards, a very gradual and far less dangerous penetration. German-speaking cantons of Switzerland today owe their language to these Alamannic colonisers, not to the Burgundians, who seem to have adopted relatively quickly the language of the Roman neighbours who far outnumbered them.

The Burgundians, like the Visigoths, remained loyal allies of Rome for a time. They fought alongside the Visigoths against Attila's Huns in 451, and against the Spanish Sueves in 456, so many of them that a Spanish chronicler said that the army resembled a whole people on the march. Like the Visigoths they supported the attempt of the Gallic senator Avitus to gain control of the western Empire, and in the interregnum which followed his death seized the metropolis of Lyons. The senators of the area negotiated a further treaty with the Burgundians; the seventh-century historian Fredegar claimed that thereby the Gallo-Romans hoped to escape imperial taxation. The Emperor Majorian retook the town and punished it for its disloyalty, but it was soon reoccupied by the Burgundians and became the chief residence of their kings.

The choice of Lyons, the great metropolis of Gaul, was typical of Burgundian royal policy. Perhaps because of the small numbers of their people and thus their weak position, the kings worked hard to achieve a willing co-operation from the Romans. They were careful to clothe their power in Roman fashion: Gundioc, as far as his Roman subjects were concerned, was not king, but Master of the Soldiers (Roman commander-in-chief), a title which he passed to his brother Chilperic I (together with the purely Burgundian title of king); Gundobad was *patricius Galliae*. The kings all worked closely with the leading Romans of the area, both laymen and Catholic churchmen. Although the Burgundians were Arian Christians until the time of Gundobad's son Sigismund, they were almost apologetically so. Chilperic I endowed Catholic churches and befriended Bishop Patiens of Lyons; Chilperic II and Gundobad both had Catholic wives and daughters. According to Gregory of Tours, Gundobad himself had become convinced of the truth of Catholic teaching on the Trinity, but all the eloquence of Bishop Avitus of Vienne could not persuade him to renounce Arianism in front of his Burgundian followers. Gregory himself is on the whole hostile to Gundobad; he reports the stories of his cruelty to his own family. Yet he does have a word of praise for him as a legislator. Two law-codes have been ascribed to Gundobad, one for the Burgundians and one for his Roman subjects. The versions we possess come from the time of his son Sigismund; the relationship between them is problematical. They contain many clauses in common, and it has been suggested that the 'Roman' law-code is in fact a commentary in Roman law terms on the Burgundian Code, made for purely private consumption. The Burgundian Code itself, later often known as the Lex Gundobada or *Loi Gombette,* is heavily influenced by Roman law, and even some of the clauses which look as if they embody Germanic legal principles may in fact derive from Roman provincial law, which is much less well known to historians than imperial law. Roman lawyers undoubtedly assisted the Burgundian legislators, from Chilperic down to Godamar. Perhaps the senator Syagrius, whose Burgundian was so fluent, according to Sidonius Apollinaris, that he used to correct the grammatical errors of his Burgundian friends, was one of these legal advisers: it would explain why Sidonius called him the 'new Solon of the Burgundians'.[9]

In the year 500, Gundobad's power stretched from the Alps to the foothills of the Massif Central; to the north it reached the plateau of Langres and to the south the river Durance, which runs east from the Rhône, cutting Provence in half. The area around Marseilles may have been won by the Burgundians, but most of Southern Provence never fell to them. Southern Provence was the last refuge of imperial power in Gaul, falling to the Visigoths in 477, just one year after the deposition of the last Emperor in the West. The province was attacked by Franks and Burgundians in the course of their joint attack on the Visigoths in 507, but was successfully defended in the name of the Visigothic kings by Theodoric the Great, Ostrogothic king of Italy.

After thirty years of administration by a praetorian prefect appointed from Ostrogothic Italy, Southern Provence was handed over to the Franks in 536–7, two years after their conquest of Burgundy.

The fate of Burgundy differed in one important respect from that of the Visigothic kingdom in Gaul: the Visigoths had been able to flee to Spain, taking with them their independence and their ethnic traditions, and leaving behind an Aquitaine with its Roman traditions virtually intact. The Burgundians had no such refuge; they and their ethnic identity continued, indeed flourished, within the Frankish kingdom. The regional name 'Burgundia', first used in a letter from Theodoric of Italy in 507, survived, coming to be used, by the early seventh century, of the south-east portion of the Merovingian kingdom. The greatest of the Merovingian kings to have his power-base firmly in south-east Gaul was Guntram, one of the four grandsons of Clovis who partitioned Gaul among themselves in 561. He clearly felt the need to have the backing of the ethnic Burgundians in his kingdom; he named his eldest son Gundobad, the first (and last) occurrence of that name within the Frankish royal family. In Guntram's day writers such as Gregory of Tours still distinguished between the Germanic and Gallo-Roman sections of the population in south-east Gaul; by the end of the seventh century 'Burgundiones' could mean 'all the inhabitants of south-east Gaul', and this became general usage in the eighth century. The author of the eighth-century text celebrating King Sigismund's martyrdom at the hands of the Franks explained that in the fifth century the Burgundians had killed all Romans who had not fled from the area;[10] a similar legend, as we shall see, served to explain how all the inhabitants of northern Gaul had become Franks.

By the eighth century, therefore, Romans and Germans in one area of Gaul had come together as a new people. The descendants of the Romans had forgotten their inheritance; they accepted this false history, and they lived according to Burgundian law. Their sense of community was probably strengthened by anti-Frankish feelings, although this is a quite unmeasurable factor. Should the struggles between the Burgundian aristocracy and the Frankish mayors of the palace in the seventh century be seen in terms of a struggle for 'national independence', as some modern historians have believed? Burgundy in the seventh century played a much greater role in the affairs of the Frankish kingdom than Aquitaine did; together with Neustria and Austrasia, it was one of the *tria regna* which made up the Merovingian body politic. At times it had its own mayor of the palace, a leading Burgundian who would act as chief minister or representative of the king in Burgundy. If there were strong particularist feelings, therefore, they did not lead so easily towards autonomy as in Aquitaine. And events of the ninth and tenth century show that the Burgundian aristocracy did not see itself, or was not able to act, as a unified force. Burgundy never became a sub-kingdom in the Carolingian Empire, like Aquitaine; in one partition after another it was divided out among two or more kingdoms. In 843 the north-western portion (including Autun, Mâcon, Auxerre and Chalon-sur-Saône) was given to the king of West Francia. (This Duchy of Burgundy, as it came to be called, was all that remained of Burgundy within the later medieval kingdom of France.) The rest found itself in Lothar I's Middle Kingdom. In 879 Lower Burgundy, including Provence, became a kingdom under Boso: in 888 Upper Burgundy, including large parts of present-day Switzerland, became a kingdom under Rudolf I. In the mid-tenth century Upper and Lower Burgundy were united under Rudolf's successors. The great variety of titles used by these kings – *rex Burgundiae* and *rex Burgundionum* alongside *rex Alamannorum vel Provinciarum*, *rex Jurensis* (of the Jura) and *rex Viennensis* (of Vienne) – suggest that they did not rest their power on any particular feeling of community among the Burgundians. In the tenth century there were some who reckoned themselves as Burgundians, others (descendants of the great families of the late eighth century) as Franks, and yet others as Romans. A number of aristocratic families in Provence still boasted of their Roman or Gallic descent, and still gave almost exclusively Roman names to their children, though in Provençal forms, such as Pons, Honorat, Maïeul and Amelius. The feeling of belonging to a separate Burgundian people was probably strongest in the north of the area, in the Duchy of Burgundy (the area barely settled by fifth-century Burgundians at all) rather than in the much more diffuse and disorganised Burgundian kingdom. The biographer of Bishop Betto of Auxerre (d. 918) speaks of 'our nation of Burgundy', and when Duke Ralph of Burgundy takes the French throne in 923, the Frank Flodoard of Rheims knows that the 'kingdom of the Franks has been transferred to a foreigner (*ad extraneum*)'.[11]

The North

THE ethnic situation in northern Gaul was quite as varied as in the south, although here there is no doubt that the Franks were the dominant group: this had been clear as early as 500. In that year the chief, though not the only, king of the Franks was Clovis, the effective founder of the Merovingian dynasty which maintained its monopoly on the kingship in Gaul for two and a half centuries. His greatness, and his importance as the creator of France, have always been recognised. Charles the Great himself, wishing to associate himself and his new dynasty with the great figures of the past, named his son and heir Clovis. (Modern conventions obscure the fact. Clovis is the modern French form of Chlodovechus; by the eighth century the guttural had been dropped, giving the form Ludovechus, modernised variously as Ludwig, Lewis or Louis, and in the latter form, of course, becoming the most common of all French royal names.)

Precisely how Clovis came to his pre-eminence in northern Gaul is not so easy to understand. It seems that the Franks on several occasions acted as allies of the Romans, and that Aegidius, a Roman general who did not recognise the authority of the emperors in the West after 462, set up a virtual state of his own based on the town of Soissons. But did he rule over the Franks for eight years, as Gregory of Tours stated? How far was his political position dependent upon Frankish support? Was his rule over the Franks a sixth-century way of explaining the by then inexplicable idea of a Roman commanding a Frankish army? Perhaps the 'kingdom of Soissons' under Aegidius and his son Syagrius is as much a part of Frankish as of Roman history. Much will undoubtedly be learnt in the future about the course of Frankish settlement in the north from the study of archaeology and place-names, but the political details are likely to continue to remain obscure.

The Franks had been an amalgamation of small Germanic peoples living near the mouths of the Rhine. In the fourth century they had provided the Roman army with many ordinary soldiers and a number of distinguished commanders: some Frankish generals such as Merobaudes and Arbogast reached positions of considerable influence in the Empire. In the middle of the century the Emperor Julian settled some Franks in Toxandria, to the south of the Rhine frontier. The Romans seem to have constructed a new system of defences further south, along the line of the important military road from

Cologne to Boulogne. The area to the north of this road was probably slowly colonised by Franks in the course of the following century: most of that area is still Germanic-speaking. At this time the Franks were ruled by a number of tribal chiefs. The first Frankish leader of any importance outside the homeland of the Franks in the fifth century seems to have been Childeric. In 463 he helped Aegidius to defeat the Visigoths; in 469 he and Aegidius' immediate successor Paul defeated the Visigoths again and took Angers from the Saxons, in a battle in which Paul was killed. The war with the Saxons continued, and Gregory of Tours said that many were killed by the Romans, while their islands in the mouth of the Loire were taken by the Franks. Was Aegidius' son Syagrius in charge of this operation, or Childeric? One later source may be relevant. The sixth-century Greek historian Procopius tells how a people called in Greek the *Arborychoi* fought in Gaul with the Franks and, neither being able to defeat the other, joined up with them and intermarried: 'They were united into one people and came to have great power.'[12] The Arborychoi can hardly be the inhabitants of the Armorican peninsula, which was being overrun by the British at this time; they must be the Romans of the Tractus Armoricanus, a late Roman military circumscription which embraced the whole north-west of Gaul, west of the Seine and north of the Loire. It is in this area that Childeric operated; Procopius' account may recall the co-operation between Frank and Gallo-Roman under his leadership.

There is one more source for the history of Childeric's reign: his grave. Discovered in 1653, it remains probably the most important archaeological find of the migration period. Buried across the river from the Roman town of Tournai, the body was identified by a seal-ring inscribed CHILDERICI REGIS: the words are Latin, and the whole concept of a seal-ring Roman. In death Childeric wore a gold cruciform brooch with three onion-shaped terminals, precisely the type of cloak-fastening presented to Roman officials at their investiture by the Emperor, and worn as a badge of office. In the grave were over a hundred coins minted in the Eastern Empire, perhaps part of a tribute paid in return for military assistance. There was little Frankish about Childeric. His sword, buckle and other personal adornments were decorated in the gold-and-cloisonné style common to all Germanic royal and aristocratic circles in the fifth century. But his grave did contain a rock-crystal ball, an amulet normally found in the graves of Frankish women, and another talisman in the shape of a small bull's head, and the very fact of burial with full paraphernalia, while not common in the fifth century, is certainly more German than Roman. Childeric's grave is that of one of the number of fifth-century Germanic rulers whose power depended upon their relationship with Rome. Nor was he the only Frank of whom this was true. The last known Roman official in the former imperial capital of Trier, for instance, was a Frank: Count Arbogast. He was a descendant, perhaps, of the Arbogast who, as Master of the Soldiers, had assisted in the pagan rebellion of 394 against Theodosius I. Sidonius' letter to Count Arbogast leaves us in no doubt that he had embraced the culture and ideals of the Roman aristocracy.

> The Roman tongue is long banished from Belgium and the Rhine; but if its splendour has anywhere survived, it is surely with you; our jurisdiction is fallen into decay along the frontier, but while you live and preserve your eloquence, the Latin language stands unshaken. As I return your greeting, my heart is glad within me that our vanishing culture has left such traces with you; continue your assiduous studies, and you will feel more surely every day that the man of education is as much above the boor as the boor in his turn is above the beast.[13]

The close relationship between German and Roman on which the Franks were to build their power was already well established before the accession of Childeric's son Clovis.

The last sixteen chapters of Book II of Gregory of Tours' *History* have always been the main source for historians of the reign of Clovis (481–511). They provided them, and generations of French schoolchildren, with memorable stories of an energetic and barbaric ruler. And they provided most of the known facts about the reign: about his sucessful campaigns against Syagrius ('king of the Romans') in central northern Gaul, the Alamans, the Burgundians, the Visigoths, and various rival Frankish kings; about his marriage to the Burgundian princess Clotild and his subsequent conversion from Germanic paganism to Catholic Christianity; and about his acclamation at Tours as *consul aut augustus*. And, because of the problems of dating and interpretation they pose, they provided, and still provide, material for endless debate. It is perhaps unfortunate that Gregory's stories, written down anything up to a century after the event, and nearly all uncheckable, should be taken as the historian's starting-point. The few contemporary documents give us an equally interesting view of the man and his achievement.

The earliest of these is a letter from Bishop Remigius of Rheims, written either on his coming to power on Childeric's death in 481, or on the occasion of his victory against Syagrius, *c.*486. Rheims was the administrative centre of Belgica II, in which both Tournai and Soissons lay. 'A strong report has come to us that you have taken over the administration of the Second Belgic province,' Remigius begins. And he offers the following advice: 'Your deeds should be chaste and honest. You should defer to your bishops and always have recourse to their advice. If you are on good terms with them your province will be better able to stand firm. . . . You possess the riches your father left you. Use them to ransom captives and free them from servitude.' [14] It is an astonishing letter to write to a pagan teenager, portraying him as if he was a Roman official and referring to *his* bishops. No doubt Remigius was as aware of the incongruity of the situation as we are, but presents it in terms which he hopes may be accepted by the new king. Remigius must have been very relieved when Clovis decided to convert to Catholicism: the relief is echoed in another contemporary letter, from southern Gaul. Avitus of Vienne wrote to Clovis on the occasion of his baptism, and compared him to the shining light of the Eastern Emperor in Constantinople: 'Your light also burns with its own brilliance, and in the person of a king the light of a rising sun shines over the western lands.'[15] Later Gregory of Tours described Clovis as a second Constantine, while Remigius was 'the equal of saint Sylvester [the bishop of Rome under Constantine] for the miracles which he performed'.[16] Like Constantine, the newly converted king seems to have been determined to master his bishops. One of Remigius' last letters, written after Clovis's death, was a strident complaint addressed to three fellow-bishops: 'For fifty-three years I have been a bishop and no one has addressed me so impudently. . . . I made Claudius a presbyter, not corrupted by gold but on the testimony of the very excellent king. You write: "What he ordered was not canonical. . . ." The ruler of the country, the guardian of the fatherland, the conqueror of nations enjoined this.'[17] In short, Remigius had been compelled by Clovis to ordain an unsuitable priest, and supports his action by the argument that the newly converted king should be master over the Church. And just as Constantine called and presided over the Council of Nicaea, so Clovis, in the last year of his life, called a Council at Orleans to regulate affairs in the conquered territory of Aquitaine. According to the preamble of the record of this council, the king himself summoned the bishops and pointed out to them where decisions were needed. In other ways too Clovis seems deliberately to have acted like a Roman Emperor. There was the enigmatic event at Tours in 508 when he wore a purple tunic and diadem and scattered coins among the crowd, and was thereafter called *consul aut augustus*. Immediately afterwards he established a 'capital' for himself in Paris, and, shortly after, issued a written law-code for his people, the celebrated Lex Salica, probably more to increase his own prestige and to show himself acting as a ruler on the Roman model than to codify the whole customary law of the Franks.

From the point of view of Frankish history, Clovis's most significant achievement was not the conquest of large parts of Gaul but the elimination of all rivals to his kingship. Gregory tells us of the murder of Sigibert the Lame, Frankish king in Cologne, and his son, of Chararic and his son, and of his own relatives, King Ragnachar of Cambrai and his two brothers, 'and of many other kings and blood-relations . . . "How sad a thing it is that I live among strangers like some solitary pilgrim, and that I have none of my own relations left to help me when disaster threatens." He said this not because he grieved for their deaths, but because in his cunning way he hoped to find some relative still in the land of the living whom he could kill.'[18] Thereafter the descendants of Clovis were, for two hundred years, not only the only Franks but the only men in Gaul who were eligible to be kings. But old tribal loyalties within the Frankish people may have survived the elimination of their leaders. The Frankish tribes who advanced south down the Rhine quite independently of Childeric's Franks, and who led the advance against the Alamans, arguably preserved their sense of identity after the death of Sigibert the Lame. In the seventh century they were given their own law-code, the Lex Ribuaria, normally a sign of ethnic identity. The rapid advance of Childeric and Clovis into Roman Gaul may also have helped to bring about divisions within the Franks. There was to be a long rivalry between Neustria in the west, where the Franks were only a dominant minority, and Austrasia in the east, which was much more Germanic in character. The fairly narrow strip of territory west of the Rhine which was the heartland of Austrasia, and from which the Carolingian dynasty was to emerge, is now German-speaking. Apart from Alamannic Switzerland and Alsace it was the only part of Gaul to submit to such heavy barbarian colonisation that the Latin language was replaced by a Germanic dialect. By the eighth century the Lex Ribuaria had come to be the code for the Austrasian Franks, while the Lex Salica seems to have been used in Neustria, and the words Neustrian (Salian) or Austrasian (Ripuarian) could be used almost if they were ethnic terms, even though both groups retained a strong sense also of their Frankish identity. But by then the meaning of 'Frank' had changed, just as the word 'Burgundian' did. In the sixth century the word 'Frank' referred to a member of a specific German people; by the eighth century it meant no more than 'inhabitant of northern Gaul'.

The development of the words 'Francus' and 'Francia' is a complex process, dependent as far as our written sources are concerned on the origins of the individual author. Foreigners and some Gauls throughout our period use 'Francia' to refer to the whole of the territory controlled by the Frankish kings: Gaul and part of Germany. But generally in Gaul itself by the seventh century it had come to mean Gaul north of the Loire and the plateau of Langres (although Tours, on the south bank of the Loire, seems to be counted as part of Francia, not Aquitaine): occasionally it was used by Neustrians or Austrasians to refer to their own territory. The politics of the ninth century produced new definitions: we find *Francia occidentalis* or *inferior* (West Francia, or France) and *Francia orientalis* or *superior* (East Francia, a name now surviving in the German province of Franken or Franconia). 'Francia' can be a political concept, the area controlled by Frankish kings; but in the ninth century we also find it used of northern Gaul or of a restricted portion of it. 'Francus' seems to change from an ethnic to a territorial sense in the course of the seventh century. By the eighth century all those living in northern Gaul (except the Bretons and Alamans) are Franks: we even find some descendants of Roman aristocratic families in Trier in the eighth century, bearing clearly Roman names, being called 'senators of the Franks'.[19] In a marginal note in a ninth-century manuscript of the *Liber Historiae Francorum* the historical process was explained: 'Clovis exterminated all the Romans who then lived in Gaul, so that scarcely one could be found. And the Franks at this time are seen to have learnt the Roman language, which they still use, from those Romans who lived there. What their national language was before this is unknown in these parts.'[20] The national language was, of course, Frankish (West Germanic, unlike the East Germanic Gothic), and in fact seems to have been spoken by some people even in areas now well within the Romance (French) areas of northern Gaul. A number of ninth-century Old High German texts were probably written in present-day France. The first Frankish king who was not bilingual in both German and Romance may well have been Hugh Capet, the founder of the Capetian dynasty at the very end of our period. Louis the Pious, brought up from a tender age in Aquitaine, spoke his dying words in Frankish, according to one source.[21] Bilingualism may have been a largely aristocratic phenomenon in northern Gaul: had Frankish survived to a considerable extent it is unlikely that all inhabitants of northern Gaul would have acquired the right to call themselves 'Frank'. The Carolingian aristocracy, largely Austrasian in origin, may have been responsible for the revival of the use of Germanic in Romance-speaking areas, and, perhaps, for the specifically German facet of Frankish pride. Charlemagne caused the old Frankish heroic literature to be written down (in a manuscript now lost), and Otfried translated the Gospels into Frankish, with a preface which asked, 'Why should the Franks not sing the glory of God in their own language? They are as bold as the Romans, and no one can pretend that the Greeks dispute with them for the prize of courage. . . . I have read, indeed, in several books, that the Franks came from the race and the kin of Alexander, who menaced the whole world.'[22] Two centuries earlier the legend of Frankish descent from the Trojans had been born: another claim to parity with the Romans. Even religion put the Franks above the Romans: in the mid-eighth century prologue to a reissue of Lex Salica it was claimed that 'they rejected with force the heavy yoke that the Romans had imposed on them [thinking here, perhaps, of the Gallo-Roman ancestors of the Franks of northern Gaul] and, having known baptism, they covered with gold and precious stones the bodies of the holy martyrs whom the Romans had burnt or beheaded or had torn apart by wild animals.'[23] When an eighth-century Frank thought of 'Romans', he would have thought not only of the former Roman Empire, but of the contemporary peoples of southern Gaul and central Italy: the men of northern Gaul, with their monopoly of kingship, their military fame and their religious orthodoxy, were worthy successors of the Emperors and worthy rulers of all the peoples of Gaul and even Italy.

The Franks were not the only people in northern Gaul, however. There were, in 500, three others in particular, although one was very minor and had no lasting impact upon the political structure of Gaul: these were the Saxons, against whom Childeric had fought on the Loire, and who had settled on the Channel coast, perhaps coming there after a period of settlement in southern England. Part of the Bayeux region was still known as Otlinga Saxonia in Carolingian times, and in the Boulogne area there are still place-names such as Bouquingham, Alincthun and Dirlinctun, recognisable doublets of Buckingham, Allington, and Darlington. But the two main peoples on the periphery of Francia were in the far west (Brittany) and the far east (Alsace).

Faced by the threat of the Germanic invasion of 406–7, according to Zosimus, 'Armorica and other Gallic provinces followed the lead of the Britons; they freed themselves, ejected the Roman magistrates, and set up home rule at their own discretion.'[24] For a number of years north-western Gaul was a centre of rebellion and social disturbance. In 417 open rebellion was temporarily crushed and, as one contemporary put it, slaves were stopped from enslaving their masters. On two later occasions the Romans had to use Asiatic Huns and Alans to defeat these rebels, or 'Bacaudae'. It was into this atmosphere of discontent and revolt that the first British immigrants arrived in Armorica – possibly encouraged by Roman authorities who hoped to bring some order to the province. The first two known Britons on the Continent both had close relations with the authorities: in 461 a British bishop attends the council of Tours, and in the late 460s the Emperor uses Riotimus, a British king, to defend Berry against Euric. He is defeated, and has to flee to Burgundy; the last we hear of him is when Sidonius writes 'to his friend Riotimus', asking him to prevent 'noisy, armed and disorderly' Britons from enticing slaves away from their owners.[25] The relationship between this British army of the Loire and the general immigration of Britons into Armorica cannot be established. Jordanes in the sixth century believed that Riotimus came directly from Britain; but he could have been a leader of immigrants as well as of warriors. So little is known about the migration from 'Great Britain' to 'Lesser Britain' that the historian has to look to the dubious or ambiguous evidence supplied by saints' lives or linguistics. The Breton linguists of Falc'hun's school suggest that 'Breton is the modern form of Gallic'. It is indeed not impossible that some Gallic speakers survived into early medieval times in the relatively under-Romanised Armorica. But clearly the new settlers, who became the leaders of Armorican society, had a great impact. For hundreds of years Breton and Cornish remained mutually comprehensible, while even the names of two of the earliest political divisions were imported from Britain: the tribal names of the Cornovii and Dumnonii give us Cornouaille and Domnonée as well as Cornwall and Devon. The numbers involved in the migration need not have been large. Northern and Central Armorica were probably sparsely populated in Roman times, and it is here, where the immigrants must have settled, that the purest Breton is found; in the south-east, the Vannetais dialect of Breton is much more influenced by Latin. No doubt the immigrants quickly assimilated any Gallic-speakers they encountered, but by no means displaced all Latin-speaking Armoricans, who continued to live in pockets in the largely Breton-speaking west of the peninsula, and in large numbers in the east. Linguistic evidence suggests that south-west Britain was the source of the migration, but southern Wales probably also contributed its quota. According to the Welsh monk Gildas, the Britons were fleeing the Saxons; modern scholars have suggested that the Irish invasions of western Britain may have been an important factor. Whatever the reason for emigration, once started it must have provided its own impetus, and may have continued from the early fifth down to the seventh century.

Together with the British immigrants came the British church. Later saints' lives tell us more about the prominent role played by churchmen in the migration, although they tell us little worth believing, and accepting the importance of the early Breton saints may distort our understanding of early Breton society. Thus the basic territorial division of early Brittany, the *plebs* (Latin) or *plou,* may later come to mean 'parish', but in its origins was probably equivalent to the early Irish *tuath* (also Latinised as *plebs*): a tribe or petty kingdom. The church in Brittany appears to have had its eccentricities, owing partly to its insular traditions and partly to isolation. Gallic bishops complain about the irregular ordinations of Breton bishops, and about the custom of celebrating Mass with the assistance of women. The West British had probably never known the system of ecclesiastical provinces, according to which bishops were grouped under a metropolitan in accordance with the Roman grouping of cities in a province, and it is thus hardly surprising that after 461 Breton bishops only occasionally acknowledged the authority of the bishops of Tours, in whose province Brittany lay. It is rather more surprising that the bishops of Tours, about whom Gregory (himself bishop of Tours from 570 to 594) tells us so much, do not seem to have concerned themselves with this loss to their prestige. By Gregory's day the virtual independence of Brittany from the rest of Gaul, in both ecclesiastical and secular matters, must have been tacitly accepted. Frankish kings from the sixth century down to the ninth made sporadic but rather half-hearted attempts to incorporate Brittany into their kingdom; usually this was a matter of forcing purely temporary oaths of obedience from Breton princes.

Little or nothing is known about the early political development of Brittany. Gregory of Tours tells us that after Clovis, Brittany was under the domination of the Franks, and that 'their rulers were called counts and not kings': a fairly clear implication that, although Franks called them by the Roman title of count, Breton rulers thought of themselves as kings.[26] In the seventh century, with Judicael, and in the ninth, with Erispoë and his nephew Salomon, we find Breton kings who submit to the kings of the Franks, and yet they retain both the title of king and their effective political independence. The power and influence of the Bretons extended at the expense of the Franks: first into the territories of Vannes, Rennes and Nantes, and then beyond. It was in the late ninth and tenth centuries that the Breton kings wielded their greatest power. Alan the Great (876–907), who started his career as count of Nantes and Vannes, in the heavily Latinised part of Brittany, united Brittany under his rule and extended its frontiers. His grandson Alan II Barbetorte (936–52) pushed back the Norman invaders, and Brittany reached south of the Loire and eastwards almost as far as Rouen. Inevitably the Gallic or Frankish element in Brittany began to predominate. It is doubtful whether the inhabitants of eastern Brittany ever came to think of themselves as Bretons, and it is perhaps significant that the rulers were called *rex* or (by Franks) *dux Britanniae,* king or duke of Brittany, not of the Bretons. Many of the institutions of tenth-century Brittany seem typically Frankish but this is probably because most of the sources relate to the east, and not to the Celtic west.

At the other end of Gaul was another well-defined geographical area which was, in the course of the fifth century, settled by a non-Frankish people: Alsace. It is a narrow territory, bordered by the Rhine in the east , the peaks of the Vosges in the west, and the Jura in the south, separated from Francia, therefore, by considerable natural obstacles. The origin of the name 'Alsatia' has been a matter of linguistic dispute, but scholars seem agreed that it has nothing to do with the name of the Germanic people who settled the area between the fifth and seventh centuries, the Alamans. These All-Men, related to the Sueves, were already well established in the former Roman territory in the angle between Rhine and Danube by the fifth century, in the land known then as Alamannia and more recently as Swabia. The first indication that they had crossed the Rhine into Alsace comes in a poem by Sidonius Apollinaris: 'The bold Alaman was drinking the Rhine from the Roman bank and proudly lording it on both sides.'[27] As in Brittany, colonisation of this area seems to have been a slow but thorough process, culminating in the imposition of a new language, although not the total obliteration of the old. Place-names suggest that the Romans continued to live in Alsace and to preserve their identity and language in its more remote areas for some time. The vines introduced by the Romans were still cultivated; in Argentorate, 'now called Strasbourg' (as Gregory of Tours wrote),[28] a factory continued to make Roman tiles, one of which has been found stamped with the name of the first known bishop, a German (presumably a Frank) called Arbogast. The Alamans pushed north too, and south, as we have seen, into the valleys of northern Switzerland, finally meeting the Burgundian settlements in the Aare valley. Their 'frontier' with the Franks was in Rheinhessen, between Mainz and Worms. Had it not been for the determined resistance shown by the Franks and Burgundians, the impact of the Alamans in Gaul would surely have been more significant. As it was, even their territory in Alsace soon fell under Frankish control. The ducal family that emerged there with Gundoin in the mid-seventh century seems to have been Frankish in origin; they were active in Frankish politics in the later part of that century, and only disappeared in the 740s, at about the same time as the independent Alamannian duchy east of the Rhine was brought under Carolingian control.

The first phase of the migrations (*die Völkerwanderung*) or invasions (*les grandes invasions*) which peopled Gaul ended in the fifth century, although Bretons, Basques and probably Alamans and Franks continued to trickle across the former Roman frontiers. The second phase began in the eighth century, with the attacks of the Arabs, Magyars and Scandinavians. The first two peoples hardly need concern us here; they made no permanent settlements. Septimania served as an Arab base from around 720 to 759, while a band of Muslim brigands held out in their stronghold of Fraxinetum, near St-Tropez in Provence, from the 890s until 973. But apart from that, the Arab impact upon Gaul was in the form of raids. Southern Gaul in general, and Provence in particular, suffered badly, especially in the later ninth century. In 869, for instance, raiders landed in the Camargue and captured

Archbishop Roland of Arles. They received a ransom of 150 pounds of silver, 150 cloaks, 150 swords and 150 slaves, and left the archbishop sitting on the beach as they sailed off: by the time his followers discovered that it was only a corpse, the Arabs were long gone. But the disruption of southern society was more catastrophic than the loss of mere wealth. And this, it has been argued, was as much a cause of the Arab successes as a result of them. The disruption of the Carolingian structure without any stable alternative being immediately established must account for the extraordinary success of the raids of the Magyars, or Hungarians, too. Although they entered Gaul only as a continuation of their main thrusts into Italy and Germany (there being thirty-three known raids there between 899 and 955), they did manage to reach Burgundy in 911, Lorraine in 917 and even Orleans in 937.

The most significant people of the later phase of migrations was undoubtedly the Scandinavians or Vikings (*les Normands* in French, which can mean either 'Norsemen' or 'Normans'). As in England they started with attacks on merchants and their towns, but in the 840s turned to a more systematic pillaging of the kingdom. They set up bases, the first being at the island monastery and trading place Noirmoutier, and raided up rivers far into Gaul, reaching Toulouse in 844 and Paris the following year. It was only in the early 860s that measures were taken to combat this threat, above all by the building of fortresses and fortifications. The civil wars of 879 to 887 allowed the Vikings to devastate large areas, particularly in the north-east. When defensive measures were again put into effect, it was a measure of the times that the initiative was taken not by the king but by the local counts and viscounts. The effects of these raids are literally incalculable. There was a movement of clerics and monks away from the coasts and towards the east, for the sources mention this, but was there a general migration, and if so, to what extent? There was rural impoverishment and a diminution of trade, but by how much? Did the Vikings create the conditions for the decline of the monarchy and the rise to independence of local aristocrats, or benefit from them? Two consequences are clear, however: innumerable fortifications sprang up all over the west and north of Gaul, which served as new political bases for the aristocracy, and a permanent Viking colonisation was made. In 911 Charles the Simple gave to Rollo (or Hrólfr) and his Vikings the area around Rouen. From there in the course of the tenth century the Norman rulers extended their power over the whole of present-day

Normandy, mostly at the expense of the Bretons.

The extent of Scandinavian settlement in Normandy is as controversial a problem as that of their contemporary settlement in England. There is almost no archaeological evidence. Place-names of Scandinavian origin are found in some parts of Normandy, although the bulk of place-names are of Gallo-Roman or Frankish type. The Norman aristocracy seems poised between two worlds. It was probably largely Scandinavian in origin, and was still apparently capable of enjoying the visit of the skald Sigvatr Thorharson, who entertained Richard II's court in 1025. And yet, three-quarters of a century earlier, Richard I had had to go to Bayeux to learn a Scandinavian language, for no one in Rouen could teach him. The Normans preserved their links with Scandinavia, allowing Vikings to use their ports as a base for attacks on England (until a peace cemented by the marriage of Richard II's daughter Emma to Ethelred the Unready) and hiring Viking warriors for their own expeditions, and yet, in the eleventh century, often referred to themselves as 'Franci'. The duality emerges in habits of name-giving: a number of Norman aristocrats are known who had two names, one Norman and one Frankish, such as Thorsteinn and Richard, or Stigand and Odo. It is perhaps significant that, on the evidence of names at least, there were few women of Scandinavian origin in Normandy. It seems likely that the settlement of Vikings was fairly small-scale; that the aristocracy was rapidly Frankicised; and that the preservation of links with their Viking past was part romantic nostalgia, part aristocratic fashion, and part commercial and military convenience.

The Viking raids and settlement obviously disrupted the Frankish structure in that part of northern Gaul considerably. The episcopal establishment and monastic life disappeared temporarily from the province, although there is evidence of a great deal of continuity in rural institutions. The Normans were generally happy enough to adopt and adapt Frankish institutions. Their rulers were content to be called counts, theoretically therefore subordinate to the king; the first to call himself duke was Richard II (996–1026) (although he also called himself *comes, princeps, patricius, marchio* and even *monarchus*!). The Frankish administrative divisions remained, although administered by viscounts appointed by the duke: the counts, generally related to the ducal family, do not seem to have had individual territories. Only a few elements of Scandinavian law came over with the settlers, including, it has been argued, a particular protection of the house and land which led to a ducal prohibition of feud; and the custom of direct inheritance by a male heir, which avoided the partition of inheritances common elsewhere. Perhaps such differences contributed to the development of the Norman duchy which, by the time of the Norman invasion of England in 1066 (and, six years later, the capture by Normans of Palermo, capital of Arab Sicily), was the best organised and most powerful state in Gaul.

Five hundred years after the disappearance of the Western Empire, there were thus in Gaul a number of distinct peoples, owing their sense of community more to a combination of cultural and political traditions and misunderstood history than to any real ethnic distinctions. All of these peoples, at one time or another, had their own leaders, called *duces*, *principes*, or, in special cases, *reges*, and although their feelings of community did not determine political developments (and indeed could be formed and re-formed by them), such feelings form an ever-present background to the political changes of the time. No doubt, as we shall see in the following chapters, there were other, smaller, communities which could form stronger loyalties. But in one area of life at least the inhabitant of Gaul might well have to take his 'nationality' into account: when he went to law.

Throughout our period the principle of 'personality' was dominant in legal thinking – 'personality' as opposed to 'territoriality'. The principle is summed up in Lex Ribuaria 3, 3 and 4: 'And thus we decree that if Franks, Burgundians, Alamans or men from any other nation are staying in Ripuarian territory and are called to law, they shall be judged according to the law of the place where they were born. And if they are condemned, they shall be punished according to their own law, not according to Ripuarian law'.[29] Thus the *professio iuris*, the declaration by which law one lived, became a part of legal procedure. Theoretically descendants of Gallo-Romans (and clerics too, according to Lex Ribuaria) would live by Roman law, while descendants of Salian Franks, Ripuarian Franks, and, presumably, Bretons and Basques as well, would live by their own law. In ninth-century Septimania there is evidence of Gothic, Roman and Salian law all being used in the courts. As we have seen, however, men did not preserve an accurate memory of their genetic inheritance; by the eighth century, descendants of Gallo-Romans in northern Gaul felt themselves to be Franks and thus bound by Salian or Ripuarian law. Thus the principle of personality tended imperceptibly towards territoriality, and was often irrelevant except when men travelled from one territory to another. In practice personality had its problems. Some of them seem to have been worked out, for instance in the case where defendant and accuser were of different nationalities. A greater problem was the ignorance of judges. A nice story is preserved in Adrevald's *Miracles of St Benedict* concerning a law case between two monasteries, held at Orleans at the time of Charles the Bald. All the legal experts present were discussing the ramifications of the case according to Frankish law, until someone got up and said that cases involving ecclesiastics had to be tried by Roman law. The judges agreed that this was so, but since no one present knew the Roman procedures the case remained unsettled.[30] It is only in the south (known later in French history as the 'land of written law') that written law-codes seem actually to have been used in the law-courts. Law elsewhere was the custom of the land; law was what was remembered by the legal 'experts'. Inevitably the system of personality broke down. In Carolingian Septimania participants proclaim themselves Romans, and then follow Germanic procedures; in the north, Franks borrow procedures from Roman law. Both Franks and Burgundians were probably using wills and Roman forms of contract as early as the sixth century; Gallo-Romans borrow the system of monetary compensation for crimes and the practice of gathering oath-helpers. Ultimately the result was that each locality had its own law, a legal chaos which lasted in France until the *Code Napoléon*. The traditional distinction between the 'land of written law' and the 'land of customary law' obscures the similarities; by the year 1000 the basic difference was rather that over much of the south, local unwritten custom derived from Roman law, whereas in the north it did not. Thus the history of law neatly reflects the history of Gaul as a whole. Roman Gaul was under imperial law (although local unwritten provincial law, so-called vulgar law, survived); with the invasions came new peoples, each with their own new legal ideas. A process of ethnic re-formation took place, and by the Carolingian period each of the new provinces effectively had its own type of law. With the fragmentation of the Carolingian Empire came the localisation of legal custom. There was no real attempt under Charlemagne or his successors to unify and standardise legal custom. We have only the lone voice of Agobard of Lyons, writing under Louis the Pious: 'How many times does it happen that five men walk or are seated together and that no man has the same law as another of his fellows?'[31] Agobard not only ridiculed the system of personality, but suggested that the whole Empire should live under a new Christian imperial law. The communities of the various peoples should be replaced by the community of Christian brethren. 'But this is a great undertaking, and perhaps impossible to man.'[32]

2. Cities and Towns

IF the English-speaking visitor to the lands west of the Rhine today is struck by their ethnic and regional diversity, he cannot fail to notice also the fierce pride of citizens for their town. More compact than most English or American towns, often possessing a well-defined boundary with the surrounding countryside, many still betray palpable signs of their Roman origins. Two in particular stand out in this regard. One is 'a very great town called Trier where, it is said, the Emperor lives; this is in the midst of land. There is also another great town which comes to the aid of Trier in all things; it is situated by the sea and is called Arles. It receives the merchandise of the whole world, and transports it to Trier.'[1] Thus a fourth-century geographer; he may have had confused ideas about Gaul, but he recognised the importance of these two cities, whose Roman monuments are preserved to such an astonishing extent to this day. Trier, at times an imperial residence and the seat of the praetorian prefect, has its towering Porta Nigra, the best preserved of all Roman town gateways, thanks to the hermit who took up residence in it and ensured its preservation as a church. From the hills on the opposite side of the Moselle one can see the brick basilica which formed part of Constantine's palace complex, still dominating one section of the town; the remains of the baths, among the most extensive in the Empire and used as a quarry by generations of Treveri; and the vine-covered hills beyond, whose slopes form the foundation for the town's amphitheatre. But far more evocative are the Roman sculptures in the Rheinisches Landesmuseum, where the whole panorama of life in the territory of Trier is displayed: the ship sailing down the Moselle with its cargo of wine-casks, the cloth merchant showing off his wares, the bailiff working out the accounts of his master's estates, the schoolboy arriving late for lessons, the bull pushing in front of it a reaping-machine, a wheeled box whose leading edge bore teeth which caught the heads of grain, pulled them off and deposited them in the box: the abortive invention, perhaps, of a north Gallic farmer. Trier flourished in the midst of its prosperous farmland, and with the presence of civil servants and the proximity of the army of the Rhine. But it was also in the front line during the Germanic invasions, and at the beginning of the fifth century the administrative capital of Gaul was transferred to Arles, another residence, a century earlier, of the Emperor Constantine. In Arles today the Roman walls, theatre, amphitheatre, temples and underground warehouses are all still in an amazing state of preservation; and the splendid array of fourth- and fifth-century marble sarcophagi, with their Christian scenes and symbols carved in high relief, witness to the prosperity and social importance of many Arlesians in the late imperial period.

The fate of these two towns in the post-Roman period may serve as an illustration of the varied history of Gallic towns, and in a general way stands for the basic differences between northern and southern Gaul. Trier clearly suffered badly in the fifth century, both from barbarian attacks and, probably, from emigration. But it did still harbour a 'Roman' official in the person of Count Arbogast in the 470s, and a bishop continued to function there. Some portion of the Roman populace must have survived too. Romans probably swelled the Frankish mob which killed the tax-collector Parthenius there in 548; they were responsible for the survival and formation of Latin place-names in the immediate environs of the city, which made it an island of *Romanitas* in a German sea; and they ensured that Trier should produce more Latin inscriptions of the Merovingian period than any other town in north Gaul. These epitaphs, of course, could commemorate the deaths of those who were brought to Trier to be buried near one of its several churches. Archaeological investigation suggests that the actual population of Trier may have been quite small in the immediately post-Roman period, consisting perhaps largely of clerics and their dependants, clustering around the cathedral in one corner of the vast urban enclosure, and around the various extramural churches. The structure of the secular Roman town had vanished, to be replaced by the 'ecclesiastical town' which was so typical of northern Gaul.

Arles too had been a prime target for Germanic attacks in the fifth century, but these Germans were more determined or better able to preserve the fabric of Roman town-life than the Franks. The town fell to the Visigoths in 477; it was besieged by the Franks and Burgundians in 507, but successfully defended by an Ostrogothic army sent by Theodoric of Italy, and it remained the seat of a praetorian prefect appointed in Italy until it was handed over to the Franks in 536/7. The career of the leading figure in Provence at this time extended over the rule of each of these three Germanic peoples: Caesarius was bishop of Arles for nearly forty years, from 503 to 542. His sermons show us the human misery caused by the prolonged siege in 507–8, but leave us in no doubt as to the vivacity of town life under the Ostrogoths. Regular markets were held in the forum, and legal cases heard there: Caesarius complained that on Sundays these rival attractions were far more popular than church. On weekdays the bishop used to hold matins especially early, so that goldsmiths, shipbuilders and other craftsmen could attend on their way to work. Sinful peasants from the surrounding countryside, carefully made-up women, and aristocrats too proud to genuflect at the appropriate times, all attended his sermons and listened to his attacks on their conduct. There were communities of Jews and Greeks in the town, and an active trade; a southern port like Arles or Marseilles must have retained its sense of belonging to the Roman world long after other parts of Gaul. The Arabs in the eighth and ninth centuries probably did much more to disturb the continuity of town-life there than the Germans three centuries earlier.

It is appropriate that memories of Roman Gaul are most vivid in the towns of modern France and Germany. The town was the most typical Roman institution, and one which Rome brought to those countries beyond the Mediterranean which it 'civilised' (which, etymologically, means 'gave town-life'). The town was the means by which Roman attitudes and customs could be introduced to newly conquered territories; it remained the physical or spiritual home of those provincials who, like Sidonius Apollinaris, had embraced the culture and ideals of Rome in their entirety. And it was also the means by which the will of the Roman Emperor could be imposed upon the surrounding countryside. The town (*urbs*) was an obvious and very Roman kind of institution, defined physically by its buildings and its walls, but it was part of a larger community, the *civitas*. Isidore of Seville made the distinction in the seventh century: 'the *civitas* is a multitude of men united by a bond of association, so-called from the citizens. . . . For although the *urbs* itself is made by its walls, the *civitas* gets its name not from stones but from the inhabitants.'[2] The *civitas* was thus not a geographical concept, but a social one: it was a 'city-community'. It was the Empire's basic administrative unit: a community with a town, the *civitas*-capital, as its political, social, religious and economic focus. Every inhabitant of Gaul belonged to one of the 115 *civitates*. Each *civitas* had its senate or council, responsible for passing on the requisite taxes to the Emperor, and each, by the fifth century, had its bishop. *Civitas* can thus mean 'community living within a certain territory', or 'territory', or, indeed, 'diocese'. But even in the time of Gregory of Tours it was coming to be restricted to its later primary meaning of 'city', that is, episcopal town. The ambiguity of the word does much to obscure the fate of the Roman concept of *civitas* in the post-Roman period. As we shall see in this chapter, the *civitas*-territory fragmented and disappeared over most of Gaul; only the ecclesiastical diocese survived to betray its former extent. But the town itself survived in almost every case, slowly being transformed into a recognisably different phenomenon, the medieval town.

The physical changes undergone by Roman towns in the centuries after Roman rule must have been very gradual. The turretted and battlemented walls which had been constructed around almost all Gallic towns in the third and fourth centuries, or around their central areas, survived. Outside the walls there was, no doubt, some habitation, particularly around the Christian churches which were often founded in the extramural cemeteries. Inside and outside the walls the Roman public buildings, theatres, baths and houses were either put to new uses or allowed to decay. The greatest physical change in the Roman town had already taken place: the destruction or abandonment of the temples and the construction and the increasing social importance of the Christian buildings: churches, monasteries, the baptistery, the bishop's house. Very few of these buildings survive today, and our best idea of what they would have been like comes from contemporary descriptions rather than excavations. Gregory of Tours and Venantius Fortunatus, the poet–bishop of Poitiers, both give us an impression of large hall-like basilicas, with rows of columns to support the roof, and walls decorated with paintings or mosaics. We know of the complex iconography of one Merovingian church whose walls were covered with mosaics of Biblical scenes and saints, thanks to a seventeenth-century description: the church itself was demolished in 1761 by the Benedictines of Toulouse, to make way for a more modern building. Now the nearest we can get to a sixth-century Gallic church is by visiting Ravenna. It would obviously be a mistake to imagine that the 'barbarian' invasions brought an end to the tradition of magnificent urban buildings. But more and more those buildings were ecclesiastical in nature, and in the course of the early Middle Ages ecclesiastical buildings must have taken up an increasing proportion of the limited space within the walls of a town. By the ninth century, when a town had its large cathedral, its new buildings for the cathedral clergy (canons), and its monasteries, the character of the town must have been totally transformed. But most Gallic towns remained towns nonetheless: a large population of clerics meant also a population of dependants, craftsmen, shopkeepers and small merchants, and the continuance of the town as a major religious centre ensured that it remained a point of attraction for the inhabitants of the surrounding countryside. Town and country were always closely interconnected. It is telling that there was no unambiguous word in Merovingian Latin for town as such: both *urbs* and *civitas* could mean the town with its rural surroundings. Authors of saints' lives or those who drew up charters sometimes had to use awkward phrases such as *oppidum civitatis* or *oppidum urbis,* 'the fortified place of the city', to make their meaning clear. Even more revealing is that literary panegyrics of towns tended to concentrate on two attributes: the size of the population and the fertility of the surrounding countryside.

In the early imperial period the *civitas* was largely autonomous; if it paid its taxes and administered justice properly it was left alone. Memories of former independence may have survived into the more centralised time of the later Empire, and played some part in ensuring that the loyalty and emotional attachment of the ordinary Gallo-Roman was to his *civitas*, not to Gaul as such, nor to one of the seventeen provinces into which Gaul was somewhat arbitrarily divided. The *civitas* was in many cases the territory which had been controlled by a pre-Roman tribe. In the third century or later many Gallic *civitates* dropped their official Roman names and reverted to the tribal names: thus Lutetia of the Parisii is now Paris, Caesarodunum of the Turones is Tours, and Augusta of the Treveri is Trier (Fr. Trèves). The boundaries of these territories, originally often dictated by the marshes, mountains or forests which separated one tribe from another, could be extremely long-lived. The limits of the tribe of the Petrocorii, for instance, were the same as those of the *civitas* of Vesunna Petrocoriorum, the same as the diocese of Périgueux and the later province of Périgord, and are perpetuated today in the boundaries of the *département* of Dordogne. The *civitates* were thus distributed in Gaul largely as the old tribes had been, clustered quite densely in the south, particularly the south-east, while in the north the *civitas*-territories were more extensive than anywhere else in the Empire south of Britain. It is impossible to tell whether tribal loyalties survived through the centuries of Romanisation. Such loyalties were likely to have been least strong among that very small section of the population whose literary works give us most of our evidence for the late Roman period. But even the élite felt a strong attachment towards their native *civitas*, stronger perhaps than that to Rome, which their political and literary heritage encouraged. 'Bordeaux is my *patria*', proclaimed the fourth-century poet Ausonius, 'but Rome stands above all *patriae*. I love Bordeaux, Rome I venerate'.[3] Sidonius Apollinaris, bishop of Clermont, declared that his Arvernians were invincible soldiers, that the soil of the Auvergne was second to none in the Empire for fertility, and that a single glimpse of its beauty made strangers forget their own land (apparently true, for Sidonius himself was born in the Lyonnais).[4] Behind the rhetoric lay a real affection, an affection which must have been still fiercer for those less educated and less travelled than Ausonius or Sidonius. Devotion to the *patria* of the *civitas* long survived the fall of the Western Empire. The average inhabitant of Merovingian Gaul, as of late Roman Gaul, thought of himself first and foremost as an inhabitant of his *civitas*; thus Merovingian saints in the *Vitae* are introduced as Turonici, Cenomannici or Arverni (inhabitants of the *civitates* of Tours, Le Mans or Clermont), even those who are Frankish rather than Gallo-Roman by birth. This patriotism need not have been based on any long-surviving tribal feelings, of course. Some *civitates* had been artificially created out of larger *civitates*, as Angoulême was out of Saintes, in the fourth century, or Carcassonne out of Toulouse, in the sixth. A *civis* was no longer the inhabitant of a territory; more and more he appears in the sources as the inhabitant of a town, the *civitas* in its narrowest sense. Thus there is no direct link, but surely there is a similarity, between the fierce loyalty of the Gauls of Caesar's day to their tribe, and the loyalty which led to the inter-city rivalry and even warfare of the sixth century, and which no doubt lay behind the growing independence of the *civitates* under their leaders in the seventh and early eighth centuries.

The town had performed a number of functions within the late Roman *civitas* and the late Roman state. It had been an administrative centre, a social and economic centre, a religious centre. Where towns survived, all these functions continued; and towns survived all over Gaul, except in those areas where the migrations had disrupted the Roman structure, as in the extreme north-east, that part of Burgundy east of the Jura, and those areas settled by the Bretons and the Basques. A few towns served as royal residences; Clovis's four sons had Orleans, Paris, Soissons and Rheims as their main residences. Paris had been chosen by Clovis himself, and was to remain the most important, even if later kings preferred to spend their time in one of the many villas or hunting lodges in the forests around the town rather than in Paris itself. Kings were buried in urban churches, and it was in towns that much royal ceremonial probably took place. Towns, with a sizeable population and impressive buildings such as churches, palaces and amphitheatres, formed a suitable setting in which to display power, as Roman Emperors had found. In the seventh century and thereafter, however, Frankish kings spent most of their time in their rural villas and hunting-lodges. Charlemagne's choice of the small Roman spa of Aachen (Fr. Aix-la-Chapelle) is hardly a return to urban residence. Charles the Bald, excluded from Aachen by the partition of the kingdom (see map 5) would often reside in one of the former Roman towns in his realm, or, more often, just outside it, in one of the great urban monasteries. At one point, according to a later tradition, he thought of following the old Greco-Roman tradition of founding a capital of his own, and changing the name of the old Frankish royal residence of Compendium (Compiègne) to Carlopolis. But in general kings probably spent little time in towns, and many towns in Gaul would never have seen a king. Authority was represented by a bishop or a count, or both.

Bishops and Counts in the Merovingian Civitas

FOR the ordinary inhabitant of Merovingian Gaul, the bishop must have loomed larger than the king. King Chilperic certainly thought so. Gregory of Tours said that 'there was nothing he hated so much as the churches. He was perpetually heard to say: "My treasury is always empty. All the royal wealth has fallen into the hands of the Church. There is no one with any power left except the bishops. No one respects me as king: all respect has passed to the bishops in their cities."'[5] The power of the bishops was nothing new. Constantine had given them legal powers in secular matters in the early fourth century; in the turmoil of the fifth it was often the bishop who defended his town against the barbarian – or against the imperial tax-collector. The presence of a bishop may even have been crucial to the survival of the town at all in the immediate post-Roman period. Towns without a bishop disappeared. Jublains, a former *civitas*-capital, was within the diocese of Le Mans, and perished; when the bishop of Aps moved to Viviers, the same fate befell Aps. The crucial role of the bishop derived in part from the absence of alternatives in a situation of declining imperial authority, but there were other factors too: the political and social power of the families from which many bishops were drawn, the spiritual authority with which they were vested, and their status as elected officials. In the early church, bishops had been elected by the people and clergy of the town or diocese, but by the fifth century the church was becoming disinclined to accept popular election. In general churchmen favoured a kind of seniority system, promotion from within the ecclesiastical structure. But laymen disagreed. Kings in the new barbarian kingdoms wanted bishops they could trust; men, perhaps, who had been in their service, and for whom a bishopric would be a suitable reward. And laymen in towns often preferred either a holy man who could obtain the ear of God on their behalf, or an eminent man who could obtain the ear of the ruler. Martin of Tours, a hermit, and Germanus of Auxerre, a military official, are two early paradigms of these opposing tendencies. Both kings and congregations, therefore, might want laymen as bishops. In Chilperic's day, Gregory of Tours laments, it was rare for a cleric to be elected bishop. Church councils might insist on a year's instruction on the duties of a bishop before the consecration of a layman, but their reiteration of this rule suggests their efforts were unsuccessful. King Guntram swore that he would appoint no laymen; yet at least five of his counts or officials received bishoprics. Such appointees were usually outsiders, which did not endear them to their towns. Bishop Dalmatius of Rodez left a will in which he adjured the king with awful oaths not to permit the election of a stranger, a married man, or a covetous man: the archdeacon of Rodez was duly elected. The Council of Clichy (626/7) actually laid down that when a bishop died his successor should be from the same *civitas:* the leader of a community should be a member of it. Normally he was, for normally the wishes of king and church corresponded with the wish of the people in the *civitas*, particularly if we understand by 'people' what the sources often mean by *populus*: the politically active and important men of the area. In short, the bishop was often a member of the local aristocracy; over much of sixth-century Gaul he was from a Roman senatorial family.

Some of these Roman families produced whole dynasties of bishops. The family of Gregory of Tours is the best-known example. His paternal uncle was bishop of Clermont; his maternal great-uncles were Tetricus, bishop of Langres, and Nicetius, bishop of Lyons; and Tetricus was the son of Gregory, bishop of Langres, from whom Gregory of Tours took his name. His mother's cousin was Eufronius, his predecessor as bishop of Tours. Gregory tells us that Eufronius was chosen by the people of Tours; Chlothar I, when asked to confirm the election, complained that he had never heard of him. But when told that he was related to Gregory of Langres, Chlothar exclaimed (according to Gregory of Tours), 'That is one of the noblest and most distinguished families in the land.'[6] Gregory himself tells us little of Eufronius. In the list of bishops of Tours at the end of the *History* he says merely that 'he came of one of the senatorial families which I have mentioned a number of times'.[7] He does not stress his own relationship; perhaps he himself had not been on good terms with him. Gregory tells us how his own episcopate was troubled by the plots of Riculf, who had been appointed archdeacon of the diocese by Eufronius. Riculf charged Gregory with an unspecified crime, and while Gregory was answering the accusation at the royal court, Riculf took over as bishop, saying, 'It is I who am in charge now, for I have purged the city of Tours of the rabble from Clermont' – that is, Gregory's family and followers, all outsiders.[8] Gregory commented: 'The poor fool seems not to have realised that, apart from five, all the other bishops who held their appointment in the see of Tours were blood-relations of my family': an astonishing statement, which it is no longer possible to check. It is not unlikely that Riculf, not Gregory, had been Eufronius' choice as his own successor. Nothing would have been more suitable than the internal promotion of an archdeacon. Perhaps Riculf had even been elected on Eufronius' death; this would explain the constant support given him by Felix of Nantes, the senior bishop of the province. Gregory, whether by design or not, was at the royal court when news came of Eufronius' death, and King Sigibert appointed Gregory. A separate election of Riculf would explain why Gregory took a long time to reach his see, his almost total silence about his own election, and the continuing opposition of Riculf and, possibly, of many citizens of Tours. It is hardly surprising that Gregory should conceal the fact that he had been appointed by royal will over the head of the canonically elected candidate; this is a procedure which he castigated on several occasions in his *History*.

The details of episcopal elections in the Merovingian period are rarely known. The delicate balance of power, the intrigue and compromise between the interested parties – king, other bishops in the province, local clergy, local aristocracy, the people – can only be inferred. Sidonius Apollinaris does describe for us two fifth-century episcopal elections, which give us some impression of the problems. In the first the metropolitan, the first bishop of the province, discovered that there were three candidates for the bishopric of Chalon. 'The first had no qualifications whatsoever, but only the privilege of ancient lineage, of which he made the most. The second was brought in on the applause of parasites, bribed to support him by the full run of the gourmand's table. The third had the tacit understanding with his supporters that if he attained the object of his ambition the plundering of the church estates would be theirs.'[9] The result of this unseemly Eatanswill was a success as far as the church was concerned: the bishops got together and, Sidonius reports complacently, 'in complete disregard of the unruly crowd they laid their hand on [consecrated] the holy John' – who had not been a candidate at all. On the second occasion Sidonius himself went to an election at Bourges. 'So great was the number of candidates that two benches would not have sufficed for the candidates for the single position. Every one of them was as pleased with himself as he was critical of all his rivals.'[10] Sidonius exploited the mutual suspicion to have the candidate of his own choice elected.

Eagerness to obtain a bishopric is easily understood: it brought power and wealth. Gallic bishops had control over the diocesan income, from offerings and church estates. The convention of early medieval hagiography that the saint only very reluctantly accepted a bishopric had an obvious foundation in political fact: those who actually sought episcopal office were likely to be the wrong men for the job, in the eyes of the Church at least. Some were so ambitious that they resorted to simony, the buying of office with money. The Irish monk Columbanus tells us it was rife in Burgundy in the late sixth century, although he may have been taking a typically rigorous position, perhaps viewing in the worst possible light the presents that any visitors to court, including bishops or episcopal candidates, would have been expected to give to the king. The dividing line between gift and purchase-price was a fine one, and impossible for an outsider to detect. Unscrupulous bishops there were, none more so than the infamous brothers Sagittarius of Gap and Salonius of Embrun. They fought against the Lombards, killing many with their own hands; they sent a gang to attack a fellow bishop. Deposed by a council of bishops, they were reinstated by Guntram, after an appeal to the Pope. After more violence, their congregations called for Guntram's intervention, and they were locked up in monasteries. But the king became convinced that the illness of his eldest son could be attributed to his action against the bishops, and he released them. After a short period of remorse they returned to their feasting, drinking and fornication. Finally they were accused by the bishops of adultery and murder; but even such crimes could be purged by penance, and so, just to make certain, treason was added to the list. They were imprisoned, and Sagittarius was eventually beheaded, after getting involved in the usurpation of the Merovingian pretender Gundovald. These brothers are among the first of the breed which was to become common in the later seventh century: local aristocrats using the income and position derived from their bishoprics to further their own secular ends.

Stories about the scandalous doings of bishops were as newsworthy in the sixth century as they are now, and generally more entertaining than descriptions of the everyday duties of the normal conscientious holder of episcopal rank. Those everyday duties could be heavy. When Nicetius of Trier was consecrated in 526 he felt a weight settling on his shoulders. He tried to shake this invisible burden off, but then he smelt the odour of heaven and 'understood that the weight he felt was the dignity of sacerdotal office'.[11] That office was first of all concerned with purely ecclesiastical matters: ordaining priests, saying Mass, baptising the faithful, and preaching. These acts emphasised the importance of the town within the *civitas* or diocese. Baptisms would normally take place within the baptistery next to the cathedral in the *civitas*: rural baptisteries were rare. Various enactments by church councils tried to persuade aristocrats and their own clergy to celebrate the major church festivals in the town, and the presence of the important relics of the diocese in the urban churches encouraged the rural faithful to continue to regard the town as the centre of their religious community despite the growing number of rural churches. The major festivals, including the feast-day of the local saint, attracted crowds of countrymen into the towns – crowds who came, perhaps, as much for the markets, the dancing and the drinking as for the ceremonies. It must have been on such occasions that the sense of belonging to the *civitas*-community was at its strongest; it was on such occasions, in the miracle stories of Gregory of Tours and others, that the blind were given sight and the demons driven out of the possessed, and that, symbolically, the erring Christian was brought back within the community.

Preaching was one of the most important of the bishop's duties. Caesarius of Arles, whose sermons survive to provide a guide to the content of sixth-century preaching at its best, claimed that the Holy Spirit spoke through the preacher and that the Word of God as transmitted by the preacher had the same dignity as the Eucharist. His predecessor Hilary of Arles had once shouted at those who were leaving the church before the sermon, 'You won't find it so easy to leave Hell!' Caesarius was more direct – he locked the doors of the church in advance.[12] Given his emphasis on preaching it is not surprising that it was a council over which he presided in 529 that first allowed ordinary priests to preach in the countryside. Hitherto, in the interests of orthodoxy, the bishop had held the monopoly, with the result, no doubt, that those who wanted to hear a sermon generally had to visit a town, or else go to hear the bishop on his annual round of the diocese. There seems to have been little follow-up to Caesarius' initiative, in the way of encouragement of preaching in the countryside, at least not until the Carolingian period. 'It was here that the Merovingian church failed so dismally. One searches through the sixth-century synods in vain for demands that priests teach the people about Christianity.'[13] In the eyes of most Merovingian bishops, the Christian community, like the *civitas*-community, revolved around and depended upon the town.

The sixth-century bishop lived and worked in the *domus ecclesiae*, his urban residence. It was law-court, boarding-school, seminary, hotel and citizen's advice bureau all in the one building. All could go there for help; the council of Mâcon in 585 forbade bishops to keep dogs, lest they deter or bite supplicants. The urban clergy often lived in the same house, ate with the bishop, and frequently slept in the same room. In a separate establishment might well have lived the bishop's wife, the *episcopa* or *episcopissa*. Men were forbidden to dismiss their wives on becoming priests or bishops, but were also forbidden conjugal relations: monks or those otherwise dedicated to the church from an early age would, of course, normally not marry. *Episcopae* might themselves have been important figures. Gregory of Tours shows us one sixth-century Mrs Proudie, sitting with a Bible on her knees, giving iconographic directions to the artists painting the walls of a new church. Perhaps she took part too in one of the bishop's main concerns: charity. Bishops were expected to give daily food to those poor who were registered on the *matricula,* or alms-list. And in times of crisis his charitable works might have to be on an enormous scale: ransoming captives and organising famine relief, often out of his own private funds. In a period in which famine was a frequent occurrence, a bishop could win much local prestige and influence by such actions. Sometimes his intervention, leading, for instance, to the arrival of ships laden with grain, was later related as if it had been a miracle. Both Desiderius of Cahors and Maurillus of Angers were credited with the even greater miracle of ensuring that no famine struck their *civitas* while they were alive. Bishops were protectors of their community in life and after death. Eutropius of Orange used to appeal to his flock: 'Pray for me that I may find a little space in Heaven with my God, for with his help I shall not cease my prayers for my townsfolk of Orange.'[14] The posthumous intervention of bishops on behalf of their citizens or their church could be fairly unnerving. When a priest complained that Nicetius of Lyons had left nothing to the church in which he was buried, Nicetius visited him in the night and pummelled him in the throat. Next morning the priest was almost unable to swallow, and he was forty days in bed before recovering.[15]

The bishop liked to have himself portrayed as the natural leader of his people, but if he wanted to keep this position he had to work at it. Even his spiritual pre-eminence in the *civitas* could be threatened, by other sources of power such as holy men or their relics. Statistics of posthumous cults give some impression of the changing position of the bishop. Of the fifty-four Gallic saints known from the fourth century, fifty-two were bishops; in the fifth century there were 123 bishops out of 175 saints; in the sixth century, of 293 saints there were only 148 bishops.[16] The bishops themselves distorted these vague statistics in their own favour; if the name of a venerated ecclesiastic is to be preserved, a cult needs to be founded and fostered, and this can most easily be done by a wealthy and continuing institution such as a bishopric or a monastery. Most of the great relics were safely housed in the episcopal towns; others were kept in basilicas built by bishops and looked after by their clerics. Bishops had collections of miracle stories written, often stressing the particular power of episcopal saints, and thus encouraging pilgrimage to cathedral towns. Gregory's own stories of miracles worked by the relics of St Martin of Tours mention the place of origin of pilgrims in 143 cases: twenty per cent came from the Touraine, seventy-five per cent from western and central Gaul, almost all from within a radius of 200 kilometres as the crow flies, and the remaining five per cent from Spain, Italy and the East.[17] The pilgrimage was thus predominantly local. But the prestige of Martin and his successors as bishops of Tours could be promoted through the distribution of relics. Few places in northern Gaul were far from a church dedicated to St Martin and containing his relics, not the actual bones, but objects which had touched the saint's body or his tomb. The custom of the division of a saint's body had not yet reached the West, but that did not prevent the occasional unseemly scramble for relics. St Lupicinus had walled himself up as a hermit in an old ruin near Clermont, and was fed with crusts of bread put through a hole in his voluntary prison. When he eventually died, the crowd tore an entrance into the tiny cell and fought each other for fragments of his clothes, before scraping from the walls the particles of blood and spittle which he had coughed up in his death-throes.[18] Manifestations of extreme asceticism were often taken by the ordinary believer as signs of great holiness; bishops sometimes had to fight to defuse such situations, which imperilled their own standing. Wulfilaic, for instance, who sat on a pillar in the manner of eastern stylites (although the climate in the Ardennes was not so amenable as in Syria, and in winter icicles hung from his beard and he lost his toenails through frostbite) was enticed down by a number of local bishops, who had the pillar demolished behind his back. Gregory of Tours puts these words in his mouth: 'I wept bitterly, but I have never dared to set up again the pillar which they broke, for that would be to disobey the commands of bishops.'[19]

The threats to a sixth-century bishop's spiritual authority are clear from the pages of Gregory's *History*; the threats to his secular authority are less certain, particularly in the case of threats from the citizens themselves. Early Merovingian towns could be as unruly and difficult to manage as late Roman ones. They possessed, of course, the same traditions, and even some of the same institutions. Stray texts refer to the continuing existence of *curiae* or town councils, and of municipal archives in which land transactions have to be registered. In Tours and Angers the *curia* seems to meet in or near the forum; in Clermont it met in the *mercatus publicus*, or market-place. The citizens often seem to have had minds of their own. They took action together with, or occasionally against, the king. They took sides in civil wars, expelling counts who did not please them and raising an army to defend themselves against invaders. They were even prepared to take the initiative themselves in attacking a neighbouring *civitas* that was ruled by a different Merovingian king, taking the opportunity, perhaps, of settling old scores. At the time of Chilperic, the men of Bourges decided to invade the Touraine; soon after Chilperic's death the men of Orleans allied with Blois to attack Châteaudun and Chartres. Townsfolk could also react violently to threats to their own well-being. When Chilperic decided to raise new taxes, some people left their cities to avoid payment; but the citizens of Limoges held a meeting and decided to kill the tax-collector. It was the bishop who saved the tax-collector, but he could not prevent the citizens from burning the tax registers. This revolt was savagely crushed by Chilperic, whose men tortured a number of the town's priests, suspecting them of being ring-leaders.

Who are these politically active *cives*? There is little doubt that they were men of some importance, for not every inhabitant of a town was a *civis*. Some may have been merchants. Other were perhaps men whose social importance rested mainly on their landed properties, yet for whom the town was still a social and political centre in the sixth century, and who still possessed houses in the town. We do hear of aristocrats, both Gallo-Roman and Frankish, who own, buy and let out houses in towns in the seventh century. King Guntram was entertained by the citizens of Orleans in their own houses; these could hardly have been hovels.

When Gregory of Tours persuaded Childebert II's tax-collectors that Tours was immune from taxation (King Chlothar I had burnt the tax registers, in honour of St Martin), to what extent was he following a lead set by his citizens? The balance of power in towns, the tensions which split towns apart, the disputes between citizens and bishops, usually lie below the surface of our sources. There are a few exceptions. Desiderius, treasurer to King Dagobert, returned at his mother's pleading to his native city of Cahors in 630, to succeed his brother as bishop, after the latter had been murdered by a faction in the town. Leudegar, nephew of Bishop Dido of Poitiers, came to Autun to be bishop after rival factions, apparently led by two local aristocratic groups, had fought over the bishopric, leading to murder and the flight of the murderer. It was no doubt during the period of episcopal vacancies that latent tensions within cities came to the surface; we hear of some of these from Gregory, including the detailed story of the rivalry of Cato and Cautinus for the see of Clermont. Once elected, a bishop had to be a skilful politician. His spiritual authority and charity towards the poor were not enough to win him support; if we are to judge from a few oft-cited cases, he may have had to use his own revenues for the benefit of the community in other ways, building defences, hospitals and bridges, as well as churches and monasteries. Sidonius of Mainz and Felix of Nantes both undertook engineering works to save their city from flooding by the Rhine or Loire rivers. Desideratus of Verdun borrowed seven thousand gold pieces from Theudebert in order to restore the commercial life of his town; he distributed the money, and was able eventually to recover it and offer to return it to the king with interest. (A number of church councils attack bishops and priests who demand interest on loans to citizens, but this clearly relates to their own capital, not the king's.) Bishop Desiderius of Cahors (630–55) seems to have been a public benefactor on a huge scale; no doubt he was determined to avoid his brother's fate. His buildings, defence works and engineering projects have to be seen in the light of the attitude of the early Middle Ages towards wealth. There were few outlets for investment, and wealth could not simply be hoarded, for that would be to court the disapproval and envy of one's neighbours. A secular aristocrat could distribute his wealth to his kin and his followers; all a bishop could do was to become a public benefactor.

Another potential leader of the *civitas*-community was the count. The origins of the office lay back in the Roman period: the *comites* were the 'friends' of the Emperor, his closest associates and agents. In the late Empire there were different types of *comes*; the ancestor of the Merovingian and medieval count was the *comes civitatis*, the count of the city, of whom several are known from imperial times in Gaul. Under the Merovingians the institution became very widespread, although perhaps not universal. In the north-east, where the territories of the *civitates* tended to be larger and where the Roman administration had suffered more in the fifth century, there might be two or more counts in a *civitas*; in that area the word *grafio* was often used rather than *comes*, a word unknown in the south or west, but used in the intervening territory, such as in Paris or Sens, for an official subordinate to the count. Other such officials were the *vicarius* and the *tribunus*, who probably controlled individual regions or *pagi* within the *civitas*. The Merovingian count was the representative of the king in the *civitas*, and combined within himself most of the king's functions; in particular he was the chief judge in the territory, and commanded the troops levied there.

Gregory of Tours is our main source for the counts of the sixth century, particularly those of his native Clermont and his residence, Tours. Seventh-century sources, largely hagiographical, tell us little;

a late seventh-century collection of legal formulae edited by Marculf mentions them frequently, so presumably they continued to exist in many towns. The most striking feature of the comital organisation revealed by Gregory is that south of the Loire the bulk of the counts came from the old Roman aristocracy. All the counts of Clermont were from the senatorial families of the Auvergne except one, Becco, a Frank appointed by Theuderic in the wake of the revolt of Clermont in 532. Another outsider was Leudast, Count of Tours, the son of a slave of Roman origins who worked in the royal vineyards on an island off the coast of Poitou. His rapacity, arrogance and cruelty did not make his relations with Bishop Gregory easy, nor did his alliance with Riculf, who was angling for Gregory's bishopric. They plotted together, and caused Gregory to be brought before King Chilperic; he cleared himself by oaths to the apparent satisfaction of all, and the downfall of Leudast and Riculf followed not long after. Such conflicts between bishop and count must have been unusual, for mostly the count was not an outsider. Counts often had close relations – indeed, blood relations – with bishops, either of their own or of neighbouring towns. Nicetius, Count of Dax, for instance, was brother to Bishop Rusticus of Aire, and then became Bishop of Dax himself. In such circumstances, neither count nor bishop is simply a representative of the interests of outside and higher institutions such as the church or the monarchy; their actions are determined much more by local and family interests. As is well known, this arrangement was regularised by Chlothar II's edict of 614. 'In no place shall a judge be appointed who comes from another province or region.' Often seen as a charter for local aristocratic ambitions, it was certainly not intended as anything of the kind, for the clause goes on: 'so that if he oppresses any individual of whatever class, restitution can be made out of his property, as is prescribed by the law'.[20] A *iudex* or judge (a term almost certainly including the *comes civitatis*) could evade any claim for compensation from oppressed citizens if his property was in a distant *civitas*. This decree was part and parcel of Chlothar's attempts to restore justice and order to his newly won kingdom. He also declared in 614 that if the king was absent it was the bishop who should punish the unjust *iudex*; this was in harmony with the Church's own feelings, for the council of Tours in 567 had urged that bishops should excommunicate oppressive judges if they did not heed episcopal reprimands.

Theoretically, therefore, the bishop was responsible for the actions of the count in the *civitas*. The logical result of this idea was, perhaps, for the bishop to replace the count altogether, or at least to control him. This may have happened in a number of cases in the seventh century; in the time of Dagobert, for instance, we are told that the bishops of Tours were given the privilege of appointing the count. And in the *Lives* of seventh-century bishops there seem to be other indications that bishops had taken on themselves comital functions, in the apparent absence of any count. Bishops repaired the town walls; Bobo of Autun had *dominium*, lordship, within the town, and Desiderius of Châlons had *principatum*. But what is happening is not so much the replacement of the count by the bishop, as the removal of the count to the countryside, which left the bishop in control of the town and its environs. In Trier we hear of the bishop actually driving the count out of the town; in other towns it was probably a slow process, brought by an increasing tendency of counts to reside on their rural estates. No doubt there were regional variations. When the power of the Merovingian kings began to wane, officials such as counts and bishops may have survived in areas such as Aquitaine and Provence, but under the control of local authorities and not the king. In north-east Gaul, the kings or their Mayors of the Palace were again able in most cases to preserve the earlier pattern. It is in the area in between, in towns like Tours, Orleans, Auxerre, Autun and Lyons, that we seem to find bishops setting themselves up as semi-independent leaders of their *civitates*. It is the same zone which provides us with evidence of the survival of Roman town councils, with written collections of legal formulae, and with Latin inscriptions: in short, the area where, thanks partly to political stability and the continuing dominance of the Gallo-Roman aristocracy, Roman ideals and institutions lasted longest. This situation continued until the Carolingian Mayor Charles Martel set about the restoration of the unity of the Frankish kingdom in the early eighth century.

In the course of the seventh century came an increasing laicisation of the episcopate; this was not so much the result of the recruitment of laymen, which was already common practice, as of the failure of these laymen to change their life-styles and ambitions upon their consecration. The canons decreed by one of the very last Merovingian church councils, at St-Jean-de-Losne in 673–5, give some idea of the state of the church. The first canon enjoined churchmen to live according to canon laws; the second forbade them to carry weapons; the fifteenth to hunt. It was prohibited for two bishops to have the same town – perhaps a situation resulting from an agreement to share diocesan revenues. Bishops were forbidden to appoint a layman as archpriest, the man who deputised for a bishop (perhaps a layman himself) in spiritual matters. Two canons mentioned with disapproval the custom whereby bishops named or appointed their successor, a custom known from earliest Merovingian times, but perhaps becoming increasingly associated with the tendency for bishoprics to be hereditary within a particular aristocratic family. Milo of Trier was, for the reforming Bishop Boniface, a West Saxon, a typical example: an Austrasian aristocrat whose father and uncle had both been bishops of Trier before him, and who acquired the bishopric of Rheims in addition to that of Trier. Such pluralism was a further sign of change, reaching its zenith (or nadir) in the person of Charles Martel's nephew Hugo, who enjoyed the revenues which flowed in from his three bishoprics of Rouen, Bayeux and Paris as well as from his abbacies of St-Wandrille and Jumièges. 'The Franks', wrote Boniface to Pope Zacharias in 742, 'have not held a council for more than eighty years, nor have they had an archbishop or established or restored anywhere the canon law of the Church. For the most part the episcopal sees in cities are in the hands of greedy laymen or are exploited by adulterous and vicious clergymen and publicans for secular purposes. . . . Certain bishops are to be found among them who, although they deny that they are fornicators or adulterers, are drunkards and shiftless men, given to hunting and to fighting in the army like soldiers and by their own hands shedding blood, whether of heathens or Christians.'[21]

By the time of Boniface, the *civitas*-capitals were in most cases aristocratic strongholds, inhabited mainly by the secular or ecclesiastical dependents of the individual lord. *Civitas*-territories were perhaps partly under that lord's control, but in most cases had probably dissolved into a number of separate lordships. The old *civitas*-community had vanished; the consciousness of belonging to a separate community which had held the inhabitants of a *civitas* together from pre-Roman times down to the sixth or seventh century had gone. In some cases deliberate administrative reorganisations may have been responsible. Thus, in the sixth century the *civitates* of Rheims, Laon (once part of Rheims), Châlons and at times Troyes had been grouped together as a duchy of Campania (Champagne): Gregory of Tours only once spoke of the men of Rheims as *Remenses*, for the inhabitants of the area were normally called, and perhaps thought of themselves as, *Campenses*. But in general the *civitas*-communities disappeared because of the dissolution of the *civitas* into smaller units. Sometimes this was the result of deliberate administrative action. Thus in the north and east of Gaul in particular, where the size of the *civitas*-territories was larger, the *civitas* split into a number of *pagi* (Gn. *Gaue*). The *civitas* of Trier was divided into four separate *pagi*, each of which was independent of the *civitas*-capital of Trier itself. Local aristocratic families founded monasteries within these new *pagi*, such as Echternach and Prüm, which served as new religious and ecclesiastical foci.

The unity of the *civitas* all over Gaul was further weakened by the extension of 'immunity'. A grant of immunity giving freedom from interference by public officials may have been a legal extension of the privileges possessed in late Roman times by imperial estates, and was used by Frankish kings from Clovis onwards. The *praeceptio* issued by Chlothar II forbade royal agents to demand payment of taxes and other public charges from those who had been given grants of immunity from earlier kings, while his *edictum* spoke of immunity being granted to both *potentes* (lay aristocrats) and *ecclesiae*. It is these grants to *ecclesiae*, especially cathedral churches and monasteries, of which we know most. The fourth formula in Marculf's collection expresses what was meant in practice: 'King X has conceded to Bishop X a total immunity for the rural properties of his church X, those that it possesses now and those that later god-fearing men may give it, so that no public agent may enter to hear legal proceedings, to take the peace-money [*fredus*], to procure lodgings or victuals, or to take sureties or, for one reason or another, to use force towards the subordinates of the Church or to demand payments.'[22] From the eighth century onwards, dozens of similar grants are known, and many more must have existed. The existence of large no-go areas within the kingdom was obviously a threat to its unity and stability, however much it may have relieved the immediate problems of administration, for the immunist was himself responsible for law and order within his territory. Charlemagne legislated to make this more effective. He prescribed that immunists had to deliver brigands to the count, and laid down the conditions under which a count might enter an immunity. And under Charlemagne too appears the *advocatus* (Fr. *avoué*, Gn. *Vogt*), the appointed representative of the immunity in any legal situation. Charlemagne made him responsible for the handing over of suspected criminals to the count, and for ensuring that those within the immunity fulfilled their military obligations to the king. The immunity possessed by many or most cathedral churches in the seventh century probably helped many bishops to consolidate their power within the *civitas*; immunities in the ninth century, both ecclesiastical and lay (and lay aristocrats, in the role of appointed *advocati*, were often able to control ecclesiastical immunities too), were an important factor in the collapse of royal power in Gaul. But from our immediate point of view, the immunity was another element tending towards the break-up of the Roman *civitas*-territory into a mosaic of separate jurisdictions and lordships.

Lords and Men in the Carolingian Town

THE reforms of Charlemagne did little to restore the unity of the *civitas*-community. Certainly the institution of count was revived, and frequently his jurisdiction corresponded to that of the diocese and hence the *civitas*, particularly in southern Gaul. But his power did not rest on the sense of common identity of inhabitants, nor were the conditions right for the revival of such a sense. Community feelings were restricted to smaller groups: to villages, or to individual lordships. Those living on a monastic estate, for instance, no doubt felt themselves primarily to be the men of the monastery, of the abbot or, indeed, of the patron-saint: thus, the serfs of St-Germain-des-Prés were described as the *homines sancti Germani*, the men of St Germanus. But there was one heir to the *civitas*-community, the *civitas* in its narrowest sense – the town. It is in the Carolingian period that we see the origins of the medieval town, a juridical organisation distinct from the surrounding countryside and having its own institutions and self-conscious identity. The town underwent a distinct revival during the reign of Charlemagne. It became again, with the reinstitution of counts and the reform of the Church, a centre of political and religious life, and must also have benefited considerably from the general peace and prosperity of the decades on either side of the year 800. Large-scale building programmes for new cathedrals and for the complexes to house cathedral canons must have altered the physical appearance of many towns, particularly when, as happened in a number of instances, the need both for space and for building materials prompted bishops to ask for royal permission to demolish the old Roman walls. New churches were added both in the centre and on the outskirts of towns. By the end of the eighth century, for instance, there were at least forty churches in and immediately around Metz, including the church which sheltered the relics of the first Carolingian family saint, Bishop Arnulf.

Independent urban institutions naturally took a long time to develop. For most of the Carolingian period towns were controlled by one or more lords. By failing to remove, and indeed by extending, ecclesiastical immunities and privileges while at the same time reintroducing counts into all or most Gallic towns, Charlemagne set the scene for endless disputes over lordship within the town. By the tenth century these disputes had ended, mostly, with the victory of one or other party. In Rheims, for instance, we hear of no count at all after the mid-ninth century: the archbishop and the *advocatus* administer the lands of the church in Rheims, that is, most of the town. According to Flodoard, the tenth-century historian of Rheims, in 940 King Louis IV ceded to the powerful archbishop the *comitatus*, the title and regalian rights of the count. Such cessions came elsewhere as a royal reward. In Cambrai, where count and bishop had shared the lands and revenues of the town, it came from Otto I in 948, after the count had been involved in a conspiracy. In Langres it came in 887, when Charles the Fat gave the bishop a diploma emphasising the important role of the bishop in the defence of the town against the Vikings and mentioning the count's inaction: in 967 the bishop was given full comital rights. Sometimes such cessions to the bishop were pious acts. Vienne was a royal city, the residence of the kings of Upper Burgundy; in 1011 King Rudolf III gave the lordship and countship of the town to his wife, who subsequently donated them to the archbishop. Occasionally the process was gradual. At Beauvais it was completed by 1015, when Count Odo of Blois, whose power had been gradually whittled away by the bishop, ceded most of his remaining goods, revenues and rights; in Noyon the bishop emerged supreme after he had succeeded by a trick in taking and destroying the tower held by the royal castellan.

In all these cases, mostly in the north of Gaul, the bishop emerged as the lord of the *civitas*; it was against the bishop that the citizens would have to fight in the eleventh and twelfth century for their privileges and freedom. In the south it was more frequently the count who emerged as lord, or his subordinate the viscount. (In southern Gaul the early Carolingians had set up a number of large regional commands, notably that under the count of Toulouse, and the individual towns were frequently under *vicecomites*, or viscounts.) Sometimes the lay authorities gained possession not only of the town, but of the rights and revenues of the bishopric too: they won the *episcopatus*, just as northern bishops frequently gained the *comitatus*. In 990 the will of William, Count of Béziers and Agde, gave to his daughter Garsinde the *civitas* of Béziers '*cum suo episcopatu*' and to his wife Arsinde the city of Agde, also with its episcopal rights. Garsinde married Raymond of Carcassonne, and both bishoprics passed to him. In 1059 the widow of Garsinde's son held the *civitates* of Carcassonne, Agde and Béziers, with the bishoprics. The viscounts of Marseilles had the bishopric in their hands from 965 to 1073. The counts of Tours were assisted in retaining predominance in their town by monopolising, not the bishopric, but the equally wealthy monastery of St Martin; the counts of neighbouring Poitiers were similarly abbots of St-Hilaire.

These developments owed much to the major upheavals of the ninth and early tenth centuries: barbarian invasions and civil disorders. Towns once again became of major military importance, and living in a large community behind walls again seemed of benefit. Old Roman walls were restored, and new fortifications erected around suburban settlements and monasteries. Occasionally the political disturbances proved too much for towns. The Saracen attacks on Marseilles reduced the population to a small community sheltering within a small citadel inside the walls, and the bishops themselves fled. When the town was revived in the late tenth century, it was around the monastery of St-Victor, not in the old *civitas*. The citadel in Nîmes was the Roman amphitheatre, already used as the residence of the count before the Saracen attacks. The Saracens left Aix-en-Provence a field of ruins, with its archbishop, count and community of canons each occupying a self-contained fortress within the former town, and similar fragmentation of the urban structure occurred elsewhere in the south. When the first documents relating to town lordship appear in the south in the twelfth century, knights are to be seen possessing single towers or sections of wall, like the castellans who each held one tower on the walls of Carcassonne, or the thirty-one knights of the Arena Castle, the amphitheatre, of Nîmes. But over most of Gaul the town survived intact; there the most significant result of the ninth-century troubles was the appearance of the 'double town'.

The area enclosed by the hastily constructed walls of the third or early fourth century town was often tiny. The average was about fifteen hectares, with towns like Trier and Toulouse leading the field (with 285 and 90 hectares) and others such as Clermont and Albi (with 2.95 and 1.30 hectares) being among the smallest. If a town was large, it was unlikely to become a 'double town'. But the majority of towns must have become heavily overcrowded in the course of the ninth century, with their more grandiose ecclesiastical buildings and the crowds of refugees from Viking or Saracen attacks, including whole communities of monks and nuns. Indeed, long before the ninth-century invasions, or even before the fifth-century invasions, settlements had grown up outside the town walls. Usually the kernel of such settlements was a church or a monastery: it was around such kernels that secondary urban settlements gradually evolved, sometimes to rival or even replace the Roman primary settlement. At Bonn, for instance, the church of St Peter within the old Roman *castrum* (in the area now called Dietkirchen) remained an important ecclesiastical centre, but settlement spread outside the *castrum*, around the church of St Remigius and in the *vicus Bonnensis* (or *on* it, for *vicus* means both village and street), and around the church of Sts Cassius and Florentius, the property of the archbishops of Cologne. The walls of the Roman *castrum* still stood, and it was still called *castrum Bonna* in the ninth century. But the real centre of the town, the houses and the market, stood outside the *castrum*, and by the early eleventh century the move was complete: the extramural settlement was now called *Bonna* and the settlement within the *castrum* referred to as '*in suburbio Bonnae*'. A similar shift of settlement, though probably much less gradual, occurred at Lyons, where the new site was in the river valley beneath the hill on which the Roman town stood.

In a true 'double town' the old settlement survived. Classic examples are Tours and Limoges. In both cases the burial place of a celebrated saint in a cemetery outside the town walls became the centre of the second settlement. The walls of Tours enclosed a fairly restricted portion of the earlier Roman town, including the forum and amphitheatre. This area did not, perhaps, prosper in the post-Roman period: recent excavations by M. Galinié have found late Roman houses and shops within the walls which were left to decay, until disturbed by rebuilding in the late ninth or tenth centuries. But in Tours as elsewhere the Romans had built their walls in the centre of the town: settlements survived outside the walls, and that around the tomb and monastery of St Martin did prosper. Charles the Bald gave that settlement a series of privileges, laying down the exceptionally heavy fine of 600 solidi for those who encroached upon them. He called the settlement a *burgus*, a word which (probably fortuitously) first occurred with this meaning in a collection of legal formulae drawn up in Tours in the early eighth century. In the ninth century it is used of extramural settlements at Lyons, Dijon and elsewhere. The inhabitants of the *burgus* at Tours certainly traded, in wine and other goods, but a *burgus* was not necessarily a commercial centre: it was distinguished from a *civitas* or an *urbs* rather, according to the Italian writer Liutprand, by its absence of walls. The word for an inhabitant of a *burgus* appears first in a charter of 1007; it shows the importance of *burgi* such as that of Tours that later on *burgensis* (burgher or bourgeois) comes to be used indiscriminately of the inhabitants of *civitates* or *burgi*, meaning simply 'town-dweller'.

The *burgus* of Tours prospered, thanks to its privileges, despite Viking attack. In 919 the monastery was rebuilt and fortified. It now appeared in the sources as a *castrum*, not a *burgus*, and came to be called Châteauneuf, to distinguish it from the old château, the *civitas*. In the 940s a third settlement around the church of St Julian between the *castrum* and the *civitas* was granted similar privileges by the king, and construction continued, so that the three settlements, all juridically separate, physically merged together. Economically the settlement around St Martin was the most successful; in the eleventh century there were bankers and cloth merchants there. Finally, a third *burgus* grew up, by the river Loire. The four settlements only came together into some sort of unity with the building of one set of walls in 1356. But in the ninth and tenth centuries the settlements lived amicably enough together, for there was only one dominant lord, the count and abbot being the same person. It was very different in nearby Limoges. There the church of St Martial, converted into a monastery in 848, was the nucleus of the new settlement. It was fortified: it is known as a *castellum* in the tenth century, and a *castrum* and *burgus* in the eleventh. The viscount resided there, but it was perhaps the wealthy abbot of St Martial who was responsible for the fortifications: in the tenth century, we are told, Abbot Stephen wanted to call the *burgus* Stephanopolis! As in Tours, the *burgus* was economically more important than the *civitas*: it was there, later in the Middle Ages, that the celebrated Limoges enamelware was produced. Above the *burgus*, the *civitas* too was fortified, and under its own lord, the bishop. The two parts of Limoges, under their different lords, remained legally distinct and frequently in conflict (to the extent of open warfare in the eleventh century) until October 1792.

The new 'monastic' *burgus*, when it evolved outside small towns such as Tours, Limoges, Périgueux or Arras, often came to equal or dominate the earlier *civitas*. *Burgi* are found outside larger towns too, such as Bourges, Poitiers, Narbonne or Toulouse, but these were never more than outlying suburbs, for there was room for the expansion of the clerical and commercial population within the Roman walls of the *civitas*. In the case of small towns the new *burgus* inevitably became a commercial centre: it was only outside the crowded *civitas* that space could be found to hold markets (from which the monastery or church could derive considerable profits) and to house the permanent and itinerant population which markets attracted. Merchants must have been important figures in these thriving new communities. The new settlement across the Meuse from Verdun was called in the tenth century simply *claustra negotiatorum*, the 'merchant enclosure'.

The great Belgian historian Henri Pirenne found it difficult to see Carolingian towns, inhabited largely by clerics, as 'real' towns. But those towns, particularly when they were also of military importance, needed a fairly large population, if nothing else of servants and suppliers of essential and luxury goods; and the economic growth of towns, which Pirenne dated to the eleventh century, can now be seen as a much more gradual process: the Viking and Saracen invasions temporarily interrupted a process already well under way. An accretion of population around an urban ecclesiastical settlement could, of course, occur around a non-urban ecclesiastical centre as well; a number of the greater Merovingian and Carolingian rural monasteries do indeed form the kernel of later medieval towns. A classic case is that of St-Omer in Picardy. The monastery founded by Audomarus at Sithiu near the Channel coast in the seventh century had four churches a century later; the last Merovingian king died there in 752, a year after his deposition. We hear of leather and cloth manufacture there in the same century, and a document of 742 speaks of its *populus*. In the ninth century there were 130 monks, and churches, hospitals, schools and workshops, and an *advocatus* was appointed in 839 to defend its 'innumerable multitude' of people. There was a market there in the pre-Viking period, and in 891 the settlement was defended successfully from Viking attack by a population of '*nobiliores*, *inferiores* and *pauperes*'. By 954 there were sufficient inhabitants for there to be a disturbance involving 'a multitude of people'; later there are mentions of *burgenses*, a guild, a fair – it is a medieval town. Sometimes the development of such towns can only be surmised, through lack of evidence. The nearby little town of Montreuil-sur-Mer, for instance, betrays its origin only through its name. It first appears in the sources as a castle called *Monasteriolum* – the little monastery – which successfully resists Viking attacks, and in the tenth century it was already a settlement which housed merchants who traded overseas.

Roman settlements other than *civitates* had also grown into towns by the tenth century. Some were already small towns in the Roman period; only a legal distinction separated a large *castrum* from a small *civitas*. Gregory of Tours' famous description of Dijon, with its high stone walls and thirty-three towers, ends with the comment, 'Why it is not called a *civitas* I do not know.'[23] A few such *castra* were elevated to the ranks of *civitates* in the Merovingian period, such as Carcassonne and Laon. But a more frequent type of settlement was the Roman *vicus*, a village or small market town. There were probably large numbers of these which survived the Germanic invasions. The Basse-Auvergne, in the best known Merovingian *civitas*, contained at least thirteen in Merovingian times, all of which were to become small market towns in the later Middle Ages. We have already met the *vicus* outside the walls of Bonn; similar *vici* are known in Merovingian times outside such towns as Paris and Clermont. The most celebrated of the Merovingian *vici* was Quentovic. It lay by the Channel coast south of Boulogne, and in the seventh century shared the economic prosperity of other *vicus* or *wik* settlements overseas: Hamwich (Southampton), Ipswich, Eoforwic (York) or Schleswig. Already by 670 Quentovic had become the natural port through which English travellers came to the Continent, and it was one of the most prolific mints in the kingdom. In 779 a diploma of Charlemagne mentioned the five great customs-collecting offices in his kingdom, situated on the five main entrance routes into northern Gaul: Rouen, Amiens, Quentovic, Maastricht and Dorestad.

By the early ninth century, at least, Dorestad had taken over Quentovic's role as the most important of these trading places. Recent excavations of this *vicus*, near the modern Wijk-bei-Duurstede, have shown that it was no mere seasonal trading post. Wharves lined the banks of the Rhine on to which boats could be dragged; behind the wharves lay rows of tightly packed houses in the long narrow plots which are so familiar from later medieval towns; further away from the river are more scattered houses, in small pieces of land surrounded by a fence: these seem to have belonged to the families who worked in the fields around Dorestad and supplied the town with its food. There may have been several thousand inhabitants in the early ninth century, among whom were craftsmen in the various industries for which archaeological evidence is present: cloth manufacture, metal working (including the production of weapons and jewellery), shipbuilding and so on. Few pots were made in the village; most that were used seem to have been produced in towns and villages further up the Rhine. The inhabitants probably traded in pottery, glass from the Cologne region, stone querns from the Mayen quarries, and other goods of which no archaeological traces remain, such as slaves. Through Dorestad no doubt came imports across the North Sea, which were carried into the heart of the Carolingian Empire up the Rhine and Moselle. In summer the town was probably busy with the presence of merchants from England, Frisia and Scandinavia – until the mid-ninth century, when the activity of the latter (i.e. of the Vikings, 'those who frequent *vici*', according to one etymology) put an end to Dorestad's prosperity. Frisians were particularly active in trade in the eighth and early ninth centuries: they had colonies in York and London, and in Mainz, where their quarter was destroyed by fire in 886, and Worms, where they were responsible for the maintenance of one section of the defences.

The economic vitality of the lower Rhine and Meuse valleys, so obvious in the twelfth and thirteenth centuries in the heyday of the Flemish woollen towns, had a long history, in which the career of Dorestad from *c.* 700 to *c.* 850 was just a brief episode. Verdun was a commercial centre in the sixth century, and, judging from the number of moneyers at work, so were towns like Maastricht, Huy, Dinant and Namur in the seventh. In the ninth century great names like Bruges, Ghent, Antwerp and Deventer made their appearance, and became important centres even before the end of the tenth century. An Arab trader of Jewish extraction who visited Mainz in 973 was amazed at the scale of commercial operation there; he found a great variety of spices, including pepper, ginger and cloves, and was surprised to find a coin minted in a Central Asian state. Some of this trade may indeed have been in Jewish hands. Although there had been Jewish communities in some towns since the Roman period, it is in the ninth century, for the first time since the sixth, that we come across references to their trading and money-lending activities. Some towns had their Jewish quarters: in Cologne it was near the Cathedral, and in Vienne it is called the '*burgus publicus Ebreorum*'. It is in the late tenth century too that we come across the first clear traces of the anti-Semitism which blackens the history of so many later medieval towns. In 992 the Jews of Le Mans were attacked, on the pretext that they had stuck pins into a waxen image of the count; not long afterwards there are the first accusations of ritual murders of Christians levelled against Jews in northern Gaul. Southern Gallic society was perhaps more tolerant of them, although life was still far from easy. Adhémar of Chabannes tells us that in 1018 the old custom of hitting a Jew in church during the Holy Week ceremonies of Toulouse had ended in tragedy: the Jew was struck so savagely that his skull was broken and his brains spilled out. Anti-Semitism is in part perhaps a measure of the increased economic importance of Jews, and their own economic activity a measure of the acceleration of trade and industry; so that the fact that many Jews in Provençal towns were still involved in landed property rather than trade in the eleventh century has been taken as a sign that economic recovery in Provence was later than elsewhere.

Our knowledge of the internal life of the Gallic towns of the ninth and tenth centuries is very limited. There is mostly only the odd reference in narrative sources or legislation, and such references are not always clear. The pastoral letter of Archbishop Wulfad of Bourges (*c.* 879), for instance, complains about the use of false measures by merchants and shopkeepers, and of usury, and of sworn 'conspiracies'. Are these 'conspiracies' the first manifestations of medieval guilds or of civic independence? Such guilds do appear in the sources from the very beginning of the eleventh century, but very probably originated earlier. We learn something about the merchant guild of Tiel, the prosperous trading town which succeeded Dorestad, from the complaints of Albert of Metz (*c.* 1020): the guildsmen lived, he said, according to their own law, being able to declare themselves free of debt by means of an oath without the necessity of an ordeal, and they had a common fund which they used to finance great banquets. The somewhat later statutes of the St-Omer merchants' guild laid down strict rules for peace-keeping at such drinking-sessions, and specified that any funds left over should be used for maintaining streets or fortifications. Guildsmen were pledged to help individual members in financial or legal difficulties; the guild acted as a substitute kinship group, safeguarding the individual in a situation where he might be travelling far from his homeland. With the guild we have a new kind of community, not unconnected with the movement over the whole of Gaul in the eleventh and twelfth centuries towards urban self-government: a community independent of any lord, distinct from the surrounding countryside.

It is again only at the very end of our period that we can detect the origins of urban liberties. One element in those origins was connected with the growth of new religious ideas in the late tenth century, specifically those created by the Peace of God and Truce of God movements: the idea that peace and co-operation were essential to the Christian way of life, and that the Church should act to enforce such peace. Communities called *burgi* or *salvitates* were founded, particularly in the south-west and south of Gaul, intended to be islands of peace in a violent and warring society. One of the earliest relevant documents concerns the *burgus* built together with a monastery by Fulk of Anjou at Beaulieu in 1007: 'Whoever inhabits this *burgus* shall never be charged with the infamy of being a serf, but all its inhabitants will be free.'[24] Elsewhere too new burghal foundations were influenced by ideas of freedom; comital officials were not allowed in, and the *burgus* possessed its own rights of refuge and asylum. Older established towns had to fight for their freedoms, against count or bishop, or else offer their lord large sums of money, as the citizens of Huy did in 1066. We have come a long way from the loose semi-tribal community of the *civitas*, with its urban core linked closely to the countryside by economic and personal ties: the medieval town was a much more self-conscious community, with its own leaders and policies, its own economic and legal personality, and rights and privileges which were jealously protected by the citizens. In a society in which, from Merovingian times onwards, the bonds of communal and family loyalty were increasingly being overlaid by loyalty to a lord, the town, often still sheltering within its Roman walls, offered a refuge and some measure of freedom.

3. Family, Kin and Law

THE family was the basic social unit in post-Roman Gaul, as in almost all human societies; as modern anthropologists have shown, the study of the way in which a society organises its structures of kinship and marriage, out of the immense variety of possibilities, is fundamental for an understanding of how the whole society works. Anthropologists have expended much energy in the investigation of kinship terminology, which can often reveal much about the network of personal relationships. But they have usually been studying static societies, or ones unaffected by the impact of western culture. Ideas about the family and the kin in the early Middle Ages were rapidly changing, as Germanic ideas of the extended kinship group with well-defined legal and social responsibilities met the Roman concept of the individual with considerable personal freedom irrespective of family obligations, and both Roman and Germanic concepts began to take account of Christian ideas of morality. Kinship terminology in this world in which Frankish and Burgundian met Gallo-Roman, classical and Biblical Latin, was likewise in a state of such confusion that no certain historical conclusions can be reached. But it is worthwhile pointing to two Latin words, whose usage begins to introduce us to the alien world of the early medieval family: *familia* and *parentes*. The first meant the household, including blood-relations, dependants and slaves; it also meant the serfs who worked for an individual lord; and it was used of that Christian substitute for the natural family, the monastic community. *Parentes* are the relations or the kin; the parents themselves are not distinguished by a collective noun.

We can obviously know very little about family life from our sources – most of which, indeed, were written by celibates. The law-codes and other legislative material give us some idea of how some people thought certain operations within the family ought to be organised – in particular marriage and inheritance. The narrative sources are most informative on the aristocratic family. The great bulk of the population lived in the countryside and worked the land as tenant farmers, freed men and slaves, and about these we can know very little. When peasants appear in the literary sources they appear as stereotypes, not as individuals. There are only three classes of people in the sermons of Caesarius of Arles, each revealed because of their sins: the clerics, whose sins are more regrettable than those of others because of their status; the merchants, a fairly small group distinguished, predictably, by their avarice; and the lustful, drunken and irreligious peasants. Leprosy in children was a sign of parental sin, and for Caesarius the fact that most lepers were peasants merely proved the inherent viciousness of the class. For the literate aristocracy of Merovingian Gaul, peasants were virtually a separate race.[1] There was a cultural divide, a linguistic divide, but, just as important, a religious and an economic divide. Sin and paganism flourished among the *pagani*, the country-dwellers. St Wandregisel, abbot of Fontanella (St-Wandrille), once came to a place 'which was in an area inhabited by peasants, who neither fear God nor do they respect any man'.[2] The clergy saw in the peasantry, if they cared to look, a record of their own failure: peasants were immoral, and they knew little about Christianity. It was not until the Carolingian period that the Church established a permanent organisation in the countryside in an attempt to ensure that baptism and some knowledge of Christianity were brought there. In the Merovingian period efforts were spasmodic. In the early seventh century Arnulf of Metz asked a beggar if he had been baptised: 'Who would be interested in giving such a benefit to a being as poor and miserable as I?'[3] This was not just a standing reproach to the Church. In a world with the widespread belief that God punished men for their sins *en masse*, by invasions or other means (a belief enshrined in the sixth-century legislation of the Emperor Justinian in Novel 77, which forbade swearing and blasphemy, 'since it is owing to offences of this kind that famines, earthquakes and pestilences occur'[4]) the existence within the community of semi-pagan and immoral peasants could be seen as a distinct social and political danger.

Clerical and aristocratic antagonism towards peasants, which so restricts our own knowledge of them, derived also from the degraded condition in which many of them seem to have lived in post-Roman Gaul. Famines, caused by appallingly low crop-yields, severe winters and plagues of locusts occur frequently in the narrative sources, often with lurid descriptions of the degradation involved, including cannibalism. Gregory of Tours described a famine in 585. 'Many people made bread with grape-pips or hazel catkins, while others dried the roots of ferns, pounded them and added a little flour. Some cut green corn-stalks and did the same..... Vast numbers starved to death for lack of food. The merchants exploited them harshly, to the point of selling a single measure of corn or a half-measure of wine for a third of a solidus. They reduced the poor to slavery in order to give them a little food.'[5] A legal formula of the seventh century shows that this was not just rhetoric: 'Everyone knows that great poverty and very bad harvests oppress me, and I have nothing with which to feed or clothe myself. At my request you have given me some money and some clothes. As I cannot repay you, I cede to you my liberty: you may dispose of me as your other slaves.'[6] The Council of Paris in 614 took account of such cases, when it said that if men could recover what they had borrowed they could return to liberty. The poverty and precariousness of peasant life seem unrelieved in our period.[7] Certainly Gaul in these years saw the introduction of many agricultural improvements – including the wheeled plough, modern animal harness, the flail, the harrow, the greater use of more easily grown crops such as rye and oats, and three-year crop rotation – but few of these introductions, which probably spread only very slowly across Gaul, made any difference to the welfare of the peasants until after 1000, and then improved climatic conditions arguably had a greater effect than such improved techniques.

The only potential sources for the peasant family apart from legal material are Carolingian polyptychs, the estate-surveys which survive for a number of monastic estates of the ninth century. They give details of the names and status of numerous peasants, together with information on the size of their families and their land holdings, and on their rents and duties to their lord. The following example from the polyptych of the Parisian monastery of St-Germain-des-Prés, drawn up under the direction of Abbot Irminon between 825 and 829, gives an idea of the kind of information given: 'Nadalfridus, a slave (*servus*), and his wife, a free peasant (*colona*), Radohis by name, people of Saint Germanus, have with them five children, Constantinus, Adalbruc, Nadalia, Radohilt, Ratberga; they hold one free estate (*mansus*), having eight *bunuaria* in arable, two parts of an *aripennus* of vines, and two *aripenni* of meadow. They owe the same as above' (that is,certain payments for the abbey in silver or kind, and certain services on the monastic land: a *bunuarium*, Fr. bonnier, is about 1½ hectares, and an *aripennus*, Fr. arpent, is an area 120 feet x 120 feet).[8] We see a slave being married to a freewoman, a family all with Germanic names apart from the somewhat startling appearance of Constantine, holding land giving them a variety of produce. Such documents have been closely studied by economic historians, but still have much to offer the historian of the family. Recent research on this same polyptych, using statistical techniques, suggests the sort of surprising conclusions that might emerge from such work: that in the ninth century infanticide of female children by peasant families may have had a measurable effect on the balance of the population.[9]

It is hardly surprising, in the light of the above considerations, of the nature of the evidence, and of the predilections of many historians, that research into aristocratic families is much more advanced. Much has been done in particular by German scholars, such as Tellenbach and his pupils, particularly K. Schmid, and by K. F. Werner and other researchers at the Deutsches Historisches Institut in Paris. There, by the mid 1970s, some three hundred thousand cards had been assembled, with names and biographical details, if known, of individuals in the Frankish world before 1000.[10] Detailed research on this mass of data is only just beginning, and will undoubtedly yield important results. So far more work has been done for regions within modern Germany; no doubt many significant regional distinctions will emerge when more study has been done for different regions within France.

The first priority for an understanding of the political and social importance of family relationships is, of course, to determine precisely who was related to whom. The early Middle Ages were the period of the single name; family identity among aristocratic families was not established by a patronymic but by the use of particular 'leading' names. At their simplest, family relationships could be expressed by taking half the name of the father and half of the mother. Thus, theoretically, the children of a Sigibert and Brunechildis would be called Brunebert and Sigichildis. These polysyllabic Germanic names naturally lend themselves to such manipulations. But names which give equal weight to both maternal and paternal kin, which betray an essential element in the kinship structures of the age, are not specifically Germanic; the Gallo-Roman aristocracy employed a similar system of name-giving which, unlike the classical Latin system, allowed equal reference to both maternal and paternal sides of the family. Thus Gregory of Tours, Georgius Florentius by baptism, was named after his maternal grandfather and his father, and took the name Gregorius when he entered the Church, in honour of his mother's great-grandfather Gregory of Langres. By the seventh century, descendants of Gallo-Romans were very frequently using Germanic names in the Germanic fashion. As in Gregory's case, of course, names were not necessarily taken from the parents alone, but from other members of the family. Thus, when King Sigibert married the Visigothic princess Brunhild, their children in fact took names which all derived from *his* family; Childebert after his uncle, Ingund after his mother, and Chlodosind after his sister. In that way Sigibert emphasised the fact that all his children were members of the royal family. Aristocratic families seem to have had a number of 'leading-names' which were typical of the family and distinguished them from members of other well known families. No one in the seventh century, for example, would have called themselves Chlodowechus or Merowechus unless they were of the Merovingian family. From this stems the possibility of being able to reconstruct aristocratic familes and the relationship between them by an exhaustive study of surviving names. K. F. Werner's article on Carolingian aristocratic dynasties provides the best example of this methodology in English, and D. A. Bullough has provided the essential warning.[11] There are obvious dangers to the method, and few ways of avoiding them. For example, Werner has reconstructed an Austrasian family of Roman origins, active in politics from the sixth century to the ninth, characterised in particular by the use of the name Gundulf. But there are other Gundulfs in the sources who are not related; are all Werner's Gundulfs in Austrasia necessarily closely related?

The uncertainty is present even in the history of the best known aristocratic families of all, the Merovingians and the Carolingians. Charles the Great gave his eldest sons typical Carolingian names such as Charles and Pippin, but the twins who were born in 778 were called by Merovingian names – Lothar (Chlothar) and Louis (Chlodowechus, Clovis). Added to the fact that Charlemagne's maternal grandfather was a Heribert (possibly equivalent to the Merovingian name of Charibert) and that his ancestor Grimoald had a son called Childebert whom he managed to maintain on the throne for a few years, some historians have thought that the Carolingian family was somehow allied by marriage to the Merovingians. Eckhardt has constructed a genealogy on these lines, aided by later Carolingian traditions (which sought to justify their family's seizure of royal power from the Merovingians by pointing to a family connection) and by a good deal of guesswork. But it remains more likely that this Carolingian name-giving was a conscious political gesture on the part of Grimoald and Charlemagne, designed to persuade subjects who associated kingship with names that had a Merovingian ring to them of the legitimacy of their rule. Leading-names may therefore not express direct blood-relationships, but may still be of political importance. We shall have to wait for further research in this field, to learn not only about political relationships within the aristocracy, but also about the history of the aristocratic family. At the moment even the broad outlines are uncertain. Karl Schmid has suggested that at the beginning of the period, among the purely Frankish aristocracy at least, the sense of family was shifting and personal, ranging to relations on both mother's and father's sides, and that by the end of the period it was more fixed, with more stress being given to descent in the male line, and possessing sometimes a rudimentary form of 'surname', the name of the lordship or castle which was the basis of the family's power. But this is a hypothesis which does not hold good for the whole aristocracy of Gaul; the further south one travelled and, of course, the further down the social scale, the more it would be at variance with the facts.

The basic institution which formed and forms the family is marriage. Here in one area we can see the interpenetration of Germanic, Roman and Christian ideas in this period. In primitive Germanic society all women were in the *mundium*, guardianship or protection, of a man. Marriage involved the transfer of the woman's *mundium* from her father or another male kinsman to her husband: this was necessarily a matter for negotiation between the two families concerned, and may well frequently have been arranged by the parents of both bride and groom, for marriages could take place very early, and betrothals even earlier. The Germanic dowry may originally have been the price the groom's family paid for the bride; in later sources we see that the dowry could consist of houses, farms and slaves as well as other goods; the woman possessed certain rights over the dowry, which was her main support in widowhood. In addition, the husband customarily gave a morning-gift on the day after the wedding, perhaps a virginity-price in its origins. It may be that a marriage which took place without a dowry but with a morning-gift was, in secular terms, a legal marriage: Germanic legal historians call it a *Friedelehe* (friendship-marriage). Since no dowry was paid, it may be that the husband did not possess the *mundium* of his wife. Dissolution of the marriage, and the wife's return to her own family (who still possessed her *mundium*), was probably quite a simple process. The Church did not recognise such marriages, and declared any offspring illegitimate.

There are a number of ways in which the slow penetration of Christian ideas affected marriage in our period. The first area is that of degrees of relationship. As Pope Gregory II wrote to Boniface of Mainz, 'Strictly speaking, in so far as the parties know themselves to be related they ought not to be joined together. But some moderation is better than strictness of discipline, especially towards so uncivilised a people [as the Franks]: they may contract marriage after the fourth degree.'[12] The normal Roman prohibition was the seventh degree; but since the measurement of degrees of relationship among the Germans and the Romans was quite different, there was scope for considerable misunderstanding, and the demands of the canon lawyers were not listened to very seriously by most Franks. Marriage between first cousins, for instance, was not unknown; even a man's marriage to his widowed step-sister or step-mother (in a natural desire both for protection of the widow and her children and to keep the dowry in the family) took place occasionally as it had done in pre-Christian days, despite the horror of the church. Christianity introduced new complications. God-parents or god-children, for instance, were often regarded by the Franks as having been adopted into the family; they had the same obligations as other members of the family, to avenge injuries done to the family. This too worried Boniface, for here canon law was not so strict as Gallic practice. He wrote to the archbishop of Canterbury concerning a man who had married the mother of his god-child: 'I cannot possibly understand how, on the one hand, spiritual relationship in the case of matrimonial intercourse can be so great a sin while, on the other hand, it is well established that by holy baptism we all become sons and daughters, brothers and sisters of Christ and the Church.'[13]

There was also the question of concubinage and the legitimacy of children. It has sometimes been said that the Merovingian kings were polygamous: Chlothar I did have seven known wives (two of whom were sisters), Charibert I four and others three. But it is quite probable that death or divorce separated these marriages, or that a number of them were *Friedelehe*. Merovingian kings did however have concubines on occasion, and not surprisingly the Church was worried about the legitimacy of the children of such liaisons. The quarrel between the Irish monk Columbanus and King Theuderic and his grandmother Brunhild which led to the monk's exile from Gaul began by a refusal to bless the king's two sons born to a concubine, born in adultery as Columbanus put it. Charles the Great himself, whose goal was, according to Ganshof, 'to make the terrestrial city as far as possible a reflection of the city of God',[14] bore children by at least eleven women, some of whom he had married canonically, one uncanonically, and some of whom he had not married at all. The court at Aachen, at least in his latter years, was indeed noted for what the church regarded as moral laxity. He lived surrounded by women, including a bevy of bejewelled and heavily made-up daughters, whom he refused permission to marry, presumably for political reasons. They had open liaisons at court, and several illegitimate children. The new Christian ideals of marriage arrived at court only after Charles' death, and when they arrived it was with a vengeance. Louis came to Aachen, and when he had dealt with his father's will, he 'gave sentence that the entire female company (which was very large) be excluded from the palace, except the very few whom he considered fit for the royal service. Each of his sisters withdrew to her own lands which she had received from her father.'[15] Devisse has recently said of Louis that he 'was the first [Frankish king] to conceive of his life as a husband according to Christian morality. Without any doubt, a good part of the difficulties which he experienced stemmed from that; his attitude surprised and shocked a society which was far from agreeing with such moral rigour.'[16] It was in his *Ordinatio Imperii* of 817 that for the first time bastards were explicitly excluded from the succession: if one of his sons died leaving only illegitimate children, the surviving sons were asked to show mercy to them – which presumably meant making sure of their inability to rule by putting them into the Church rather than by killing them. Indeed, Charlemagne himself may have had similar feelings on that score. His eldest but illegitimate son Pippin the Hunchback was put into a monastery after his revolt, and later illegitimate sons ended as Bishop of Metz and Abbot of St-Quentin.

The attitude of the Church to marriage was, of course, ultimately that of St Paul: that it was better to marry than to burn. The true Christian would not marry at all; he would sever all family ties and enter a monastery. When the Church did eventually put forward the idea of a layman as a saint, when Abbot Odo of Cluny wrote the *Life of St Gerald of Aurillac* in the tenth century, it was only possible to do this by making that layman a celibate. Born of a chaste marriage, in which his father has to be reminded by a heaven-sent vision to set about the conception, Gerald only once came near to succumbing to temptation. Luckily God intervened, and the attractive serf-girl on Gerald's estates suddenly appeared so deformed to his eyes that he resisted. Even so, God punished him by a cataract for having strayed. Later in life Gerald lived the life of a monk, though privately and secretly, hiding his self-inflicted tonsure under his cap. This was a *Life* written by a enthusiastic monk, of course; his attitude may have been more rigorous than that of most clergy. And in fact the Church did have some effect on lay attitudes to marriage in the course of the ninth century. The indissoluble nature of the ecclesiastical marriage ceremony was emphasised by an increasing recognition of marriage as a sacrament. The success of this policy can be judged by the extraordinary troubles faced by King Lothar II (of Lotharingia) in his attempts to divorce his barren wife Theutberga. Hincmar of Rheims, much involved in this controversy, stressed the duties which the husband owed the wife in marriage. His elaboration of the ceremony of coronation of queens (the first ever was in 856, when Charles the Bald's daughter Judith was crowned as part of her marriage to Aethelwulf of Wessex), whereby queenship was for the first time seen as an office, like kingship, has been seen in part as a public rebuke to Lothar II, who was denying that both partners in a marriage were equal in the eyes of God.

The coming of Christianity thus gradually, very gradually, gave new definitions to the family. And as far as the Franks are concerned – that is, by the eighth century, most of the inhabitants of Northern Gaul and many of the aristocrats who were administering other parts of the Frankish kingdom – the intermingling of Roman law with their own laws and customs had also made important changes. There is no surviving source which tells us more about relationships within the family and between the family and the rest of society – about the rights and responsibilities of the kin at law, for instance, or the rules governing the inheritance of property – than do the Frankish law-codes. And, because Frankish legal history is both complex and a great area of controversy, it will be necessary, before considering the evidence provided by the law-codes, to look briefly at their nature and development.

The earliest law-code was the Lex Salica, whose fame in academic circles derives partly from the fact that it is the oldest of the West Germanic law-codes, and certainly the most Germanic in character, and partly from the history of its editing, which has been more prolonged and controversial than probably any other medieval text. It survives in eighty-seven manuscripts, spread today over eleven European countries. Each differs from all the others, to a greater or lesser extent. One is of the eighth century, and the rest of ninth-century date or later; the scholarly position was such that in 1947 Stein could argue that Lex Salica was a concoction of the ninth century associated with Hincmar of Rheims, a claim which produced a flurry of academic indignation and, eventually, a great advance in our understanding of the origins of the law-code. The conclusions of its most recent editor, K. A. Eckhardt, are not accepted by all, but do offer a useful and plausible hypothesis. There are four manuscripts which preserve a text substantially the same as that set down in writing towards the end of Clovis's reign. The Pactus Legis Salicae (so-called to distinguish it from later Carolingian versions of Lex Salica) mentions the Loire and the Carbonarian Forest (in Belgium) as the limits of the bulk of the Frankish people, and implies that there is only one king. Since a written code is mentioned by Childebert in an edict of before 558, the only date possible is between Clovis's conquest of Aquitaine in 507 and his death in 511. The shorter of the two prologues which some manuscripts bear relates that the Franks and their leading men decided that 'because they excel the peoples near them in the strength of their arm, so also ought they to excel in the authority of the law, so that criminal acts shall be resolved by legal skills. There were chosen from among them four men from many, Wisigast, Arogast, Salegast and Widegast, who in villas beyond the Rhine, in Bodheim, Saleheim and Widheim, met together in the *malli* [public legal assemblies] to discuss the origins of all cases and decided on each in the following manner.'[17] Eckhardt proposes that Clovis issued this Pactus, adding a few capitula to the first sixty-five titles of the Code before his death; as the no doubt largely fictitious story in the prologue suggests, it was done through desire for prestige by an imitation of Roman imperial habits as much as anything else. The second version, which can be partially reconstructed from a sixteenth-century printed edition of a lost manuscript, was probably issued by Clovis's son Theuderic I. The last Merovingian reissue of the Pactus may have been under King Guntram, with a completely new version being produced in Carolingian times, by Pippin and then, shortly after the imperial coronation, by Charlemagne. The short prologue dates from Guntram's time: his reissue may be associated with Asclepiodotus. He was an educated Roman, perhaps of senatorial origins, who became referendary – secretary and legal officer – to Guntram, and may have drafted the Edict of Guntram of 585 as well as the treaty of Andelot in 587, which is preserved verbatim in Gregory's History. After Guntram's death Asclepiodotus entered the service of Childebert II as referendary, and his name appears at the foot of Childebert's decree of 596. He ended his career as *patricius* of Provence, in which capacity he received two letters from Pope Gregory I. Asclepiodotus is an ideal example of the way in which Gallo-Romans could prosper under the Merovingians, and of how the Franks used Roman expertise in their government. Perhaps trained in Roman law, he may have become actively involved in the production of Germanic law. He may not have been the first Roman legal adviser to the Franks: the Pactus Legis Salicae was, after all, unlike the somewhat later Anglo-Saxon and Irish laws, drafted in Latin, and legal historians have detected elements of Roman provincial legal custom in some of its provisions.

The shape of the Pactus has some consistency. The first clause, probably added later in the sixth century, concerns the penalties facing those who did not answer a summons to the *mallus*. The second is concerned with the stealing of pigs – pigs before weaning, one-year-old pigs, one-year-old pigs stolen from a locked enclosure, two-year-old pigs, two-year-old pigs stolen from a locked enclosure, and so on. The whole of the first section involves the theft of farm animals; there is no barbarian law-code quite so unremittingly agricultural. After clauses on cows, goats, sheep, birds and bees, and cornfields, it eases gradually into cases of violent attack on human beings with the clause, 'If anyone steals another's slave, slave-girl, horse or draught-animal, he shall pay 1400 denarii, which makes 35 solidi.'[18] The great bulk of the code is in fact concerned with violent crime of one sort or another, and civil matters such as inheritance or details of legal procedure occupy a very small part; nevertheless, as we shall see, enough remains to outline the importance of the family or kin in Frankish legal thinking.

The deficiencies, contradictions and old-fashioned character of the Pactus were recognised in the sixth century, and a number of Clovis's descendants, either in reissues of the Pactus or in separate decrees, attempted to remedy the problem. In *De apsoniis*, for instance, the cases of genuine necessity which might excuse a man from attending the *mallus* were defined, thus removing the ambiguities of the first title of the Pactus. The entry of the Franks into the Christian world was marked by recognition of church sanctuary, and the existence of several independent Merovingian kingdoms acknowledged by an agreement allowing the *posse* of one king to enter the kingdom of another in hot pursuit of a criminal. But in practice Salic law was no doubt adapted and modernised in the courts, and modified in accordance with local custom. We can see such modifications, often incorporating ideas from Roman law, in the collections of legal formulae made in the seventh and eighth centuries, and we can see them in the second major compilation of Frankish law, Lex Ribuaria. As we have it, this is a Carolingian text, but almost certainly goes back to a Merovingian original. The term 'Ribuaria' or 'Ribvaria' refers to the area around Cologne, the former Gallia Ripensis, settled initially by a Frankish king independent of the Merovingians. The law-code seems to assume the existence of a sub-king in the region (the *staffulus regis* or 'royal law-stone' of the text has been identified as a perforated stone pillar that used to stand between Cologne Cathedral and the old Roman praetorium which in Frankish times was used as a royal palace), and may have been drafted under Dagobert or his son Sigibert III, both kings of Austrasia. The most obvious 'modernisation' of the Lex Ribuaria is the integration of Christian and Roman realities into the law. A series of penalties are laid down for the killing of clergy, ranging from 100 solidi for a simple cleric to 900 solidi for a bishop. There are clauses dealing with the slaves and freedmen of the Church, and with the practical problems resulting from judging clerics according to Roman law and men of other nationalities by their own law. This principle of personality (see above p. 39) must have resulted in the steady diffusion of different ideas and principles of law throughout Gaul, and we can see this in Lex Ribuaria, as in the procedure for the freeing of slaves. The Franks could do this by throwing a coin on the ground in front of the king: this was manumission *per denarium*. Manumission among the Romans could be by written document or in a church with a priest as witness. All three procedures appear in the formulary compiled by the monk Marculf, and the Lex Ribuaria specifically lays down the procedure involved for 'any free Ribuarian who wishes to free his slave, for the good of his soul or for a price, in a church, according to Roman law'.[19]

One of the most important changes in Frankish practice relating to the family concerns inheritance. Family solidarity in early Frankish society seems to have been formidable. An individual had very little freedom to bestow his property on whom he wished. The will did not exist, and the order of inheritance was laid down: the children inherit (if one is to translate *filios* as 'children' rather than 'sons', as I think one must); if there are no children, the father or mother; if no children or parents, the brothers and sisters; then the sisters of the mother; then the sisters of the father; if none of these survive, then the nearest other relatives on the father's side. This is an interesting view of what the family meant to the ordinary Frank – or to the ordinary Frankish lawyer – and a rather puzzling one, for it seems to favour female members of the family. It was possible to disinherit the family, but only by renouncing all kinship ties: this was performed in a picturesque ceremony involving the breaking of four elder sticks above the head of the judge or *thunginus*, and throwing them to the four corners of the law-place. No doubt too, as in other barbarian law-codes, there was some procedure whereby a father could disinherit one of his children for some serious breach of familial loyalty or morality. He could also, if he wished, adopt someone as his son, a procedure possibly borrowed from Roman practice, and in the Pactus Legis Salicae the only way for a man to bequeath property to someone outside his family. Classical Roman law had emphasised the total freedom of the individual to bequeath his property as he wished, although by the fourth century this had been modified to ensure that parents did not abandon their offspring completely. Roman practice seems to have had a rapid influence on the Franks, or at least upon the Frankish aristocracy. They start making wills, and formularies and charters invoke Roman law in support of this principle of free disposition. The major beneficiary of this development must have been the Church; it is difficult to see how it could have won itself such a powerful position in Frankish parts of Gaul had it not been made possible for Frankish magnates to bestow property on churches and monasteries. A similar development took place in England under the aegis of the Church, with the introduction of bookland, property secured by charter and freely disposable by the possessor, which gradually replaced the traditional folkland, property owned by the possessor but in which the kinship group still had important rights.

Clause 6 of Title 59 of the Pactus, '*De alodis*', states that daughters should not inherit 'Salic land'.

> In terram Salicam mulieres ne succedant,
> No woman shall succeed in Salique land:
> Which Salique land the French unjustly gloze
> To be the realm of France. (*Henry V*, Act I, Scene II)

Shakespeare was right to remark that this passage was unjustly glossed, even though the long, learned and ingenious explanation which follows is quite misguided. *Terra Salica* cannot mean all land within the Frankish realm, for the preceding five clauses of *De alodis* refer to occasions when a woman can share in the inheritance. Clearly *terra Salica* is something special. Some have argued that it was land taken in conquest and held by military service, which women could not perform: others that it is communal land, or the kernel of the ancestral estate. A comparison with Lex Ribuaria makes the matter clear, for that later code makes a similar distinction, and in less ambiguous terms. Title 56 stipulates that children (*liberos*, less ambiguous than the *filios* of the Pactus) should inherit, and if no children, then the parents, and so on: but that while the male sex survives, no woman may succeed to *hereditate aviatica*. This must be ancestral land, as opposed to the simple *hereditas* – moveables and land acquired by conquest, purchase, gift or theft – which a women could inherit. Indeed, wills such as that of Burgundofara, foundress of the monastery of Faremoutiers-en-Brie, show us that women could own a good deal of land in their own right: she specifies that some estates came to her in a partition of her father's estates with her two brothers and sister, while others were directly bequeathed to her in her father's will. It is possible that later Frankish jurists were as puzzled by the phrase *terra Salica* as Shakespeare or more recent scholars. The Edict of Chilperic (561–84) feels it necessary to state that daughters can inherit the land if there are no immediate male heirs, and sisters inherit from their brothers, while a formula preserved in Marculf's collection states his opposition to what he feels is the old custom very firmly: 'A long-standing and wicked custom of our people denies sisters a share with their brothers in their father's land; but I consider this wrong, since my children came equally from God . . . . Therefore, my dearest daughter, with this letter I hereby make you an equal and legitimate heir with your brothers, my sons.'[20] The idea, of course, that such a written document could overrule the custom of the people was an important innovation. Under the influence of Roman law such documents as wills and charters entered Frankish legal practice. It was, perhaps, always an uneasy and half-hearted adoption. Unwritten custom and the unwritten word had as much force legally as the written word; the Carolingian capitulary was a record of the words of the sovereign, and they, and not the document, had legal force. The old Frankish enthusiasm for visible and concrete gestures to signify the legal act also continued. It was not the writing or witnessing of a charter which transferred property from one person to another, so much as the physical acts sometimes mentioned in Carolingian charters, which took place before or after the writing of the document: pieces of land were transferred by handing over a piece of turf, a bag of earth or a branch;

a house by a roofing-tile or a bell-cord; a dowry by means of a glove. The occasional rare and bizarre record of such procedures survives: a parchment charter with a twig sewn at its foot.

The importance of the family as a basic social unit among the Franks is revealed most clearly in the criminal law. This was, as is often said, typically Germanic; it is very similar in its essentials to the laws of the Lombards or the West Saxons – but also to contemporary Irish law, or ancient Hindu or Hebrew law. Comparative lawyers have suggested that such systems are to be associated not with specific ethnic groups but rather with a specific stage in the cultural development of a people. The most typical element is the monetary compensation for each crime. In cases of homicide the criminal had to pay the *wergild* or 'man-money' of the victim. The wergild-lists in the Pactus show the mathematical precision with which society was graded, in the minds of the lawmen who drew it up if no one else. The murderer of a highly trained and valuable slave such as a gold-smith was liable to pay 75 solidi; of a *litus* (half-free man) or Roman freeman, 100 solidi; of an ordinary Frankish freeman, 200 solidi; of a Roman who was *conviva regis*, companion of the king, 300 solidi; of a Frank in the *trustis* or retinue of the king, 600 solidi. There are interesting distinctions within these main categories. A free boy under twelve years old (and in no position to defend himself, therefore) and a woman of child-bearing age both had wergilds of 600 solidi. Moreover, the wergilds of free Franks were tripled if they were killed while on military expeditions, or in their own house by a man with a gang of followers, or if their corpse was hidden, at the bottom of a well, or under branches: it is only this latter form of homicide that is called 'morter' or murder in the Frankish (Germanic) glosses to the Pactus. In cases of homicide the wergild was shared between the king and the kin of the victim: both parties thus had an interest in pursuing the culprit.

How did the system work in practice? The procedure can, at least in part, be pieced together from the Pactus and later sources. Let us trace it through from the moment of the crime. The body of a dead man has been found in a village, and a particular villager falls under suspicion. Villages were close-knit communities (the Pactus says that a stranger was forbidden to settle in a village if even one voice was raised against him), and the identity of the murderer would in most cases be perfectly obvious. It was generally felt that it was the duty of the kin of the dead man to avenge the victim, but few would be willing to unleash the whole series of reprisals and counter-reprisals which is occasionally reported in the narrative sources. The kin's duty to blood-feud would normally be sublimated into an incentive to find the murderer and bring him to justice, while the threat of blood-feud might well persuade the kin of the murderer to co-operate, at least if they felt him to be in the wrong. One of the dead man's family would lodge an accusation against the suspect at the local *mallus*, presided over in the early years by a *thunginus*, perhaps a royal appointee but more probably a figure of some local power and importance. (Already in the sixth century it was becoming common for the count to preside over the *mallus*; in Carolingian times it was often a subordinate, a viscount or *centenarius*.) He was advised by a number of men who knew the law: *rachinburgii*. There had to be at least seven of these, chosen from among the local freemen. One of the earliest additions to the Pactus declared that if the *rachinburgii* were asked by one of the participants in a trial what Salic law said about the matter in hand, and they were unable to answer, they were to be fined: an indication that the Salic law was largely customary, for there are many matters not dealt with in the written code. Charlemagne attempted to professionalise the system still further, by introducing permanent doomsmen or *scabini* to replace the *rachinburgii*. The *mallus* met in each *pagus* every forty days. Various procedures were laid down for finding a suspect and bringing him before the court; in this case we shall assume that he came of his own free will, to declare his innocence.

There were two major methods of proof used when criminals were not caught red-handed. The accused could purge himself by an oath, taken together with a suitable number of his neighbours or friends who were willing to swear to his innocence, or he could undergo an ordeal; the latter was only resorted to if the former had failed to settle the matter. Both these methods of proof can be found throughout our period all over Gaul. As early as the time of Gregory of Tours we hear a story about a Catholic priest who 'proved' the truth of Catholicism in the face of Arian criticisms by plunging his arm into a cauldron of boiling water in order to fish out a small object; his arm was undamaged, and when the Arian tried his flesh fell away from the bone.[21] This is the method of proof by boiling water which is mentioned in the Pactus; already by the mid-sixth century the principle had been accepted by Romans in southern Gaul. Both oath and ordeal fitted well into the thought patterns of the time, and indeed both rested on precisely the same belief: that God was determined to see justice done. Even if both methods are of Germanic origin (which is not certain), the Church quickly accepted them. The ordeal was given an elaborate liturgy, which made it into an impressive ecclesiastical ceremony, and oaths were normally sworn in church, in front of an altar. Gregory of Tours tells a number of stories which warn his readers of the horrors that face perjurors: they fall down and break their head on the stone floor of the church, or they stand rooted to the spot like a bronze statue. A particular church in the Touraine, dedicated to St Julian, was an especially good place for oath-swearing, said Gregory, for perjurors were almost always punished there. Gregory must have been as aware as any judge of the strong possibility of an accused man perjuring himself; but the procedure did demand that the accused find a number of other men prepared to perjure themselves on his behalf – which must have been much more difficult, unless his innocence was fairly certain, or his social position such that he could call on considerable local support. To avoid this danger, those of high social status were required to find more oath-helpers: Queen Fredegund had her word concerning the legitimacy of her son Chlothar II supported by the oaths of three hundred aristocrats and bishops. For a known criminal, escape by means of perjury must have been impossible. In 596 Childebert II tightened up the procedure still further, decreeing that if five or seven men of standing declared that a person was *criminosus* (a habitual criminal), then he should die. If he was a free Frank he should be brought before the king; otherwise he would be executed on the spot, without even the chance to perjure himself.

The growing popularity of the ordeal as a method of proof may have been due to uncertainty about the oath. At the very beginning of the sixth century the Burgundian law-code had declared that 'many of our people are corrupted through inability to establish a case and because of instinct of greed, so that they do not hesitate frequently to offer oaths about uncertain matters and likewise to perjure themselves about known matters. . . . if the party to whom oath has been offered does not wish to receive the oath, but shall say that the truthfulness of his adversary can be demonstrated only by resort to arms . . . let the right of combat not be refused.'[22] The judicial duel, or ordeal by battle, was to remain a common method for settling difficult disputes between free men for long after our period. It was one of the very few ordeals which involved both participants (or their champions). One other, and one of the few ordeals which was specifically Christian in origin, derived probably from a peculiarly Irish form of penance: the two participants in the dispute stood with their arms outstretched in the form of a cross, and the first who faltered lost the case. Charlemagne seems to have approved of the idea, but Louis the Pious declared it to be blasphemous, and after his capitulary of 818/9 it disappears for ever. Other forms of ordeal were more long-lasting, and more familiar: boiling water, the hot iron, cold water (in which the water, abjured by the priest, rejects the guilty man, so that he floats), and ordeal by lot (the picking of marked tallies while blindfold). The Council of Worms in 868 recommended that bishops and priests should use the ordeal of the host: if a consecrated host was swallowed by the accused cleric without difficulty, then he was innocent. Given sufficient ceremony to awe and unnerve a guilty party, this ordeal might have been very effective, at least judged in the light of anthropological observation of very similar ordeals still used in West Africa.

The judicial duel was the most controversial of the ordeals, because of the bloodshed involved, and scepticism was expressed from any early date. Outside Gaul we find the pessimism of Liutprand of Italy: 'We are uncertain about the judgment of God, and we have heard of many persons unjustly losing their cause by wager of battle.'[23] In ninth-century Gaul, Agobard of Lyons expressed similar doubts, while the resourceful Hincmar of Rheims proved capable of justifying it in theory while banning it in practice from his own diocese. Such doubts were almost certainly expressed about other forms of ordeal as well; it was to counter these that Charlemagne proclaimed in 809 that 'all men should believe in the judgment of God without any doubts'.[24]

Ordeals must have been exciting, but rare, occasions for the Gallic populace. They were resorted to only when all other methods of proof had failed, when the family and friends would not come forward to defend the accused, or when they were unable to do so because the accused was far from home. And procedure did allow for less colourful methods of proof. Salic law, like Roman law, allowed for the calling of witnesses, and Louis the Pious extended this privilege, formerly restricted to the prosecution, to the defence as well. Once guilt had been decided to the satisfaction of the judge and his advisers, there were a number of options open to the accused. He could make an accusation of false judgement, or demand to have the case retried: Charlemagne's frequent prohibition of the latter procedure suggests that it was a common method of appeal, and was being misused. Alternatively, the guilty party could agree to pay the monetary compensation for his crime. The Pactus lists these compensations in solidi and their equivalent in denarii, at the rate of 40 *d.* to the *s.* This has caused a good deal of debate, for at the time there was no coin of the value of a solidus (the gold triens being a third of the solidus) and no denarius either. But a passage in Lex Ribuaria suggests that penalties were often paid in kind; it lists a series of equivalents: 'a healthy ox is worth two solidi; a cow one solidus; a stallion, seven solidi; a mare, three solidi; seven solidi for a sword with a scabbard' and so on.[25] The wergild for the lowest kind of Frankish freeman was thus equivalent to a herd of 200 cows. Even taking into account that the amounts expressed in the law-codes were no more than bargaining points, and that the whole family of the guilty party would help him find the money, this must have been an enormous sum for the ordinary Frank. It is hardly surprising that the authors of the Pactus thought it necessary to describe procedure for those who could not afford the prescribed penalty. Title 58, *De Chrenecruda*, describes how the insolvent criminal must go to his house, scoop up earth from each of its four corners, stand on the threshold facing into the house, and throw the earth over his shoulder, first on to those members of his kin standing behind him who are on his father's side, and then on to his kin on the mother's side, thus ritually transferring all his responsibilities on to them. Then, without a cloak or shoes, and carrying only a staff, he must leap over his fence, abandoning all his property, or, in our terms, declaring himself bankrupt. The ritual obviously assumed the willingness of the kin to shoulder the man's debts. Some manuscripts point out that this ancient custom was no longer observed; others that it was observed in pagan times. In historical times it may have been more common for the criminal to 'pay with his life', which meant, not execution, but enslavement to the man he had injured, or to the kin of the man he had killed, perhaps for as long as was needed for him to work off his debt.

The kin or the family were central to the operation of Frankish law, although they may appear in the written law only by implication. The wergild which the murderer paid went largely to the kin of his victim, and might be paid largely by his own kin. Criminal acts were thus not the responsibility of single individuals, but of whole groups of people within the locality, and ultimately it was their business to ensure that a successful and honourable conclusion was reached. Compensation-money, according to the Pactus, was divided into three parts, the *fredus*, *faidus* and *debitum*. The *fredus* or peace-money was paid to the king or his representative, perhaps, as some German historians believe, as compensation for the breaking of the 'king's peace', but more likely as payment for his or his agent's role in the arbitration. The *debitum* went to the heirs of the victim, including females and children, and the *faidus*, or feud-money, went to the male relatives of the victim, those whose social duty it was to revenge injuries done to their relative. The institution of the blood-feud was a mechanism which, in a primitive society with no police force and limited governmental resources, helped to ensure that criminals were brought to justice. In a small and largely rural society with different kin-groups in an area being linked by marriage, it was probably rare for feud to end in bloodshed. Nor was it likely that the injured kin would insist on payment of every denarius specified by the written code; that might only have led to the continuance of bad feelings and the possibility of further disorder. Feelings of honour might fuel further hostilities, as in the case of Sichar and Chramnesind, reported by Gregory of Tours: Sichar had killed Chramnesind's relatives, and had paid the monetary compensation, and one day in his cups pointed out to Chramnesind how grateful he ought to be that Sichar had murdered his kin and thus enriched him. Chramnesind said to himself, 'If I don't avenge my relatives, they will say that I am as weak as a woman,' and split Sichar's skull in two.[26] But in general the threat of feud, forcing opposing factions to come to arbitration, must have been more important than the pursuance of feud; and this had been so since the earliest description of Germanic society, by Tacitus in the first century AD: 'It is incumbent to take up a father's or a kinsman's feuds no less than his friendships; but such feuds do not continue unappeased: even homicide is atoned for by a fixed number of cattle and sheep.'[27] By the Carolingian period this was probably true for much of the population of Gaul, for this social mechanism, or the sense of family solidarity and personal honour which enabled it to function, seems to have been accepted by Romans as well as Germans. But its validity was questioned by those who believed in higher loyalties than those of the family, as we shall see in subsequent chapters, by those who abandoned earthly ties in obedience to God, and by those who emphasised the prior claims of kings and lords.

4. The Christian Community

MOST people in Gaul in the centuries after the barbarian invasions belonged to a community wider than nation, city or family, a community with its own initiation ceremonies and meeting-places, membership of which gave people a sure knowledge of the world, both visible and invisible, and a chance of eternal happiness. The initiation ceremony was baptism, involving triple immersion in sunken pits or fonts in specially built baptisteries (both fonts and baptisteries often octagonal in shape, for the number 8 signified eternity and rebirth), and was usually performed by a bishop, at Easter, Christmas or on another suitable day such as the feast of St John the Baptist. Already by 500, child, rather than adult, baptism was the norm; in Carolingian times the child might be one or two years old. By then it had become much easier for parents to obtain the sacrament for their children: parish priests would perform the ceremony, using a small font inside their parish church. In theory, continuing membership of the community required fulfilment of the oaths sworn at baptism; in practice it required only a minimum participation in the sacraments. The Council of Agde in 506 laid down that every Christian should take communion at Christmas, Easter and Pentecost; Carolingian bishops decreed that every Christian should make confession of sins once a year, before Lent (hence Shrove Tuesday, from 'to shrive', meaning both to hear and to make confession). But Christians were urged to attend church each Sunday, and even more forcibly urged to refrain from work on that day, thus clearly distinguishing themselves from members of other religious communities, from pagans, who (if they were Roman by tradition) celebrated Thursday or Jupiter's Day (preserved in Fr. *jeudi*), and from Jews, who celebrated Saturday.

Christians and Pagans

CLEARLY there were still pagans in Gaul in 500. Caesarius of Arles referred to pagans who were actually rebuilding temples which had been destroyed by Christians, and this presumably in south-east Gaul, the home of Gallic Christianity. There is, in fact, a large body of evidence from the Merovingian period of continuing pagan practices. It is often difficult to know whether it is Gallo-Romans or the newly settled Germans who are involved, but it seems logical to assume that paganism was more likely to last among the indigenous inhabitants of Gaul than among the newcomers: the Germans seem to have lost their pagan religion in proportion to the extent of their uprooting from their traditional homes and from familiar sacred landmarks. The Franks, of course, had migrated less than many Germans, and occasionally the surviving evidence refers to paganism within their settlements in north-east Gaul. But much of the paganism of Merovingian Gaul may be found in the villages, mountains and forests of areas barely touched by Germans and only thinly Romanised under the Empire.

There are various kinds of evidence for paganism. There is some royal legislation, such as an edict attributed to Childebert (d. 558) which ordered the destruction of idols and temples, and threatened with punishment those who did not comply as far as their own lands were concerned, or those who tried to prevent the bishop from carrying out the edict in his diocese. But ecclesiastical legislation is far more abundant: many Merovingian councils issued canons condemning various pagan practices: 'It is not permitted to dress up as a calf or a stag on the Kalends of January or to present diabolical gifts. . . . it is forbidden to discharge vows among woods or at sacred trees or at springs . . . nor let anyone dare to make feet or images out of wood. . . . it is forbidden to turn to soothsayers or to augurs, or to those who pretend to know the future, or to look at what they call the "lots of the saints", or those they make of wood or of bread.'[1] Similar evidence is to be found in a missionary sermon preserved in the *Life of St Eligius*, who preached to pagans in his own diocese. Pagans are exhorted to stop worshipping Neptune, Orcus, Diana and Minerva, and to stop observing Thursday as a day of rest. They must not go to sorceresses and diviners, make wishes at wells, venerate sacred stones or trees, wear amulets (even if they do contain a saying from the Holy Scriptures), shout during eclipses of the moon, pass their flocks through holes in trees, dress up as stags on the Kalends of January, or invoke the name of Minerva while performing household tasks.

Occasionally pagans appear in the narrative sources. An inhabitant of the Auvergne was on a boat sailing to Italy, and the ship suddenly found itself in danger of being wrecked. All on board immediately called for supernatural aid, and the Arvernian found himself to be the only Christian. Gregory of Tours says that his companions called on Jupiter, Mercury, Minerva and Venus: he, on the other hand, prayed to St Nicetius of Trier – a nice illustration of the way in which saints performed functions formerly carried out by the gods – and the sailors echoed him, saying 'O God of Nicetius, help us.'[2] The ship was, of course, saved. Gregory of Tours did not seem surprised that there should have been *multitudo paganorum* aboard. Another interesting anecdote comes from the *Life of St Eligius*, bishop of Noyon from 641–60. The bishop went one St Peter's Day to a place in his own diocese, and there preached against 'diabolical games', 'wicked dancing' and 'other superstitions'. The notables of the place, some of whom were men of Erchinoald, the mayor of the Neustrian palace, decided to kill the interfering cleric. The saint was warned of their plot but said that he desired martyrdom: he went out to preach accompanied by just two priests and a deacon. 'Roman that you are,' the crowd's spokesman said to Eligius, 'although you are always bothering us, you will never uproot our customs, but we will go on with our rites as we have always done, and we will go on doing so always and forever. There will never exist the man who will be able to stop us holding our time-honoured and most dear games.'[3]

There are a number of difficulties in the interpretation of texts like these. The pagan gods that are mentioned are all given classical Latin names, just as when Clotild made fun of her pagan husband Clovis for worshipping such gods, quoting from Virgil's *Aeneid* as she did so. Were the classical gods worshipped, or were the Celtic or Germanic gods dignified by Latin names in the usual conventions of literary Latin? More important, how far do the names and the details of pagan customs recorded in these sources form part of a common literary tradition, representing what pagans were expected to do rather than what pagans in a Merovingian context actually did? There are striking resemblances between the customs described in the sermon attributed to Eligius and those in a tract attacking paganism written by Martin, Bishop of Braga, in north-west Spain: this says more about literary borrowing than it does about paganism. Both these writings form part of a tradition which can be traced, through the sermons of Caesarius of Arles, back to St Augustine's *De catechizandis rudibus*. The crucial question, however, is whether the pagan practices described in these sources were consciously pagan at all as far as the participants were concerned. The inhabitants of the village near Noyon where Eligius risked martyrdom thought that their festivities were justified because of the ancientness of the custom; there is no indication that they worshipped pagan gods, and it seems probable that they were Christians who still continued rituals closely bound up with the rural processes of sowing, harvesting and so on – particularly given that there was a basilica in the village, and that they were men of Erchinoald, himself a patron of Christian monasticism. Were the pagan companions of the Arvernian on board ship for Italy simple pagans, or were they like the Arian whom Gregory of Tours met, who said, 'We have a saying that no harm is done if, when one passes between the altars of the Gentiles – of the pagan gods – and the church of God, one pays respect to both.'? Gregory's comment, and that of many a missionary, was, 'I saw the stupidity of the man.'[4] But the Arvernian's pagans remind one irresistibly of Helgi the Lean in an Icelandic saga, 'who believed in Christ and yet invoked Thor for sea-voyages and in tight corners and for everything that struck him as of real importance'.[5]

The theological confusion and religious syncretism of the ordinary inhabitant of Merovingian Gaul was naturally unacceptable to the missionary mind. 'One cannot worship God and the Devil at once,' as Martin of Braga wrote, for the benefit of his Galician peasants. 'How can any of you, who have renounced the Devil and his angels and his evil works, now return again to the worship of the Devil?'[6] Clearly Martin, like many early medieval missionaries, is concerned with those who have been baptised, renouncing 'the Devil and his angels', yet who still continue the worship of the Devil: observing the first days of the month, burning candles at trees and springs, marrying on the day of Venus (Friday), invoking the names of the demons, and so on. To take just the last practice, it is perhaps relevant that Martin talks of 'the Devil and his angels'. The cult of angels, popular throughout Christendom (though always under suspicion because of its connections with the Gnostic heresy), was probably widespread in Gaul. There is a sarcophagus of *c.* 700 in the funerary chapel of Abbot Mellebaudis in Poitiers which was decorated with pictures of the angels Raphael and Raguel, and a fragment of a stone mould from Gémigny, near Orleans, with representations of eight angels, including Raguel, Raphael, Uriel and Michael, surrounding a central medallion figuring Christ. Gems and other archaeological finds bear witness to the cult offered to other angels. Yet in 363 the council of Laodicea had condemned the private cult paid to angels as idolatry; the council of Rome in 492 had said that the wearing of amulets inscribed with the names of angels was demon-worship; and a council of Rome in 745 condemned a prayer written by a Frank called Aldebert which invoked Uriel, Raguel, Michael, Adamis, Tubuas, Sabaoth and

Simihel, and claimed, without much scriptural backing, that 'with the exception of that of Michael, all the names of angels mentioned in this prayer designate demons from which the accused asked aid and protection'.[7] The missionary mind tends to view the world in black and white: what is not orthodox Christianity is paganism. The historian has often been all too willing to follow that lead. In fact the variety of beliefs held by those within the Christian community – that is, by the baptised – was probably very considerable, thanks partly to residual pagan beliefs and partly to the general lack of interest among most Merovingian churchmen in religious education and to the consequent ignorance among the laity and, probably, even among the clergy.

Something of the religious world of Merovingian Gaul may be recaptured by the archaeologist, through a study of burial customs in particular, and of the popular art on the objects buried with the dead. Decorated buckles and brooches from the period exist in their thousands in the museums of France and the Rhineland. The decoration owes very little to Christian art, save in certain exceptional cases. The geometrical symbols used – swastikas, crosses, rosettes – all belong to an international repertory of folk motifs which goes back for centuries in both the Celtic and Germanic worlds. The representation of animals is common – horses, griffons, hippocamps, double-headed serpents, interlaced serpents – and these too belong to no obviously Christian tradition: some archaeologists have concluded that large parts of western Europe remained largely pagan until the eighth century, until the time, that is, when objects cease to be placed in the graves with the corpse. (In fact, no cleric ever seems to have objected to the fashion of burial fully dressed, and these objects went on being worn after the eighth century – it is just that the archaeologist very rarely finds them if they are not placed in tombs.) Occasionally Christian motifs do appear on these objects. There is a series of buckles from Burgundy, for instance, showing a man between two beasts: the man is plainly identified as Daniel on two of them, by the crude inscriptions DANFE PROFETA and DANINIL. Daniel, shown also on many Roman and post-Roman sarcophagi in southern Gaul, probably has a specifically funerary significance, recalling a phrase in a prayer from the burial service: 'Save me, O Lord, as you saved Daniel from the lion's den.' But the motif of the man between two beasts is found in a pagan context too, in contemporary Scandinavia, and may be symbolic of man's threatened position in the world and after death, from which he hoped to be rescued by magic or divine power. It is very noticeable from a study of the decoration of Merovingian jewellery that those pieces bearing human figures are almost always ambiguous. Is the menaced man always Daniel? Is the horseman with a lance, common on openwork brooches, the Christian knight, the St George already appearing in Egyptian art, or is he Woden? The most famous example of this ambiguity is the gravestone from Niederdollendorf, showing, on one side, a standing warrior with a lance and a kind of halo (variously interpreted as a heroised representation of the dead man, or as Christ), and on the other a figure with a sword, surrounded by serpents, and raising his right arm above his head, perhaps in prayer. It is impossible to characterise such iconography (which can be closely parallelled for around AD 600 in both Aquitaine and Kent) as either Christian or pagan: it belongs to the vast area of common ground shared by adherents of both Christian and non-Christian religious, which has more to do with rituals of daily life and social activity than with theological or moral teaching.

Missionaries were active within Merovingian Gaul, particularly in the north-east, combating both Frankish and Roman pagans, but also in their own dioceses. Remigius of Rheims sent Vedastus to convert the *civitas* of Arras: if Vedastus was from the Limousin, as his *Life* states, then he was the first of several great missionaries from western Gaul to work in the north-east. They included Nicetius of Trier, Eligius of Noyon, Remaclus, the founder of the monastery of Stavelot-Malmédy, and, the greatest of them all, Amandus. The missionary career of Amandus ranged from the Basque province to the Low Countries: he spent nearly forty years in the north-east, until his death in 675. His *Life* tells us that 'in places where he destroyed temples he built monasteries or churches' – a phrase which gains rather than loses in historical significance when it is realised that it is lifted straight from the *Life of St Martin of Tours* by Sulpicius Severus.[8] Martin, the first great missionary in the Gallic countryside, remained an inspiration to Aquitanian churchmen throughout the sixth and seventh centuries. But individual churchmen can only have had a limited impact upon the theological or ethical understanding of the populace, particularly when the rural clergy remained ill-educated or simply non-existent. It was not until the late eighth and early ninth centuries that the Carolingian Church made a serious attempt to bring Christianity to the rural population. Minimum standards of clerical education were laid down, an attempt was made to ensure that the rural clergy lived disciplined lives, under the watchful eye of an overhauled diocesan organisation, and the importance both of the Mass and of preaching were emphasised.

For the Carolingian churchman, participation in the Mass was a symbolic and a physical means of confirming membership of the Body of the Church, by partaking of the Body of its founder. The liturgy of the Mass, borrowed from Rome in the eighth century and replacing the traditional Gallican forms, was more elaborate and dramatic, involving, for instance, the greater use of incense and of processions. And at the same time the Mass became more remote from the people: certain elements were added which were intended only for the officiating priest, the clergy took over the singing of parts of the Mass which had formerly been chanted by the congregation, and, above all, the Mass remained in Latin which, by the eighth century, was comprehensible to few in Gaul: in the north-east and east the people spoke Germanic dialects, and over the rest of Gaul (outside Brittany and the Basque lands) Latin had evolved into an early form of Old French or Old Occitan. The decision to retain Latin as the language of the Church and government, inevitable because of ecclesiastical tradition, the international nature of Charlemagne's Empire and the lack of expertise in the writing of the vernacular, had important consequences within the medieval Church, leading to an ever-increasing gulf between the clergy and the laity. Later this gulf was deliberately maintained: when an application was made in the late eleventh century to celebrate Mass in the vernacular, Pope Gregory VII held that 'not without reason has it pleased Almighty God that Holy Scripture be a secret in certain places, lest, if it were plainly apparent to all men, perchance it would be little esteemed and be subject to disrespect; or it might be falsely understood by those of mediocre learning and lead to error'.[9]

Carolingian churchmen held that the only legitimate sacred languages were Hebrew, Greek and Latin. The Synod of Frankfurt in 794 had to state that it was permissible to pray in the vernacular. Later in Charlemagne's reign, however, a conscious attempt was made to reach the laity; the reforming councils of 813 decreed that preaching should be in the vernacular, either *in rusticam Romanam linguam aut Theotiscam*, 'in the rustic Roman (i.e. Romance) tongue or in German'. A good number of texts in Old High German from this period survive: translations from the Bible, prayers, sermons, and religious poems. But there are no comparable texts written in Old French or the equivalent, presumably because it was more similar to Latin and written translations were unnecessary. The priest would be able to improvise in the vernacular from whichever of the many collections of sermons or homilies he possessed.

A good idea of what the Carolingian Church expected of the parish priest by way of the instruction and edification of his community can be gathered from the two books of the *De synodalibus causis* of Regino, abbot of Prüm (*c.* 900). The priest should own liturgical books, a collection of homilies (a homiliary), an explanation of the Lord's Prayer and the Creed (which all his flock had to learn by heart), and a martyrology, listing the feasts of the Church. He should also possess a penitential, so that he could prescribe appropriate penances for those sins which were confessed to him: this despite the various condemnations of the mechanical penitential system in ninth-century councils. The priest should be able to read these books without mistakes, but he should know certain texts – including the whole of the Psalms – by heart. He should perform the various offices of the day, and offer Mass daily; on Sundays all his parishioners should attend Lauds, Mass and Vespers, and hear the sermon which the priest was to preach. He himself was to offer to his congregation a model of Christian living: he was not to get drunk, to pawn the church vessels to inn-keepers, to hunt, to have women in his house, to take part in weddings; he must be hospitable to travellers, visit the sick and look after the poor; he must keep his church in a proper condition for the worship of God, not using it as a granary, or allowing women to dance there. Each year the bishop was to visit his parish, and ascertain (by means of a ninety-six point questionnaire which Regino includes) whether or not the priest lived up to these standards; members of the congregation could even appear before the bishop at a synodal tribunal to speak against their priest.

There is little that is original in Regino of Prüm. He assembles and organises the decrees of earlier church councils and earlier writers: his ideals were thus the ideals of the Church at large. But to estimate to what extent those ideals were put into practice is difficult, indeed impossible. Much depended on the energy of the individual bishop; the success of Regino's programme at a parish level also depended upon a minimum level of priestly education. Clearly the Carolingian Church was much better equipped to reach the ordinary Christian than the Merovingian Church. The whole country was now covered by a network of parishes and parish churches; there was, from the days of Charlemagne, a programme for clerical education monasteries and pilgrimage centres throughout Gaul acted as points of attraction for the laity; and the monastic ideal, as we shall see, widely accepted as the best means for the Christian to attain salvation, was an ever-present reminder to lay men and women of the ethical and spiritual ideals of the Christian community. Nevertheless there are signs that the message of the Church was not accepted in its entirety. We have already seen how the laity was reluctant to accept the church's ruling on marriage; the history of the relationship between the Christian and Jewish communities in early medieval Gaul provides another example of the Church's failure, or, at least, of the prolonged nature of its struggle.

Christians and Jews

THE church councils of the sixth and early seventh centuries enacted a number of canons concerning the Jews, most of which were no more than re-enactments of earlier ecclesiastical or imperial legislation. They are concerned above all that the Christian community should be protected from the Jews, so that their Christian beliefs should not be contaminated and, ultimately, so that they might not be persuaded to convert to Judaism. This had been a very real problem in earlier centuries, when Roman converts to Judaism may at one time have been almost as numerous as converts to Christianity. Most Jews in Merovingian Gaul were almost certainly descendants of converts, and not descendants of men and women who had left Palestine in the Diaspora. Even in Frankish times Judaism was a proselytising religion of which the Church had to be wary. The marriage of a Jew and a Christian was forbidden, since it might lead to conversion. Likewise Jews were forbidden undue authority over Christians, either as judges or other royal officials, or as slave-owners: the attempts of Jews to convert their slaves (as they were required to do by Jewish law) were a recurring theme of Christian legislators. Christians were also forbidden to attend feasts held by Jews, that is, presumably, those feasts held on religious festivals, or to follow Jewish practices with regard to the Sabbath. A Roman law had forbidden Jews to attack 'any person who has left the disgusting Jewish superstition and has become a Christian':[10] it may be that Avitus, bishop of Clermont, was relying on this law when, in 576, one of the town's Jews tipped rancid oil over a new convert to Christianity as he walked to the cathedral in his white baptismal robe. The Christian crowd destroyed the synagogue, and Avitus, according to Gregory of Tours, persuaded over 500 Jews to be baptised. The remainder of the Jewish community migrated to Marseilles. The destruction of the synagogue at Clermont was not an isolated instance. At roughly the same time the synagogue at Orleans was destroyed also: Gregory tells us that when King Guntram visited the town in 585, the Jews welcomed him and sang his praises in Hebrew, hoping (thought Guntram) that he would rebuild it at his own expense.

In general the relations between Christian and Jew seem to have been good, hence the constant efforts of ecclesiastical legislators to sever or control those relations. The danger of conversion to Judaism was increased by the strong emphasis the Church in the early Middle Ages itself placed upon the Old Testament (the legal and political structure of ancient Israel was close enough to that of Frankish Gaul to make it an obvious inspiration), and also by the proximity and frequency of Jewish communities. Most towns seem to have had their Jews. In southern Gaul, by the ninth century but probably from a much earlier date, Jews had considerable amounts of rural property too. Septimania seems to have had particularly large Jewish communities. Julian, bishop of Toledo and author of a theological treatise against the Jews, called that province 'a brothel of blaspheming Jews'.[11] Even at the height of the persecution of the Jews by the Visigothic kings, an inscription could be raised in Narbonne to the memory of the three children of Paragorus, a Jew: it is dated to the second year of King Egica (688), and includes the phrase 'Peace be unto Israel' in Hebrew characters.[12] In Gaul, as in Spain, there seems to have been little popular support for the sporadic attempts of kings or churchmen to whip up animus against the Jews.

The most marked discrepancy between ecclesiastical doctrine concerning the Jews and the practice of ordinary Christians occurred under Charlemagne and Louis the Pious. There were Jews at Aachen, involved not only in supplying the court but also possibly in such activities as minting. A Jew called Isaac ended up as Charlemagne's ambassador to Harun al-Rashid in Baghdad. Charlemagne (whether consciously or not) acted to abolish the inequity in Roman law whereby the participation of Jewish witnesses in cases involving Jews and Christians was limited. According to the principle of personality of laws, Jews themselves apparently lived according to Jewish law; when the case involved a Christian, Roman law was followed. To facilitate the legal proceedings Charlemagne even laid down that

Jews should take an oath wrapped in a prayer shawl, holding the Torah in their hand (in Latin if a Hebrew version could not be found), and swearing by 'the God who gave the law to Moses on Mount Sinai'.[13] Under Louis the Pious Jews seem to have been granted more privileges, if we are to believe the most vocal opponent of Louis's Jews, Agobard, Bishop of Lyons. 'The Jews are especially popular at the court and it is said that the emperor values them highly because of the patriarchs [?]. Important people at the court seek the prayers and the blessings of the Jews. . . . All the time the Jews go around showing people the imperial orders that they have been given under the imperial name and seal which protect the privileges granted to them. They are permitted to build synagogues, against the law. Indeed, the Jews brag about the glory of their ancestors, their wives show off clothing which they claim to be gifts from royalty and from the ladies of the palace. Some Christians even say that the Jews are better preachers than the priests.'[14]

Agobard's dispute with the court arose after he had baptised a pagan slave belonging to a Jewish woman in Lyons. The slave was now a Christian; Jews were forbidden by law to possess Christian slaves. But the Jew refused to hand the slave over. Louis's *magister Judaeorum*, the official in charge of Jewish affairs, supported her. Agobard seized the slave; three high court officials declared against him, and Louis dismissed him from court.

> Indeed, I have suffered because of those at court who support the Jews. They are angry because I preached that Christians should not sell Christian slaves to Jews and that Jews should not be permitted to sell Christian slaves in Spain [to Muslims]. They are also angered because I have preached that Jews should not be permitted to hire Christian domestic workers and because I have tried to stop the Jews from having these women who are Christians work on Sundays and celebrate the Jewish Sabbath. I also preached against Christians who dine with Jews and eat meat during Lent because of this. Further, I preached that Christians should not eat meat that was slaughtered and skinned by the Jews . . . . Yet, imperial agents have changed the market day from Saturday to Sunday so that the Jews will be able to keep their Sabbath.[15]

Agobard joined the revolt against Louis in 833; he was dismissed and replaced as archbishop by the great liturgical scholar Amalarius of Metz, who, according to Agobard, said Mass in Lyons surrounded by a crowd of Jews, so many that they hardly allowed the faithful room to come to the altar. Agobard's attitude, a product not of fanaticism but of the rigid interpretation of canon law, was in the eleventh century to become the standard attitude of churchmen; it is one of the great tragedies of European history that it did so. But the influence of the Jews at court cannot be all in Agobard's imagination. In 838 an Alamannic nobleman called Bodo, well educated and destined for the high clergy, left Louis's court, ostensibly on a pilgrimage to Rome. Instead he went to a town in southern Francia with a large Jewish community (possibly Ausona, near Barcelona), was circumcised and took the Jewish name of Eleazar; he sold his entourage into slavery, except his nephew, who also converted to Judaism. Because of his eminence, the event created a scandal throughout the Frankish world. But the attractions might have been there for many Christians: Agobard and his successor at Lyons, Bishop Amulo, certainly thought so. The latter complained that many in Lyons preferred Jewish sermons to Christian ones, sermons which offered dangerous arguments against the divinity of Christ.

In the early Middle Ages the Church clearly had problems in persuading the Christian community to think of itself in exclusive terms. The boundaries between pagan and Christian and between Jew and Christian, as established by the Church, were often ignored by ordinary Christians. As far as paganism was concerned, the church itself gave up the struggle. As the memory of the pagan gods grew dim, it became impossible to maintain that certain daily rituals or customs did in fact involve the worship of pagan gods or the Devil. To take but one example: sixth-century missionaries claimed that to name the days of the week after the pagan gods was Devil-worship: today every European country except Portugal still names the days of the week after the pagan gods. But if pagans did not survive, Jews did. Already by the end of our period there are signs that Christians were beginning to see themselves as a community, defined partly by its relationships with outsiders, Jews and Muslims. One of the earliest appearances of the myth of the magical attack by Jews on Christians was in Le Mans in 992; some of the earliest pogroms seem to have been in the years between 1007 and 1012, a foretaste of the massacres which took place in northern Gaul and the Rhineland on the eve of the First Crusade. According to Guibert of Nogent, the crusaders from Rouen declared that they were travelling huge distances to attack the enemies of God in the

East, 'although the Jews, of all races the worst foe of God, are before our eyes. That's doing our work backwards':[16] they slaughtered all who would not accept Christianity. the laity had accepted the clergy's view of the exclusiveness of the Christian community, and taken it to one of its logical conclusions.

The Monastic Community

WITHIN the Christian community there were numerous small communities or *familiae*, within which men and women could attempt, separately, to live a Christian life. Monasteries were – although not all of them, and not all the time – the main centres of spirituality, of learning and of education; they were also important landowners and centres of commerce and, at times, of political influence. Perhaps most interesting of all, monasteries were places within which new forms of communal living could be developed. The history of monastic life in early medieval Gaul reveals the conflict between Christian idealism and the inexorable demands of secular life, between the desires of some to abandon their natural family and give themselves to God, and the unwillingness of others to allow monasteries to secede from the real world. The opposition between the natural kin and the artificial monastic *familia* runs throughout our period.

One of the clearest statements of the early monastic ideal comes from the sixth-century *Lives of the Fathers of the Jura*.

> So great then was the rigour of observance in this monastery that any virgin who entered it renouncing the world was never again seen outside, except when she was carried to her tomb, on her last voyage. And when a mother had a son at the neighbouring monastery, or a sister had her brother there, neither of the two knew, at first hand or by hearsay, if the other was still living, for each of them considered the other as already buried. It was feared that the sweetness of family memories would break, little by little, by a kind of softening, the bonds of the monastic life.[17]

Frequently the strength of family ties meant that monks had double loyalties, to God and to their kin, and if their families were royal or aristocratic, there could be important consequences on the observance of the monastic life. Those family feelings might mean that aristocrats who founded monasteries on their land, perhaps with one of the family as the first abbot or abbess, were very reluctant to relinquish control of that monastery. Moreover, in part because monasteries were often regarded as in a sense the possessions of individual aristocratic families – what German historians call *Eigenkirche* – their extensive landed estates could often be the prey of secular ambitions or power struggles. The greater the reputation for piety a monastery had, the more land it was given and the wealthier it became, and the more liable to interference from the lay world.

The earliest 'monks' (a word deriving from the Greek *monachos*, one who lives on his own) did not have these problems: they were 'hermits', who lived in the desert (*eremia* in Greek). In Egypt they lived on their own in cells on the fringes of the Sahara, often only a few miles from the flood-plain of the Nile; in Gaul the desert was more likely to be a forest or an uninhabited mountain region such as the Jura. But by the time monastic ideas reached Gaul, above all with Martin of Tours in the late fourth century, it was recognised that living a solitary life was a useful spiritual exercise for exceptional people only. The ordinary sinner was better advised to live a communal or 'coenobitic' life, in which his companions would aid him to avoid sin by example, and an abbot by discipline, and by enforcing a rule. The stories about the early monks inspired them, and their ambition was the same: to conquer the desires and passions of the body, to sever ties with the world and to concentrate the mind upon God. Inherent in monasticism was the feeling that by hard effort a monk could make himself worthy of salvation; it is not surprising that western monks in the fifth century were tempted by the ideas of the heresiarch Pelagius, who taught that men could obtain salvation by their own efforts. Even after this had been declared a heresy, largely thanks to St Augustine, the ideas lingered, notably in southern Gallic monasteries such as Lérins, which had been founded by Honoratus of Arles on an island off the Provençal coast. Bishops fought against Pelagianism; hagiography was composed to combat Pelagian ideas. The *Life of Germanus of Auxerre*, who went to Britain in 429 to confront Pelagians there, reports how his mother had had a vision of Germanus' future glory even before his birth: sainthood was predestined, not created by an individual's free will. In monasticism, a striving for individual asceticism became less important than the effacement of personality in humble obedience to the Rule and the will of the abbot. The goal was now communal, not personal: to create a community living according to Christian principles, a model for the outside world. Watching over the abbot was the bishop. The surviving acts of the Gallic church councils of the later fifth and sixth centuries show how determined bishops were to control abbots and monasteries. 'No one shall presume to begin or to found a monastery without the permission and approval of the bishop'; 'the bishops are responsible for the monasteries and for monastic discipline in their dioceses'.[18]

Such episcopal supervision was not always welcome to abbots and abbesses, even those of indisputably holy intentions. It was not unknown for bishops to exploit their position, and to demand hospitality or gifts from wealthy monasteries within their diocese, or to attempt to intervene in the election of abbots or other internal matters, or indeed to lay their hands on the property of the monastery. We can see some hostility between bishop and monastery in the course of the celebrated revolt of the nuns of Holy Cross in Poitiers, an event which was fully reported by the neighbouring bishop, Gregory of Tours, and so forms one of our best pictures of the internal life of a monastery in the sixth century. Its foundress, Radegund, the daughter of the king of Thuringia, had been captured as booty by Chlothar I. Not too long after their marriage, she left to set up her monastery, providing it with Caesarius' Rule and relics of the True Cross from the Byzantine Empire. She herself, in true humility, had Agnes appointed as abbess rather than herself, and followed the rule to the letter, to the extent of doing all the manual work required of other nuns. The revolt after her death was led by two of the nuns, Chrodieldis, daughter of King Charibert, and her cousin Basina, daughter of King Chilperic, and part of their complaint lay in the fact that their royal status was not recognised in the monastery: 'We are humiliated here as if we were the offspring of low-born serving-women, instead of being the daughters of kings!'[19] As the daughter of a king, Chrodieldis naturally felt that she should have been chosen as abbess rather than Leubovara, Agnes's actual successor. The complaints of the two suggest that they, like many aristocratic nuns or monks, were able in the same breath to complain about the harshness of the monastic rule and about infringements of it by others. The episcopal commission appointed to settle the dispute (made up of the bishop of Cologne, Maroveus of Poitiers and Gregory of Tours) reported that 'they said that they could no longer endure the poor food, the lack of clothing and, indeed, the harsh treatment. They disapproved of the fact that other people shared their bathroom. The Abbess played backgammon. Lay visitors ate with her. Occasionally engagement parties were held in the nunnery. She was so lacking in reverence that she made dresses for her niece out of a silken altar cloth.'[20] The defence of the Abbess to these charges is interesting. There was always enough food, even in these difficult times; the nuns had plenty of clothes, indeed, more than was necessary. The bathroom had been newly decorated, and Radegund had decided that the monastic servants could use it until the smell of the new plaster had disappeared. She played backgammon, just as she had done when Radegund was alive; there was nothing in the Rule or the canons of the Church against it. She never ate with lay people. She had held a marriage party for her niece, but the bishop, some of the clergy, and the town worthies had been present. The dress had been made from silk which was left over after the making of the altar cloth. As for the transvestite, whom Chrodieldis said lived in the nunnery and slept with the abbess, he lived miles from Poitiers and wore female clothing because he was impotent. The eunuch who lived in the monastery as a servant, 'just as if this was the Imperial court',[21] as Chrodieldis said, had been castrated for medical reasons, without the knowledge of the abbess.

Some of the problems at Holy Cross were doubtless the fault of Radegund and Agnes. They had allowed their monastery to become a comfortable home for retired or otherwise unemployed gentlefolk, and they had not preserved a suitable barrier between themselves and the outside world. The poems of Venantius Fortunatus, then living in Poitiers and not long afterwards to become its bishop, give us another glimpse of Radegund and Agnes; some read almost like love-letters ('I fear, alas, for I see in it the danger that the least insinuation by wicked tongues may restrain the expression of my feelings'[22]), while others are thank-you letters, bearing witness to the constant interchange of dinner invitations and small presents – fruit, flowers, and baskets. Even more indiscreet was the coolness which Radegund and Agnes had allowed to arise between themselves and Bishop Maroveus of Poitiers. 'They put themselves under the protection of the king,' said Gregory, 'for they aroused no interest or support in the man who should have been their pastor.'[23] Radegund's own letter to the bishops had set out more clearly than any other sixth-century document what she feared from her own bishop: that he, or another, might break the Rule, interfere with the election of the abbess, claim new jurisdiction of some sort over the nunnery, or appropriate some of the property bestowed by Chlothar I and his royal sons. Maroveus had kept his distance from the affairs of the nunnery within the walls of his own city, and not without reason: tangling with nuns who had such influential relatives would have been impolitic. But his inaction allowed the laxness within the nunnery to turn into revolt, and indeed to fights between the ruffianly gangs of rival supporters both inside and outside the monastery itself.

Needless to say, Holy Cross was hardly typical. But its story illustrates the tensions that could exist between bishop and monastery, as well as between the monastic ideal and the obligations of kinship and status. There proved to be no real solution to the latter; but relations with the bishop could be eased by means of a privilege, a document which was commonly sought by monasteries in the seventh century. By such a document the abbot obtained a guarantee of the integrity of the monastic estates, of free election, of freedom from unwelcome episcopal visits, and sometimes a guarantee that the bishop would consecrate priests or dedicate altars within the monastery without demanding fees or gifts. Monasteries in the seventh century and later were thus sometimes able to escape the close episcopal control which sixth-century church councils had attempted to impose.

In the course of the sixth century, scores if not hundreds of monasteries were founded, ranging from those founded by wealthy bishops, aristocrats or kings to tiny ones created by pious clerics or laymen upon a portion of their estates. Some were dependent for their impetus and survival on the presence of a holy man; others were more formalised institutions with written regulations providing for all eventualities, institutions which could survive for centuries. Sometimes rules were borrowed from other monasteries, as Radegund borrowed hers from a nunnery in Arles whose rule had been written by Caesarius; sometimes abbots compiled their own, like Filibert, who in the early seventh century went from one monastery to another collecting ideas, like 'a prudent bee flitting from flower to flower', gathering nectar where he could. Sometimes it is possible to trace the slow movement of particular customs from one monastery to another across Gaul, as with the liturgical practice of *laus perennis*, or 'perpetual praise', where a community was organised into three or more choirs which worked a shift system, so that there was always one group of monks or nuns at prayer. This custom seems to have come from Constantinople, firstly to the monastery founded in 515 by the Burgundian king Sigismund near the relics of St Maurice at Agaune. From there it spread all over Gaul: in 585 to King Guntram's monastery of St Marcellus in Chalon-sur-Saône; in the seventh century to St-Denis, near Paris; by the eighth century to Tours, St-Riquier and many others. This particular liturgical development is symptomatic of a change in the nature and social significance of monasticism. The private spiritual development of the monks became still more unimportant; monasteries were institutions which could offer up perpetual praise to God and prayers for the souls of the founders and benefactors. And monasteries were no longer just places in which, conventionally at least, monks lived a poor and humble life of dedication to Christ; they became centres of considerable economic importance, endowed with impressive buildings and much treasure, glorifying God and the family of the founder.

This change has often been associated with the coming to Gaul, around 590, of an ascetic monk from Bangor in north-east Ireland, Columbanus. He left Ireland as a voluntary exile: cutting all ties with kin and country was the highest form of asceticism in the early Irish church. Columbanus founded a number of monasteries on the Continent, above all Luxeuil in Burgundy, which was an inspiration for numerous monastic foundations in the seventh century. According to his hagiographer, St Eligius of Noyon declared that before the foundation of Luxeuil monasticism in Gaul was moribund, and was thus responsible for a historical myth which has survived right into the twentieth century. Luxeuil was a model for later monastic foundations in a number of ways. Before Luxeuil, the larger and more important monasteries had been urban monasteries; seventh-century monasteries were much more frequently rural monasteries, endowed with considerable lands. This had a particular impact upon female monasticism. Nunneries in the sixth century were invariably urban, living off rents and offerings, and borrowing the male priests necessary for the liturgical life of the nunnery from neighbouring monasteries or from the episcopal clergy. When rural nunneries were founded in the seventh century, priests and men for manual labour had to be provided, and the result was the double monastery, housing both men and women (carefully segregated) and ruled generally by an abbess. The move away from urban monasticism had wider geographic repercussions too; it involved a move away from the more Romanised and urbanised south and west towards the north and east: it was Frankish aristocrats in the north-east who took over from Gallo-Roman ecclesiastics the role of the monastic founder. One element of Luxeuil's monasticism which was particularly attractive to the aristocratic founder was its independence from the bishop. Luxeuil itself was geographically far removed from the influence of the bishop; Columbanus had founded and organised his monasteries without reference to the bishop, and had further encroached on episcopal prerogative by laying down private penances for sinners. Its privilege, confirmed by the king, protected its independence. Such privileges were often given to monasteries in the later seventh century. Balthild, the Anglo-Saxon slave who married Clovis II and later acted as regent, founded monasteries herself, such as Corbie (whose first abbot and monks were brought from Luxeuil), and the double monastery of Chelles. But she was also behind the reform of old monasteries along the new monastic lines: St-Denis, St Medard of Soissons, St Martin of Tours and others. The new privilege of St-Denis ensured that the bishop of Paris would no longer be able to exact payment for his liturgical duties or dip into the monastic funds when he needed; Landeric of Paris acquiesced because, as he said, 'the request of the king is for us like a command which it is extremely difficult to resist'.[24] If the bishops lost ground, the founders of monasteries gained. A monastery was, for an aristocratic family, a reservoir of wealth and land which could be borrowed and which, since church land could not be alienated, would not suffer from partition and fragmentation like most of a family's estates. It could provide hospitality and suitably grand surroundings in which to display the family's power; it could accommodate elderly, incompetent or dangerous relatives; it could provide the family with saints to increase its prestige; and it could become the religious centre of an entire district, attracting the local population and further increasing the family's influence.

The fate of most monasteries in the obscure period in the late seventh and early eighth centuries is unknown. Many may have lost the struggle to serve both God and their founding family; they survived as institutions owning considerable properties (although many of the properties may have been let out on long lease), but their wealth was used for secular purposes, and monastic discipline declined or disappeared under the rule of lay abbots. This was a common fate in eighth-century Europe, notably in the numerous kingdoms of England and Ireland. In southern Gaul, monasteries suffered not only from secularisation, but also from the brutal effects of both Saracen and Frankish invasions. In a handful of northern monasteries, notably those under the protection of the king or his mayors of the palace, monastic life survived, and indeed flourished. In some of those monasteries were the seeds of the cultural revival that was to be encouraged and fostered by Charlemagne – the so-called Carolingian Renaissance. At Corbie, Laon, Chelles, Fleury, St Martin of Tours and elsewhere, monks and nuns were studying and copying manuscripts: it was in monasteries such as these that the first short-lived Merovingian manuscript art was devised, a lively and colourful parade of animals and geometric patterns. When, under the patronage of the Carolingians, men like Boniface and Chrodegang of Metz began to bring the Frankish Church back to some standards of moral rectitude and canonical observance, they found men in these monasteries already versed in the latest ideas on canon law.

The intellectual and educational resources of the monasteries were exploited by the Carolingians in their effort to govern their considerable dominions; they were mobilised to enable Charlemagne to use a grammatically correct Latin as the language of government in his multi-lingual Empire. From the early eighth century onwards the Carolingians were using clerics in their administration, to a much greater extent than the Merovingians had ever done. There were other ways to exploit the monasteries. They could be used as royal residences: it was difficult for a monastery to refuse a royal request for hospitality, especially if it was under royal protection, as many important monasteries were in the ninth century. Chelles was so frequently used that it constructed a special building, the *palatium*, for royal visits. More simply, monastic land could be expropriated. The reforming councils of the 740s recognised that this was a political necessity; they insisted only on the ultimate rights of the church over the lands it had held. Laymen who held monastic land *de verbo regis*, by the word of the king, paid a proportion of the revenue to the Church; Carolingian kings could not afford to alienate their supporters by insisting upon the physical restitution of this land. And, finally, Carolingian kings could reward their followers or placate their relations by giving them abbacies. Pluralism was not uncommon: Alcuin of York was Abbot of St Martin of Tours, St Lupus of Troyes, Ferrières, Flavigny, and perhaps other houses. Laymen too could become abbots: Einhard, the biographer of Charlemagne, became under Louis the Pious Abbot of St Peter and St Bavo in Ghent, St Servatius in Maastricht and St-Wandrille at Fontanella, and spent his last years with his wife Emma at his own foundation of Seligenstadt.

Lay-abbots are an important factor in the Carolingian world, although their detrimental effect has no doubt been exaggerated. Sometimes a count was given an abbacy – an 'abbot-count' (Latin, *abbacomes*): a monk would be in charge of the spiritual life of the monastery, while the count would control the revenues and protect the monastery and its estates, a function for which he was obviously well suited. Under Louis the Pious a portion of the monastic revenues, or *mensa*, was set aside for the monks, so that an unscrupulous layman could not expropriate the total amount. Some lay-abbots were unscrupulous, others were active reformers and patrons of the monastic life. It is often, in fact, difficult to know who the 'lay-abbots' are. Not all monks had made a full profession of vows; until they had done so they were laymen themselves; an abbot could thus be a 'lay-abbot' even if he had spent his life in a monastery. There is controversy over whether Einhard was in fact a layman. Angilbert, ambassador to Rome on three occasions, celebrated poet (known as 'Homer' at Charlemagne's court), lover of Charlemagne's daughter Bertha and father by her of the historian Nithard, is often said to have been a lay-abbot (probably because of his life-style), while in reality he was a priest attached to the imperial chapel at Aachen.

Angilbert provides an intriguing introduction to Carolingian monasticism. He was Abbot of St-Riquier, near Abbeville on the Channel coast, which he reconstructed and reorganised in the 790s. Our sources consist of his own description of the liturgy, relics and altars of the monastery; a description of the monastery and its possessions drawn up on the orders of Louis the Pious (both of these surviving in Hariulf's twelfth-century history of the monastery); and two seventeenth-century copies of a lost eleventh-century drawing of the monastery. The drawing shows the three monastic churches, disposed in a triangle and connected by perhaps 700 metres of covered walkway. St-Riquier was a grandiose conception. The main church, with its two massive towers, numerous relics and altars, and with four *imagines* (apparently free-standing sculptural groups on the floor of the church, possibly of gilded and painted stucco) representing the Nativity, Passion, Resurrection and Ascension, was on a scale unknown before. And the liturgy was on a scale to match, with an elaborate processional element ('a liturgical choreography' as one modern commentator has called it[25]) involving the movement of the monks around the various altars and *imagines* of the main church and along the covered walkways to the other churches and even around the surrounding villages on certain days in the year. The processional liturgy was probably borrowed from Metz, where a similar system had been established by Bishop Chrodegang some years earlier. In Metz the processions had been from one church to another, as in Rome, the ultimate inspiration. Rome may have inspired the architecture at St-Riquier too: the main altar was at the west, as in San Salvatore in the Lateran and St Peter's in the Vatican. It was part of that great importation into Francia in the eighth century of the practices of the Roman church which was an integral part of the Carolingian programme of unification and standardisation.

The three churches at St-Riquier were dedicated to the Saviour, to St Mary and to St Benedict. In the monastic sphere the Benedictine Rule was the Roman rule; it was under Louis the Pious that it was established as the standard rule for all Gallic monasteries. This crucial step in the history of European monasticism was primarily the work of Witiza, the son of a Gothic count of Maguelone in Septimania. Born around 750, he spent some time at the Carolingian court before being attracted by the monastic life. He refused the abbacy of a monastery near Dijon because he thought the monastic discipline there too loose. He founded a monastery at Aniane, on his own ancestral land – a disastrous experiment, because the rule he imposed was so severe that all his monks deserted. Around 787 he built a new monastery, larger and with the luxury and decoration he had hitherto despised; it was probably then too that he adopted the more humane Benedictine Rule and, like the Northumbrian monastic founder Biscop a century earlier, took the name of Benedict himself, to indicate the source of his inspiration. Benedict of Aniane's fame grew, and he visited many monasteries in southern Gaul, to preach and to reform. Soon he was doing this officially, as monastic supremo for Louis the Pious, at that time King of Aquitaine. He met opposition: he was accused before Charlemagne of being a disturber of the peace, and of usurping the goods and rights of others. The new monastic ideas were hostile to traditional Frankish practice, by which aristocratic families had retained rights over or even control of 'their' monasteries. Royal support of the principle of free election of abbots by the community, for instance, could be seen as a direct attack upon aristocratic privileges, and royal protection, which more and more monasteries sought under Charlemagne and Louis the Pious, was primarily protection against those aristocrats who felt they had rights over monasteries.

Benedict of Aniane played a major role in the long series of reforming councils which Louis the Pious held at Aachen between 816 and 819. The Synod of Aachen in 816 was mostly concerned with implementing Chrodegang of Metz's ideas for communities of cathedral clergy, but it also produced twenty-five decrees on monastic discipline, which were supplemented in succeeding years. The first and most significant was that the Rule of St Benedict was to be followed in all monasteries: a system of inspectors was later established to make sure that this was carried out, and representatives from each monastery urged to come to Benedict of Aniane's new monastery of Inde (now Cornelimünster), near Aachen, to see how the ideal monastic life should be lived. But there were also some major, and some minor, changes to the Benedictine Rule as originally compiled in the sixth century by Benedict of Nursia. Above all, very much more of the monks' time was to be taken up with the liturgy, and that liturgy was more prolonged and elaborated. The liturgical developments had been in process since the seventh century, but now they were incorporated into the monastic way of life, with inevitable consequences for the way in which monasticism was viewed: the monastic community was coming to resemble a Buddhist prayer-wheel, in which the fate of the wheel itself mattered less than that of the person who set it in motion.

There were a number of other significant changes to Benedictine practice. Benedict had allowed abbots to entertain guests in a special room apart from the other monks; in 816 it was decreed that abbots and guests should eat in the common monastic refectory; in 817 that no laymen might eat in the refectory at all; while in 818/19 it was conceded that lay nobles might eat with the monks. Abuse of monastic hospitality had taught abbots caution, but there was little agreement on detail. Novices should give all their property to their relations before final vows, rather than giving it to the poor or to the monastery, as Benedict of Nursia had specified. Presumably the family of the monk were to be given no excuse to claim rights to any portion of the monastic property; but the result may have been to encourage families to put relations in a monastery in order to acquire their property. The intent throughout this legislation is not only to obtain uniformity of custom, but also to ensure that those customs were followed, by emphasising discipline and by trying to remove the possibility of lay interference. Thus Benedict of Aniane gave the abbot more means of supervising and disciplining his monks than his predecessor, even instituting a monastic prison, but in other areas the powers of the abbot were reduced: he was given a deputy with very considerable powers, the prior, and the consent of the community was required before the abbot might appoint any of the major officers of the monastery.

There were critics of Benedict of Aniane's ideals, notably the influential abbot of Corbie, Adalard, Charlemagne's cousin, who was exiled to the island-monastery of Noirmoutier when Louis the Pious came to Aachen, and not recalled until Benedict's death. Some important monasteries resisted reform: Hilduin, the powerful Abbot of St-Denis, St Medard in Soissons and St-Germain-des-Prés, did not manage to reform St-Denis until the early 830s. The mid-ninth century was a troubled time for monasteries, with the invasions of Vikings and with civil war. The problems of a serious-minded abbot, attempting to preserve a canonical monastic life, can be seen most clearly in the 133 surviving letters by Lupus, Abbot of Ferrières-en-Gâtinais, some forty kilometres west of Sens. He became abbot in 840, at the wish of Charles the Bald, who had caused his predecessor Odo to be deposed for his support of the Emperor Lothar I: he died in 862 or shortly after. He wrote letters on the pronunciation of Latin, the difficulties of writing history, irregular verbs, predestination, and much else. He requested the loan of copies of Livy, Cicero or Boethius, or the gift of lead for the church-roof (this from King Aethelwulf of Wessex), of some cloaks and vestments to present to the Pope, or of some cups suitable for use when travelling. But many of his letters petitioned for the support of the great men of the kingdom on behalf of his own position or the welfare of his monastery. He wrote begging Charles the Bald to return to Ferrières the estate of St-Josse, which the king had granted to his vassal Count Odulf, and he begged Hincmar of Rheims to support his plea, describing in pitiful (and perhaps exaggerated) terms the poverty of Ferrières, with its monks wearing patched garments and their servants almost naked. Nor could Lupus devote all his time to his monastery or to his scholarship. Abbots and bishops, like counts, were royal servants as far as the Carolingians were concerned; he was obliged to go on military expeditions and to be present at the court regularly, and was sent as *missus*, inspector-general, to Burgundy in 844–5, and as ambassador to Rome in 849. He was also obliged to attend synods and councils of the Church, in some of which he acted as secretary. His last letters were overshadowed by what he called 'the imminent ruin of our monastery, which is menaced by our own sins and by the proximity of the pirates [Vikings]'.[26] Among his very last letters is one thanking the monastery of St-Germain in Auxerre for sheltering the monks of Ferrières in their flight from the Vikings, and one to the Archbishop of Sens, urging him to ward off the vengeance of God by leading a campaign against the sins of the day.

The Viking attacks undoubtedly brought terrible dislocation and destruction to monastic institutions, particularly those near the Channel and Atlantic coasts. Surviving monks sometimes fled with their relics and books to safer places inland. The best known migration is that of the monks of Noirmoutier (which in the 840s was used by the Vikings as one of their first permanent bases) who eventually brought themselves, and the relics of St Filibert, to Tournus in Burgundy. The destination of refugee monks from various Breton monasteries has recently been traced from the survival of manuscripts in places like Angers and Fleury which have marginal glosses in Old Breton. Where a monastery survived, and where it was restored, it was sometimes no more than an economic institution operated for the benefit of a local aristocratic family, sometimes being given walls to protect it and its considerable population of laymen and clerics from enemy attacks. But a communal life of learning and prayer often survived; this too had its uses for the lay aristocrat, who needed literate men for his administration, and prayers for his salvation. A tradition of scholarship was preserved in a number of monasteries, and there were always those prepared to strive for monastic reform.

One monastery stands as the fulfilment of Benedict of Aniane's vision, and may stand for the changed face of tenth-century monasticism: Cluny. Founded by William the Pious, Duke of Aquitaine, in 910 and given to the austere Abbot Berno, it emerged as a leading centre of monastic life under its second abbot, St Odo (927–42). Odo, like Benedict of Aniane before him, was asked by a number of monastic proprietors to reform their monasteries; within a century, scores of monastic houses had been reformed by or founded by Cluny, and were ruled by priors under the authority of the abbot of Cluny. Constant visitations from Cluny helped preserve monastic discipline; the structure was not unlike that envisaged by Benedict of Aniane and Louis the Pious, but with Cluny in place of the Emperor as the centralising force. Cluny's greatest asset was not so much its series of very able abbots, most of whom had very long tenures (only three abbacies separated Odo, d. 942, from St Hugh, 1049–1109), as its undoubted independence. Men were willing to call on Cluny for advice, or to give it land, in the knowledge that its abbot was not merely acting for some secular overlord. Cluny was founded by the Duke of Aquitaine, but in his lands in the Mâconnais, in Burgundy, a politically fragmented county by the late tenth century. Moreover, Cluny's orthodoxy was unquestionable; it was placed under the direct protection of the Papacy, and maintained frequent contact with Rome. Scores of properties were given to Cluny and its dependencies, by landowners of all degrees of wealth and importance, in return for prayers to be said for the donor and his family. This was an important development in the history of Christian piety, and one actively encouraged by Odo: as we have already seen (p. 80) he was the first to write a hagiography which showed how men could achieve salvation without joining a monastery. By showing itself to be a stable institution whose well-disciplined monks spent much of the day in prayer and in praise of God, Cluny could provide laymen with the hope of salvation. The names of all those who made donations to the monastery were carefully kept, so that they could be prayed for, and the importance attached by Cluny to prayers for the souls of the dead can be seen in its introduction of a new festival to the Christian calendar: the Feast of All Souls. The liturgy at Cluny reached heights undreamt of, or perhaps even unwished for, by Benedict of Aniane: on feast-days, according to Odo's biographer John of Salerno, the monks chanted 138 psalms. The liturgy was the weapon of the *milites Christi*, the soldiers of Christ, and, they believed, a very effective one. Abbot Odilo was told of a hermit who had had a vision in which he saw demons complaining that the souls of the damned were being freed from Hell: 'They chiefly made mention and greatest complaint about the members of the Cluniac congregation and its abbot.' It was upon hearing this report, according to an eleventh-century Cluniac, that Odilo instituted the new Feast.[27] This participation in the cosmic struggle between God and the Devil was carried out within some of the most grandiose architecture ever conceived by the Christian Church. Not only the physical surroundings, but the whole ethos and nature of monasticism had changed almost beyond recognition since the days of the first Gallic monks.

Cluny is, of course, only the most prominent of innumerable attempts at monastic reform in the late ninth and tenth centuries. Some of these were on a small scale, such as the monastery of Aurillac founded in the 890s by Count Gerald (as described in his *Life* by Odo of Cluny). In northern Gaul Gerard of Brogne was acting as a professional reformer in the Flemish monasteries, and the monastery of Gorze in Lotharingia provided an inspiration for monastic reform which reached as far as England. The basic difference between Gorze and Cluny was in the political circumstances in which they found themselves. Gorze was in a stable and unified kingdom, and all her dependent monasteries were under the effective protection either of the German king or of a bishop. Cluny was in the midst of a totally fragmented political landscape; neither the descendants of the founder nor any other political power was in a position to dominate the monastery, and thus it was able to preserve its total freedom, as William's foundation charter put it, 'from our power, from that of our kindred, and from the jurisdiction of royal greatness'. Otherwise Cluny and Gorze lived in the same world; one which accepted that the only certain way to salvation (and, indeed, education) was to join a monastery; in which all levels of the Christian community had accepted that donation of gifts to a well-run monastery would ensure that prayers would be said for their souls; and in which it was becoming increasingly more possible for a monastic community to live out its communal ideals undisturbed. The monastic community stood before the lay world in Gaul, offering it a way of life which was almost a direct inversion of its own: a life of peace and prayer, which ignored the lures of wealth and lust, broke away from the demands of the kin, and accepted the rule of a humble man. The ideal was seldom fulfilled; but that such an ideal could be accepted tells us much about early medieval Gaul.

PART II

Authority

Introduction: Kings and Aristocrats

THE political history of Frankish Gaul, traditionally interpreted as the doings of kings and aristocrats, is not easy to understand, either for the scholar, frustrated by the difficulties of penetrating the records to find the living personalities and the everyday issues which concerned them, or for the ordinary reader, overwhelmed by the unfamiliar names and the apparently aimless manoeuvrings. It is possible to give body to the brief narratives of historians or annalists, or understand the significance of land charters, by studying structures and ideas; thus, work in the post-war period on the nature of kingship and on the development of the Frankish aristocracy has enabled historians to get a better understanding of the actions of individual members of the class of ‘kings’ or ‘aristocrats’. And historians now are not so prone to fall into the centralist trap of actually imagining that what kings did necessarily involved or affected many of their subjects. As we have already seen, some of the most crucial Merovingian political activity took place at the level of the *civitas*, the city-state; in the Carolingian period it often took place at the equally obscure level of relations between lords and their men.

The authority of the king, and his ability to enforce obedience, naturally depended upon a number of variables: the personality of the king, the extent to which he could reward loyal followers, his level of information and interest in what was going on in all corners of his kingdom, and, ultimately, his willingness and ability to impose his will by armed force. We must not make the mistake of assuming that kings necessarily wanted to have complete control over events in their kingdom. Like most Roman Emperors or medieval kings, a Frankish king did not govern or administer – he reigned. He acted as king and did what kings were supposed to do: give presents and favours and, when appropriate, lead armies. He would also, of course, take part in legal procedures, if called upon to do so; he might even, if his bishops pressed him, publicly declare the need for morality and justice in his kingdom. But if the customary taxes and dues were paid, the cities and localities would frequently be left to a kind of self-government which was not unlike that enjoyed by the *civitates* of the early Roman Empire. In the countryside the estates of great landowners, clerical or lay, were frequently equally free of royal interference or influence.

It was only under Charlemagne and his immediate successors that the Church achieved brief recognition by kings – though by no means by all their subjects – that kings had the Christian duty to govern strictly and ensure the spiritual and moral welfare of their subjects, as a bishop did that of his flock.

At all times, Frankish kings depended for their power upon the acquiescence of the aristocracy, or a part of it. From the earliest times, the kings seldom acted alone. The earliest Merovingian decrees all issue from decisions made jointly by the king and by the *optimates, potentes, meliores* or whatever other word was used of the great men of the kingdom gathered at the royal court. The king was powerless without these men. By simply living on their estates and ignoring the court they could effectively diminish the authority and prestige of the king. Even at the height of Frankish royal power, in the mid-sixth or early ninth centuries, there were aristocrats who could be tempted to act in direct contravention of royal will and to pursue their own political interests.

Historians have often been tempted to see the history of the Frankish monarchy in terms of a power struggle between monarchy and aristocracy; it could equally appropriately be described as a story of continuing co-operation. After all, the Frankish monarchy is unique among the monarchies of early medieval Europe for the unswerving loyalty bestowed upon its royal families. In only a handful of cases before the tenth century did an aristocrat from a non-royal Frankish family dare to put himself forward as king, and in no case save that of the Carolingians themselves did the usurper prosper. Even among the other peoples of Gaul who recognised Frankish authority, only the Bretons, a very special case, had their own kings. The Merovingians and subsequently the Carolingians had a monopoly of royal power, and aristocrats were prepared to respect that monopoly; not, however, for any mystical or theoretical reasons, but because on the one hand those kings were of use to them, and on the other they did not inconvenience them. The history of Gaul from 500 (and earlier) to 1000 is indeed the history of a slow and virtually uninterrupted annexation by the aristocracy of powers of justice, taxation and lordship that had belonged to the emperors and then to the Frankish kings, and also the history of the broadening of that aristocracy, so that by 1000 Gaul was a patchwork of scores of petty states. But that annexation was neither premeditated nor deliberate; in many cases aristocrats were not wresting privileges from the king so much as fulfilling functions that kings were unable or unwilling to provide. Moreover, in a world in which political support depended upon constant generosity, wealth and thus power naturally flowed in one direction: once the resources of the Merovingian and then the Carolingian dynasties had been exhausted by distribution to the aristocracy, the kings had nothing left save their (often considerable) prestige.

The history of the changing relationships between kings and aristocrats, and the changing foundations of royal and aristocratic power, falls into four main periods: the period of Merovingian supremacy, from Clovis to the sons of Dagobert I (*c.* 500 to the 650s); the period during which the Carolingians emerge as the leading aristocratic family and unite Gaul under their authority (650s to 750s); the period of Carolingian supremacy (750s to 850s); and the period of the rise of independent principalities and lordships and the break-up of Carolingian power (850s to *c.* 1000). In the four chapters which follow I shall continue to use the words 'aristocracy' and 'aristocrat', however etymologically inappropriate they may be. The words 'nobility' and 'noble', like the German word *Adel*, have the connotation of a legally defined, self-conscious and hereditary class. Much of the debate over the existence or non-existence of an early Frankish *Adel* has been created by the connotation of the word; the latest contribution to the debate sensibly substitutes the German word *Oberschicht* or 'upper class'. No doubt there was a nobility in fifth-century Gaul – members of the Roman senatorial class – and most scholars would admit the existence of a nobility in Gaul by the year 1000. But for the period covered by this book there was no well-defined noble class. Individual aristocrats were no doubt readily identifiable, of course: by their life-style, their dress (which often revealed their wealth), their landed property, their proximity to the king, their political and military activity, and their family connections.

5. The Merovingian Supremacy

IN the early Merovingian period there were two predominant aristocracies in Gaul: Roman and Germanic. Their traditions were not so different as might be supposed. By 500 Visigothic and Burgundian aristocrats had been Roman landowners, living side by side with Roman senators, for two or more generations, and in the north the Frankish aristocrats had been near neighbours and fellow-soldiers of the Romans for far longer. Soon after the Frankish conquest of Gaul the Frankish and Roman aristocracies began to intermingle and intermarry. The intermarriage which, outside Aquitaine at least, was eventually to eliminate the consciousness of Roman descent, has been illustrated by recent prosopographical research. Thus, we know much about Bertram, Bishop of Le Mans from 586 to some time before 626, from his will, which lists 135 properties scattered over Gaul between Brittany and Provence, some 300,000 hectares in extent, about half the size of a modern French *département*. His family connections can also be pieced together, from a variety of sources. He was the nephew of Bishop Bertram (Bertechramnus) of Bordeaux, who was related to the Merovingian royal family through his mother Ingitrudis. Bertram of Le Mans was the product of a 'mixed marriage', his father being Frankish and his mother Roman, from Aquitaine: she was related to Avitus of Clermont, whose name shows his descent from the most distinguished senatorial family of Roman Gaul. Bertram's extensive estates came to him from both his Frankish and his Roman ancestors. Sometimes such intermarriage and intermingling of traditions can be seen in the name-giving habits of the aristocracy. Waldalenus was a duke in Burgundy in the late sixth century; his wife Flavia was clearly a Roman, and his two sons, Donatus (later Bishop of Besançon) and Chramnelenus (later duke), were given Roman and German names respectively. The chronicler Fredegar said that Chramnelenus was '*ex genere Romano*', and the likelihood is that Waldelenus himself, despite his Germanic name, was of Roman family. Names such as Chramnulfus and Waldebertus are prominent in later seventh-century Burgundian history, perhaps illustrating the continued importance of this aristocratic clan. The frequency with which Romans in Frankish and Burgundian areas adopted Germanic names naturally obscures for us the question of the survival of Roman aristocratic families in these areas. Only rarely can we detect their survival, above all in areas of strong Roman tradition. We have already come across Germanus, first abbot of Granfelden near Basle (d. *c.* 675), who came from a family of 'Frankish senators' near Trier, as his hagiographer put it. Their names, such as Germanus and Numerianus, show us that by 'Frankish' the author simply means 'north Gallic': around the former Imperial capital, at least, Roman aristocratic families remembered their traditions. Outside the Frankish north, such memories were far more resilient. Indeed, the consciousness of belonging to a great tradition seems even to have been heightened in southern Gaul in the seventh century, as we can again see in name-giving fashions: we have names like Hector, Patroclus, Orestes, Virgil, Plato and Cato. That this fashion was more the result of nostalgia than of learning is suggested by the appearance in the sources of four bishops called Dido, whose parents had presumably not progressed far enough into their Virgil to realise that Dido was a Carthaginian princess: one is reminded of the eighth-century monk who thought, logically enough given the *-us* ending, that the goddess Venus was a man.

In Southern Gaul, of course, the aristocracy retained more than just their names to remind them of the past. They retained, if not increased, their social position, their hold on the church, their landed property, and their cultural predominance. The latter had always been an important criterion, and in the confused conditions of the fifth and sixth centuries may have seemed even more so. 'Since old grades of rank are now abolished, which once distinguished the high from the low,' wrote Sidonius Apollinaris in 478, 'in future culture must afford the sole criterion of nobility.'[1] But public schools did not outlive the Roman Empire, and increasingly it must have been more difficult for a layman to obtain an education, and less socially useful for him to do so. Nevertheless, we have our sixth- and even seventh-century imitators of Sidonius, such as Dynamius, a late sixth-century *patricius* of Provence, who corresponded with Pope Gregory the Great and the Italian immigrant poet Venantius Fortunatus (who ended his life as Bishop of Poitiers): more interestingly, a poem by Dynamius' wife Eucheria survives, and a poem in praise of the monastery of Lérins by their grandson, replete with classical allusion. In the sixth century it even seemed fitting for a Frankish aristocrat to take up these literary pursuits. The high palace official Gogo wrote both poetry and prose; his letters have been described as 'pretentious and obscure',[2] in short, the height of late Roman fashion. More famous are the literary and scholarly aspirations of King Chilperic I, who wrote Masses and hymns and a treatise (of considerable unorthodoxy) on the Trinity, and who wished, like the Emperor Claudius, to insert some additional letters into the Latin alphabet. Most Frankish aristocrats must have been perfectly fluent in Latin: there is not a hint in the *History* of Gregory of Tours that there were any translation problems between the Roman and Germanic elements of the aristocracy, nor that the Roman senators and bishops themselves spoke a word of Frankish.

The Roman aristocracy, as we have seen, continued to monopolise the offices of bishop and count in southern Gaul, right into the eighth century. Under the Merovingian kings of the sixth century, at times they even held important military positions. Eunius Mummolus, son of Count Peonius of Auxerre, was one of the most successful Merovingian generals, defeating the Saxons and the Lombards in Gaul (scattering the latter by his very presence, so terrified were they of his prowess, according to Gregory of Tours), and leading the armies of Guntram against his royal brothers. For four years after his break with Guntram, from 581 to 585, he remained unassailable within his base of Avignon, an effectively independent power. Romans were to be found not only leading Merovingian armies, but also at the royal courts, acting as advisers, administrators and legal experts, just as their predecessors had done in the fifth-century courts of the Visigoths and Burgundians. But in general the influence of the Roman aristocracy was above all ecclesiastical and local: the highest posts in the Merovingian armies and at the Merovingian courts were reserved for Franks.

The origins of the Frankish aristocracy are obscure. In the Pactus Legis Salicae the only Franks distinguished by a higher wergild were those actually on military service or those who were in the royal *trustis*, the sworn followers of the king. Some scholars have therefore concluded that the Frankish aristocracy owed its position entirely to its relationship with the king. Bergengruen has argued that it was not until the later part of the sixth century that the Frankish aristocracy ceased to be a court and service aristocracy and that its members became, like the Roman senators, landowners on a large scale. It is only then, the theory runs, that Franks began to consolidate their local political power and, for instance, to found monasteries upon their estates. This theory rests partly on the silence of the earliest Salic law concerning an independent aristocratic class, and partly, almost unconsciously, on nineteenth-century ideas of an early Germanic society made up of democratic communities of free peasants. But the Pactus Legis Salicae was a fairly disorganised and incomplete collection of Frankish customary law, perhaps partly out of date even at the time of its compilation, and drawn up on the orders of a king, deliberately emphasising the central role of the king in early Frankish society. Other evidence, notably archaeology and Gregory of Tours' *History*, suggests that from the very beginning there was a powerful aristocracy among the Franks, and that its power was by no means dependent upon the king.

In the late fifth century the first *Reihengräberfelder*, or row-grave cemeteries, began to be established in the Gallic countryside. Characterised by neat rows of graves containing single bodies, often buried fully dressed and with equipment (notably, in male graves, weapons), this burial type spread in the course of the sixth century from north-east Gaul throughout much of the world dominated by Franks, both Germany and Gaul. Even in southern Gaul some communities imitated this Frankish fashion. In the first two generations of this kind of burial practice, on either side of the year 500, our first Frankish aristocrats appear. A very few seem by their wealth and by the kinds of objects buried with them to be very near in rank to the Frankish king Childeric (d. 481) or to the boy-prince buried under Cologne Cathedral. The boy, aged about six, was lying within a stone-built chamber on a wooden cot; near him on a chair with lathe-turned back and leather seat, rested his child-sized helmet, and beside them were placed the long-sword, spears, bow and arrows and battle-axe of an adult, and a lathe-turned wooden staff or sceptre about half a metre long which may have denoted his royal status.[3] One such aristocrat was buried in grave 1782 in the huge cemetery of Krefeld-Gellep, outside a former Roman fortress on the Rhine. This grave contained a full set of weapons (sword, throwing-axe or *francisca*, barbed spear or *ango*), a helmet, a pair of knives with rilled gold-foil handles (possibly eating-implements), a silver spoon, personal jewellery and horse-harness decorated with gold and garnet cloisonné work, and vessels including glassware, a bronze jug, bronze hanging-bowl and bronze-bound bucket.[4] At a lower social level, perhaps, are those graves in which helmets are rare and vessels fewer, but in which the swords still had gold-and-garnet decorated pommels, and gold still decorated scabbards and belt-fittings. An example is grave 319 from Lavoye, best known for its bronze jug decorated with Christian scenes. The third archaeological group consists of what one might call the graves of lesser aristocrats: without helmets, well equipped with undecorated weapons, and with gold-cloisonné personal jewellery. This group may be typified by three graves at Mézières (Ardennes).[5] The oldest, no 68, was that of a warrior who died around 500, a Frankish chief, suggests the excavator M. Patrick Périn, installed by Clovis at this strategic point in the river Meuse. Tomb no 66, somewhat more recent, contained a long-sword with a silver pommel supplied with a loop and an interlocking ring; these ring-swords, found in England too, have been seen as symbolic of the link between a superior and the inferior who wears the sword. Perhaps this lesser aristocrat was the man of some great court aristocrat, or an 'antrustion', a member of the royal retinue, living on land granted by his lord. Around him and his two companions at Mézières spreads the later cemetery, consisting of the graves of some five hundred individuals buried in the course of the sixth century. None of these individuals was as wealthy (after death, at least) as the three warriors. This phenomenon of rich graves at the core of a cemetery is quite common. The most plausible explanation is that the rich graves, male and female, are those of the 'founders' of the cemetery, which is subsequently filled with the bodies of their dependants and servants and, sometimes, descendants. The cemetery was attached to a landed estate, property either deserted long before by the Roman landowners or else acquired by some means or other during the period of conquest. Those who worked on the estate may have been either Franks or Gallo-Romans, or both; in any case they copied, although in a diluted form, both the dress and the burial customs of their lord.

By the middle of the sixth century these rich graves have become much rarer in Gallic cemeteries. Like the Merovingian kings themselves, the obvious trend-setters, the aristocrats are having themselves buried in churches. One of the earliest of such burials is at Flonheim in Rheinhessen, a small church apparently used by one wealthy family for its dead from the time of Clovis right down to the mid-seventh century; the church of Arlon in Belgium is another, used like Flonheim for about a century and a half. Such finds are not common; often aristocratic families must have buried their dead not in tiny rural churches on their estates, but in the great urban or monastic basilicas, where they could benefit from the very best post-mortem care provided by the relics of powerful saints. Almost all of these have been so disturbed and so rebuilt in subsequent centuries that discovery of aristocratic tombs underneath them is very unlikely. Indeed, the wealth in these tombs may have jeopardised their survival for more than a few years. Gregory of Tours relates how the servants of the powerful aristocrat Guntram Boso, possibly acting on their lord's orders, went to a church near Metz and removed the precious objects from the tomb of one of his in-laws, on the day after her funeral![6]

The vast wealth of the greatest aristocrats is stressed again and again by Gregory of Tours. When King Childebert II had Duke Rauching killed he found a great amount of gold on his person; when his wife was informed of his death, she was riding through the streets of Soissons, 'bedecked with fine jewels and precious gems, bedizened with flashing gold, having a troop of servants in front of her and another one behind', on her way to Mass; while 'those who had been sent by the king to sequester Rauching's property discovered more things in his coffers than they could have expected to see in the public treasury of the king',[7] A vast hoard of gold, silver and precious objects was found when Guntram Boso was killed, in the same year, 587; two years earlier 250 talents of silver and more than 30 talents of gold were found in the hoard of Mummolus, a Gallo-Roman aristocrat. Aristocrats were, of course, bound by the same political necessities as kings. The foundations of power lay in land, for that provided the basic resources of food and men; but political power depended on supplies of treasure. Loyalty had to be bought; an ungenerous lord was an unsuccessful lord. And a lord who had nothing to give away but land was, ultimately, equally unsuccessful.

A treasury, then, was the keystone of political power. Aristocrats had them, and kings, and so indeed did queens. When Rigunth, daughter of King Chilperic and Fredegund, left in 584 on her ill-fated journey to Spain to marry the Visigothic prince Reccared, her father gave her an immense dowry. The mother added to this a vast weight of gold, silver and clothing. Chilperic was appalled. But Fredegund turned to the assembled Franks and said: 'Do not imagine, men, that any of this comes from the treasures amassed by your earlier kings. Everything you see belongs to me. Your most illustrious king has been very generous to me, and I have put aside quite a bit from my own resources, from the manors granted to me, and from revenues and taxes. You, too, have often given me gifts. . . . None of it has been taken from the public treasury.' Gregory adds that 'there was such a vast assemblage of objects that the gold, silver and other precious things filled fifty carts'.[8] It is an instructive passage, and equally instructive is the fate of the treasure. Much of it disappeared, together with some of the escort, at the first stop outside Partis. The rest was taken in Toulouse by Duke Desiderius, Chilperic's chief commander in Aquitaine, as soon as he had heard of Chilperic's assassination. Rigunth herself was brought home to mother. Gregory's last mention of her is ironic, given the role played by treasure in her brief life: she and her mother quarrelled (because of her promiscuity), and Fredegund tried to kill her by slamming down the lid of one of her treasure chests on her neck.

Like Fredegund, kings found their treasure in various ways: 'manors . . . revenues and taxes . . . gifts'. The Merovingian kings in the course of the conquest of Gaul had acquired estates everywhere, either by inheritance from the imperial fisc, or by confiscation. They had inherited also much of the structure of tax and customs collection from their Roman predecessors, and endeavoured to exploit it as best they could. There were taxes on both men and land, based on registers of tax-assessments, which periodically had to be revised. In 590, for instance, Childebert II ordered the tax assessments of churchmen in Clermont to be renewed, and in the meantime remitted all arrears; tax collection had been impossible, since many of those on the register had died, and much of the property had been divided and sub-let. Franks themselves seem to have been immune from such personal taxation, or at least to have considered themselves to be so. Tax collectors who tried, with the support of kings, to tax them suffered when their support vanished; Parthenius was stoned to death when King Theudebert died in 548, and Audo lost all his property and had to take sanctuary in the cathedral of Paris when Chilperic was assassinated in 584. Gallo-Romans seem to have been submissive enough, save when kings attempted to raise extraordinary taxation; Gregory mentions only one great tax-revolt, when the people of Limoges nearly killed the collector Marcus, and brought down the wrath of Chilperic upon themselves. In general, the ability of the Merovingian kings to raise taxes seems in the sixth century to have been quite considerable, and no doubt very profitable. But already the kings are treating their possession of the power to raise taxes as another of their possessions, to alienate if it seemed appropriate. In the sixth century the churches of St Martin in Tours, and St Martial in Limoges were exempt from direct taxation, with all their men and property; in the seventh century privileges which either freed particular institutions from customs dues or else gave them the right to collect them for their own benefit became more and more common.

Perhaps the most vital revenue-raising expedient whose returns diminished rapidly in the course of the seventh century was war. War was profitable for the ordinary soldier as well as for thc king, and kings were on occasion forced into it by their men. In 532 Theuderic refused to go with his brothers against Burgundy, and his Franks threatened to desert him unless he changed his mind. They were placated when he led them to his own province of the Auvergne, whose loyalty he suspected: there 'you will be able to lay your hands on so much gold and silver that even your lust for loot will be satisfied. . . . You may capture as many cattle and slaves and seize as much clothing as you wish.'[9] Later, and for the same reason, his brother Chlothar's Franks forced him to go on what proved to be a totally disastrous expedition against the Saxons. But in general the expeditions of the Merovingians in the sixth century, in Germany, Italy, Spain, and within Gaul itself, if often militarily far from successful, were at least financially well worthwhile. Italy, in particular, a graveyard for the armies of the Franks and their allies, was a source of constant profit for the Merovingian kings who sent them in, for they were recipients of massive bribes from all sides in the wars waged by the Byzantine Emperors against first the Ostrogoths and then the Lombards.

Even the wars which resulted from the family arrangements of the Merovingians themselves were of profit. The Frankish kingdom had been divided into four portions on the death of Clovis in 511; during the succeeding hundred years they were reunited only once, by Clovis's surviving son Chlothar I, from 558 to 561. The fraternal warfare, which Gregory so bewailed, brought booty and confiscated land to the kings and their Frankish supporters; the only losers were the Gallo-Roman populace, who were denied the stable conditions needed for successful agriculture and commerce. Politically speaking, partition probably ensured the survival of the Merovingian dynasty. Elsewhere, in contemporary England or Spain, the inevitable political opposition gathered around a powerful magnate; successful rebellion brought a new and normally short-lived dynasty. In Francia, discontented aristocrats clustered around one of the royal brothers or nephews, or occasionally around a man who claimed Merovingian blood: the dynasty itself was safe. Above all, partition neatly solved the problem of what to do with younger sons on the death of their fathers. Family solidarity might dictate another solution, however. In 523/4, on the death of one of Clovis's sons, Chlodomer, the three surviving sons could have organised the division of Chlodomer's kingdom among his own three sons. Instead Childebert and Chlothar murdered two of them, and would have murdered the third, Chlodovald, had he not escaped, tonsured himself and entered a monastery, to become the first Frankish royal saint, St Cloud.

Chlodovald was saved from death by the intervention of *viri fortes*, powerful men: possibly the first political intervention of the aristocracy in our sources, and the first of many on behalf of a boy king. When Theuderic died in 534, Childebert and Chlothar again intervened to partition his kingdom between themselves; but Theudebert, Theuderic's son, 'with the help of his *leudes*', succeeded to the throne. *Leudes*, the sworn followers of a king, members of his armed retinue, may or may not at this time have constituted the aristocracy of Theudebert's kingdom. The terminology of our sources, notably of Gregory, is often ambiguous. Sometimes 'the Franks' themselves seem to have a politically important role. Is this the people assembled in the army, or just the wealthy, the aristocrats? Who are the *Franci* who murder Theudebert's Gallo-Roman tax-collector Parthenius, or who force Theudebert to give up his wife Deuteria – the first and last Gallo-Roman to be married to a Merovingian king? Theudebert was one of the most flamboyantly successful of early Merovingian kings, using his north-eastern kingdom as a spring-board for campaigns against Saxons, Thuringians, Ostrogoths and Greeks. According to the Greek historian Agathias, he planned to march on Constantinople; he certainly did go so far as to mint gold coins with his own name on them, a hitherto respected imperial prerogative. The letter he wrote to the Emperor Justinian between 539 and 547 expressed his confidence and his ambitions, speaking of his realms stretching 'from the Danube and the borders of Pannonia to the shores of the [Atlantic] Ocean'.[10] Perhaps Theudebert's thoroughly Roman approach to his rule upset his Frankish supporters, who came mainly from the north-east, later known as Austrasia, where purely Frankish influence was much stronger than in the other *Teilreiche*, or 'portion-kingdoms'. On his death in 548 his son Theudebald, still a young boy, was looked after by the *proceres et primi regni*, the magnates and first men of the kingdom: the first entry of the aristocracy as a sustained political force, and indeed the first political appearance of the Austrasian aristocracy, from whom the royal successors to the Merovingians would emerge.

Rather more is known about a later Austrasian minority, that of Sigibert's son Childebert II. In 575 Sigibert, king of Austrasia, had been assassinated by order of his sister-in-law Fredegund. This was one round, and one of the most effective, in the long vendetta that had begun when Fredegund inspired Chilperic to murder his wife so that she could take her place. The wife, the Visigothic princess Galswintha, had a powerful avenger: her sister, Brunhild, Sigibert's queen. Sigibert's assassination left Brunhild temporarily defenceless; she was captured by Chilperic. But her five-year-old son Childebert II was rescued by Duke Gundovald, who had him proclaimed king by the Austrasians. For ten years, until he reached his majority, his kingdom was controlled by the magnates, and his mother Brunhild largely excluded from power. The magnates sought to protect their infant king by looking for an alliance with one or other of Sigibert's surviving brothers, Chilperic, king of the Neustrian *Teilreich*, and Guntram of Burgundy. At first, under the influence of Gogo, Childebert's *nutritor* or governor, the Austrasians looked to Guntram. In 577 the childless Guntram met Childebert (with *suis proceribus*, his magnates), and adopted him as his son. But in 580 Chilperic, too, lost his last children, and began to urge a group of Austrasian magnates to overthrow the Burgundian alliance, using as his spokesman Childebert's Bishop of Rheims, Egidius, who seems to have been receiving Chilperic's money. The coup came in 581: a new alliance with Chilperic was agreed by the Austrasian opposition, Gogo died, and his supporters were ousted from their positions. Lupus, Duke of Champagne, for instance, was forced to flee to Guntram's kingdom by Ursio and Berthefried. Brunhild tried to protect her supporter: 'Leave us, woman,' replied Ursio. 'Let it be enough for you that you held the kingdom under your husband. Now your son rules, and his kingdom is under our protection, not yours.'[11]

The hostility shown by Gregory of Tours to these Austrasian magnates – Egidius of Rheims, Guntram Boso, Ursio, Berthefried and others – has ensured that they have generally been regarded as villains. Guntram Boso's high-level intrigues in particular attracted Gregory's attention. He was, Gregory concluded, 'an unprincipled man, eager in his avarice, covetous beyond measure of the property of others, giving his word to all, keeping his promises to none'.[12] Gregory's view may well have been shared by the rank-and-file of Childebert's kingdom: for the first time we can see an apparent division between the magnates and the bulk of the people. 'The lesser people raised a great murmur against Bishop Egidius and the royal dukes, and began to shout and to proclaim publicly: "Take away from the king's presence those who are selling his kingdom, who are giving his

1 A nineteenth-century impression of the treasure found in the grave of King Childeric (*d* 481/2) at Tournai in 1653. Most was lost in a theft from the Bibliothèque Royale in Paris in 1831. Courtesy: the Bodleian Library, Oxford.

2 The ivory belt-buckle reputedly worn by St Caesarius of Arles. It represents the soldiers guarding Christ's tomb – a suitable symbol of resurrection to be placed in a saint's tomb.

3 The front and back of the gravestone from Niederdollendorf. One side shows a warrior, perhaps in his tomb and being threatened by evil serpents; the other may represent Christ in Glory.

4 Two of the incised stone slabs from the funerary chapel of Abbot Mellebaudis at Poitiers (*c* 700). The upper one represents St Matthew, St John and the Archangels Raphael and Raguel.

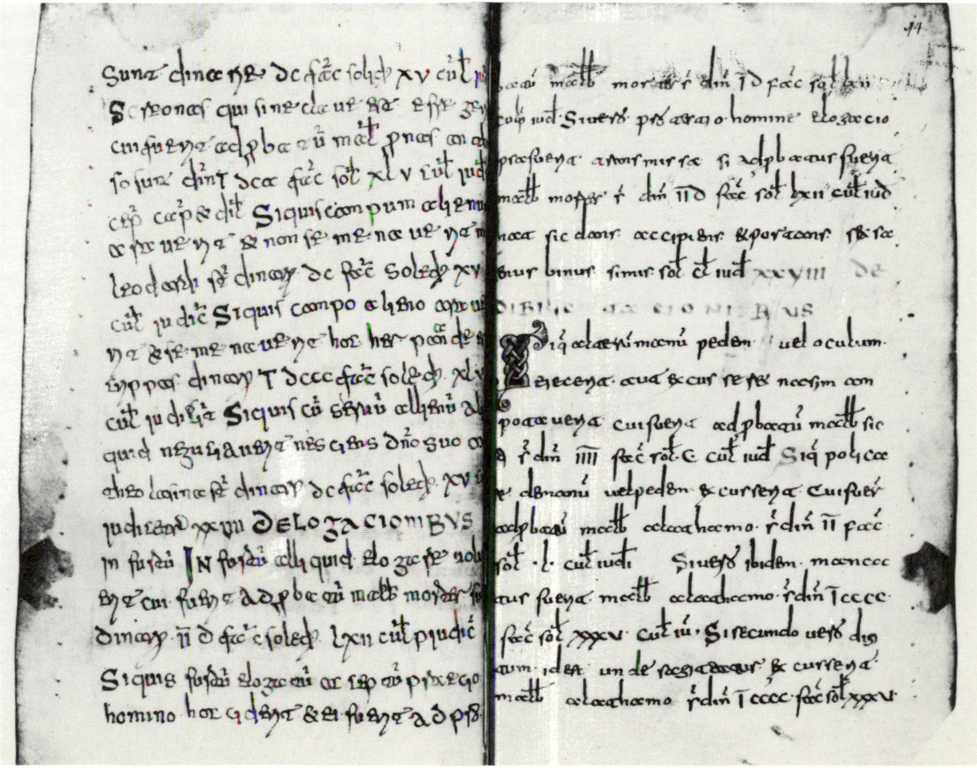

5 The text of laws 26–28 in the earliest surviving manuscript of the Lex Salica. This opening shows clearly where one scribe ends and another begins: both write in typically eighth-century styles. Courtesy: the Ducal Library, Wolfenbüttel.

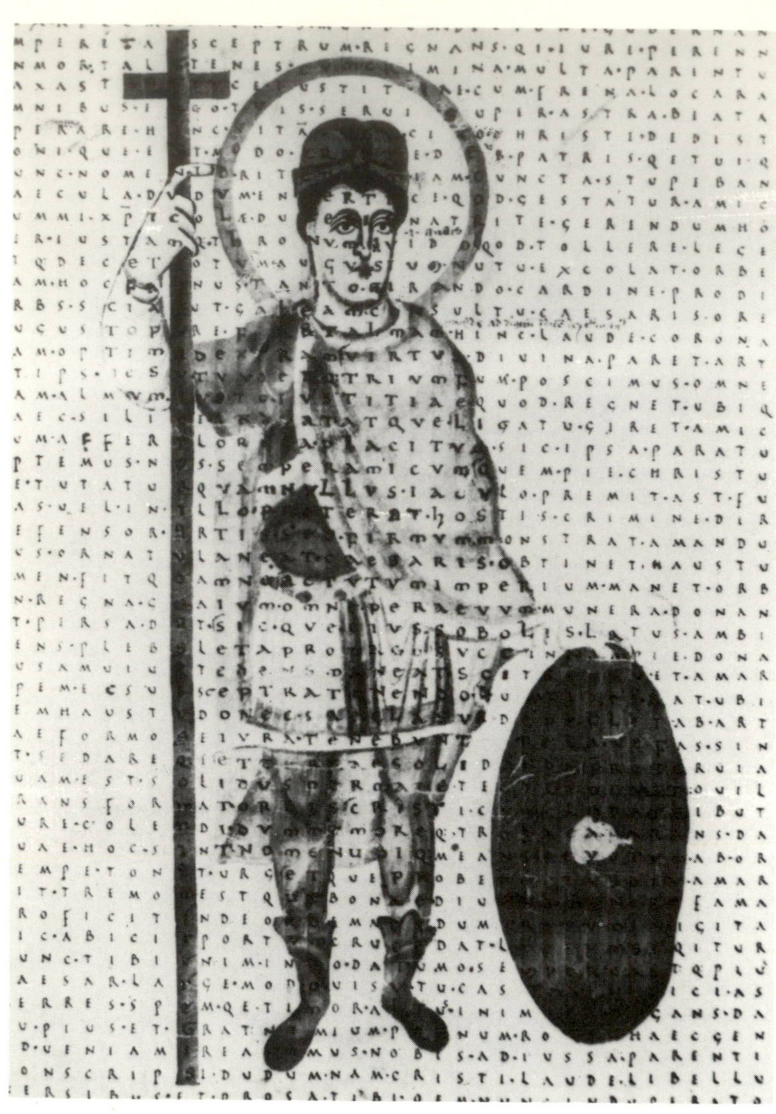

6 A contemporary portrait of Louis the Pious incorporating the text of a poem – a scholarly conceit of the Late Roman period revived during the 'Carolingian Renaissance'.

7 The reading-desk which may once have been used by St Radegund. It is preserved today in the monastery of the Holy Cross in Poitiers along with other relics of the saint.

8 A seventeenth-century engraving of an early drawing of the great Carolingian monastery of Centula or St-Riquier.

civitates over into the lordship of another, and surrendering his people into the jurisdiction of another prince!"'[13] The mob attacked, and Egidius had to flee for his life. These Austrasian magnates were behind one of the most interesting political episodes in the sixth century: the attempted usurpation of Gundovald. He claimed to be a son of Chlothar I; Chlothar denied him, but others certainly believed his story, and it may indeed have been true. He had gone to Italy, and thence to Constantinople; it is possible that his attempted usurpation was supported by the Byzantine Emperor. In 582 Guntram Boso went as spokesman to Constantinople, to put the Austrasian plan to Gundovald. According to Gregory, Gundovald later explained how Guntram Boso had appealed to his sense of family solidarity: indeed, in 582, with Guntram and Chilperic both childless and the young Childebert by no means assured of survival, the plight of the Merovingian dynasty was a plausible enough pretext for Gundovald's intervention. It throws an interesting light on the ambitions of the Austrasian aristocracy, or the dominant portion of it. They did not want a weak king; they did not want to act as a council of regents. A weak king threatened their own position, and under a weak king the stream of benefits was liable to dry up. Above all, perhaps, the magnates wanted a renewal of the profitable eastern campaigns. Chilperic's kingdom was ill-placed geographically for such enterprises, and Guntram was too cautious to get involved.

Support for Gundovald nevertheless dried up when he landed at Marseilles in late 582, perhaps because shortly beforehand a son had been born to Chilperic. Gundovald had to turn tail, and Guntram Boso arrested Bishop Theodore of Marseilles, attempting to remove attention from himself by blaming another for Gundovald's arrival. By 584 conditions were suitable for Gundovald's return. Chilperic's heir had died, and Chilperic himself had been assassinated, at Brunhild's instigation. No one as yet knew that Fredegund was bearing Chilperic's son, the future Chlothar II. With Guntram the only surviving adult Merovingian, the future of the dynasty looked precarious; many may have thought that recognition of Gundovald would strengthen the dynasty. Gundovald led his supporters on a triumphant progress through Aquitaine, during which he had himself raised up on a shield as king. But his rising had come too late. Chilperic's son Chlothar was born. Guntram appealed to his subjects: 'I beg you, all men and women who are present, that you preserve your loyalty to me and that you do not kill me as you killed my brothers.

Give me at least three years in which to bring up my nephews, whom I have adopted as my sons, lest it happens, God forbid, that I die while they are still small children. At the same time you would perish, for there would be no fullgrown man of our family left to protect you.'[14] Not long afterwards, in 585, Childebert II reached the age of fifteen, and his majority. Brunhild took over control of affairs, and began a purge of her former opponents among the Austrasian magnates; and there was a reconciliation between Childebert II and Guntram. The rebel Gundovald was crushed at St-Bertrand-de-Comminges.

For almost another thirty years the Visigothic princess Brunhild dominated Frankish affairs. Precisely how she did it, and the real significance of her career, are very difficult to assess. Gregory of Tours *History* ceases in 592, before the death of Guntram and the emergence of Childebert and his mother as rulers of the greater part of Francia; Gregory himself is dead before the death of Childebert, at the age of twenty-six, when Brunhild became regent for her two young grandchildren, Theudebert and Theuderic. Our only informants from then on are notably hostile to Brunhild: a Burgundian chronicler usually known as Fredegar, and the authors of two lives of saints 'persecuted' by Brunhild: the Visigothic king Sisebut's *Life of Desiderius of Vienne*, and Jonas of Bobbio's *Life of Columbanus*.[15] The key point in Brunhild's career after Childebert's death was 600, when her grandson Theudebert came of age and, presumably together with his Austrasian advisers, deprived Brunhild of any influence in his kingdom. She was welcomed to Burgundy by Theuderic and, eventually, twelve years later, persuaded him to attack his brother Theudebert (who was, she now claimed, a gardener's son, and no Merovingian at all). Theuderic won a decisive victory; Theudebert was imprisoned and his small son assassinated. When Theuderic himself died shortly afterwards, Brunhild tried to put Sigibert, her great-grandson, forward as the new king. But Chlothar II, the son of her old enemy Fredegund, who had been restricted to a few *civitates* on the Channel coast by his cousins, was invited into Austrasia by the magnates. The Burgundian magnates too revolted against Brunhild. She was 'brought before Chlothar, who was boiling with fury against her. He charged her with the deaths of ten Frankish kings . . . . She was tormented for three days with a diversity of tortures, and then on his orders was led through the ranks on a camel. Finally she was tied by her hair, one arm and one leg to the tail of an unbroken horse, and she was cut to shreds by its hoofs at the pace it went.'[16] Brunhild was about sixty-five when she died. Chlothar II had reunited the Merovingian kingdom, for the first time since the death of his grandfather Chlothar I, in 561.

A traditional picture of Brunhild's career sees her as a 'Romaniser', relying on Romans to help her in her policies of centralisation and tax reform, both of which antagonised the Austrasian and Burgundian aristocracies. That is what the daughter of a Visigothic king ought to have been doing. Certainly she did rely on such Romans as Protadius, her lover according to Fredegar, who was 'monstrously cruel, extorting the last penny for the fisc, and with ingenuity both filling the fisc and enriching himself at the expense of others'.[17] And certainly she tried to maintain good relations with her bishops, most of whom were Gallo-Romans. The two churchmen she exiled, Desiderious (who was killed, probably without her knowledge, on his way into exile) and Columbanus, were exceptions; they had attacked her at her weakest point, by emphasising publicly that Theuderic's children were illegitimate. She did not want her grandson to have a queen, to supplant her in her role as controller of the royal household. But there is nothing to suggest that her attitude to rule differed from that of her Frankish predecessors. Despite some hostility there was no active opposition from the magnates until after the defeat of Theudebert and death of Theuderic. Then they were faced with a choice between an aged regent acting in the name, again, of a small boy, or the vigorous twenty-nine-year-old Chlothar II. As at the time of Gundovald, thirty years earlier, they chose rather to have a strong and vigorous king. Although the desires of the magnates have not changed, it looks as if the periods of minority have left them more organised and determined. Warnachar, the later mayor of the palace in Burgundy, seems to have been able to act as spokeman for the Burgundian aristocracy. In Austrasia the leading figures were Arnulf, Bishop of Metz, and Pippin, later to be mayor of the Austrasian palace. They came from two of the wealthiest aristocratic families in the area, with land in the Moselle valley in particular. Pippin's daughter was to marry Arnulf's son: the dynasty which resulted from the union of Arnulfing and Pippinid would be known as that of the Carolingians.

A further presage of the future was the way in which the newly reunited kingdom was organised. Although there was only one king, the *tria regna* of Neustria, Austrasia and Burgundy continued to function separately, with the fourth part of Gaul, Aquitaine, being divided among the three kingdoms as before. Warnachar was made mayor of the palace in Burgundy after he, or the Burgundian aristocracy as a whole, extracted an oath from Chlothar that he would never be deposed. Warnachar had considerable power within his kingdom, even summoning a synod of his bishops shortly before his death in 626. Fredegar gives the impression that royal visits to Burgundy were infrequent under Chlothar II and his son Dagobert, and distinctly unwelcome to the magnates. Dagobert visited in 628: 'the profound alarm that his coming caused among the Burgundian bishops, magnates and others of consequence was a source of general wonder; but his justice brought great joy to the poor.'[18] A similar, and equally unwelcome, sorting-out occurred in Burgundy three years after Dagobert's death, when his widow Nantichild came with the young king Clovis II. The Austrasian magnates, on the other hand, still welcomed strong and accessible kings. In 622/3 the Austrasians were given Dagobert as their own king, and did not turn against him until he inherited Chlothar II's entire kingdom and decided to settle in that Neustrian den of iniquity, Paris: 'he forgot the justice he had once loved. He longed for ecclesiastical property and for the goods of his subjects. . . . . He surrendered himself to limitless debauchery.'[19]

Both Chlothar II and Dagobert I attempted a new beginning for the Merovingian monarchy after the appalling civil wars that had ended Brunhild's career. The Edict of Paris of 613 is the best-known public enunciation of this desire: a mixture of pious wishes for law and order, and decisions to continue the taxation policies of his predecessors. The historian Mitteis thought that the Edict was the price Chlothar had to pay for the aristocracy's support: 'Not without some exaggeration, this edict has been termed the "Magna Carta" of the Frankish aristocracy.'[20] Like Magna Carta, it is a much debated and much misunderstood document, but that is where the similarity ends. Mitteis, and others, seized upon the clause proclaiming that judges should be drawn from their own localities, and saw it as a concession to aristocrats who were already building up and consolidating their local power bases; it is, in fact, as it explains, a provision which would enable amends to be seized from the properties of a corrupt judge – not a concession, but an attempt to organise the kingdom justly. Nor are 'judges' in this context necessarily counts, as many have supposed, for the term probably includes lesser officials. A more significant clause of the Edict of Paris relates to the appointment of these judges, in which both bishops and magnates can clearly have some responsibility: 'Bishops and *potentes* who possess properties in several regions, should not appoint judges or itinerant officals from other provinces, unless they are from that place in which they render justice and perform their services.'[21] The king relies upon the aristocracy for the administration of the kingdom, but he is attempting, again, to diminish corruption by making local officials liable to have their property confiscated.

The Edict of Paris, like any other written proclamation in the early Middle Ages, no doubt had little significant effect upon what went on within the kingdom. Kings enforced their will not so much by proclamation as by their presence and their contacts with the leading men of the kingdom. We know of one means by which Chlothar endeavoured to spread his ideas and influence among the aristocracy, a means no doubt used by earlier Merovingian kings: he attracted the youth of the aristocracy to his court for their education. The aristocracy cannot have needed much persuading. A member of the family permanently resident at court must have been a useful asset, as well as an investment for the future. In the mid-seventh century a whole group of men who had been educated at the court of Chlothar remained active in the royal interests, and in preserving their old friendships: Desiderius, treasurer and later Bishop of Cahors, whose letters are our source of information about this group; Audoen, referendary and later Bishop of Rouen; Eligius, treasurer and later Bishop of Noyon; Abbo, Bishop of Metz; Sulpicius, Bishop of Bordeaux; Paul, Bishop of Verdun. Chlothar and Dagobert seem deliberately to have used bishops loyal to the monarchy as a means of holding their kingdom together. The Edict of Paris had upheld the king's right to appoint to bishoprics. This was not necessarily a centralising factor, in the sense of appointing men from the royal court to the provinces regardless of their own connections. Desiderius, for instance, became Bishop of Cahors in succession to his brother, in an area in which the family held considerable property. Eligius, however, also from Aquitaine, was appointed bishop in north-east Gaul, not perhaps to the satisfaction of all in his diocese: his hagiographer reports one confrontation in which his opponents address him as 'Roman' (i.e. Aquitanian) almost as if it were an insult.[22] As bishops, these men could in some ways be more useful to the king than when serving as treasurer at court, for they could act as royal agents and informants with areas in which often the kings themselves had only rare contacts.

Chlothar and Dagobert were prepared to develop other tested means of controlling their kingdom. The 'sub-kingdom' had been known in the sixth century, but largely as a way of getting rid of a spare but energetic royal son; it seems now to have been used as a specific element of policy. Chlothar made Dagobert king of the Austrasians, under his own general authority; Dagobert made his younger brother Charibert king in southern Aquitaine – a brief revival of the 'kingdom of Toulouse' – primarily in order to contain the Basques, who were thrusting deeper into Frankish territory. Under Dagobert the Frankish aristocracy must have benefited from the revival, after years of neglect, of the traditional campaigning against their enemies: Basques, Bretons, Visigoths and Slavs. The Slav campaigns went badly, according to Fredegar because of the demoralisation of the Austrasian contingents, who were discontented with Dagobert's rule from Neustria. Not long afterwards Dagobert gave the Austrasians his infant son Sigibert III as their king. Dagobert's two under-kingdoms are an interesting presage of future events. The Aquitanian kingdom he abandoned after Charibert's death in 632, and his own assassination of Charibert's young son Chilperic, possibly because of the lack of co-operation from the Aquitanian aristocracy. The Austrasian aristocracy, on the other hand, pleaded for their own king. The Austrasians and the Aquitanians had two of the most clearly developed 'national' identities in the early seventh century, the one, the bearer of Frankish traditions, loyal to the monarchy, and the other, still mindful of its Roman past, hostile or indifferent to it. In the next century these two peoples would produce the two most highly organised and successful political entities in Gaul.

The sixth-century Merovingian kings seem to have demanded a general oath of loyalty from their subjects. Chlothar and Dagobert may have attempted to strengthen this oath by insisting that the oath be sworn in their presence, like the oaths taken by their antrustions. Bishop Bertram of Le Mans talked of the 'indissoluble oath' which he had sworn to Chlothar; Eligius, on the other hand, refused to swear such an oath to Dagobert. Here we may have a distinction which was to prove so important in future centuries between north and south, between Frank (Bertram) and Roman (Eligius). Among the Franks it was common to take an irrevocable oath of loyalty to an aristocrat, or for aristocrats to take such an oath to a king. Such an oath bound them to service (often in their youth, in the armed retinue or following of their lord), and did not necessarily result in gifts of land in return: it was the oath given by an inferior to a superior. Romans seem to have regarded those bound by such oaths as little better than slaves: Gregory of Tours referred to the (perhaps aristocratic) retainers of

Merovingian kings as *pueri regis*, the king's boys, or slaves. Hence Eligius' refusal. The Roman institution whereby men could enter the service of a *patronus* was a contract between equals (later known as a *convenientia*), revocable by either party. Hence the common Frankish epithet for southerners: faithless oath-breakers. Both Frankish and Gallo-Roman aristocrats, like Merovingian kings, could have their armed retinues, but the basis of their recruitment was very different. In the later Merovingian and Carolingian periods, when such personal bonds between lords and men became fundamental political institutions, the resulting societies in north and south would be very different in character.

6. Mayors and Princes

DAGOBERT I died in 638, the last energetic and effective Merovingian king; there followed over one hundred years during which '*rois fainéants*' ruled in Francia – 'do-nothing kings'. This traditional picture is misleading: there is a great deal of difference between the immediate successors of Dagobert and the misty figures of the early eighth century. If some seventh-century kings were 'do-nothings', it was because of dynastic accident: they were minors, under the domination of their mother or of the mayor of the palace. The period has often been seen in terms of the gradual and inevitable rise of the Carolingian mayors of the palace; but perhaps more significant in the long run (and far more inevitable) was the way in which the monarchy lost control of much of Gaul. The Carolingian reconquest of Gaul in the eighth century only brought a temporary pause in the movement towards regional and local autonomy.

On Dagobert's death the kingdom of the Franks was split once again, between his sons, the nine-year-old Sigibert III and the five-year-old Clovis II. Austrasia went to the eldest, together with the traditionally Austrasian portion of Aquitaine (roughly the eastern half); Clovis II was given the rest, including Neustria and Burgundy (which, after Warnachar, only very sporadically had its own mayor). In Clovis's kingdom, effective power was held by the Neustrian mayors, first Aega and then Erchinoald. The latter 'was gentle and good-natured, humble and kindly towards the bishops . . . and quite without pride or greed', wrote Fredegar. 'He was certainly clever, but open and straightforward about it; he lined his own pockets, to be sure, but quite moderately; and everyone was very fond of him.'[1] In Austrasia Pippin remained mayor, and he and Bishop Cunibert of Cologne 'with blandishments drew the Austrasian notables into their orbit, ruled them generously, won their support and knew how to keep it'.[2] When Pippin died, around 640, Sigibert III's tutor Otto became mayor. But Pippin's son Grimoald 'swore friendship with Bishop Cunibert and considered how he could succeed to his father's office'.[3] It did not take him long; Otto was slain by the Duke of the Alamans, at Grimoald's instigation, and Grimoald became mayor.

The greatest asset of the Pippinids, apart from considerable political skill, was undoubtedly their landed wealth, in the heart of Frankish

Austrasia. Pippin is sometimes known as Pippin of Landen, his grandson as Pippin of Herstal, both after family estates near modern Liège. The estates of Pippin I's ally Arnulf lay near his episcopal town of Metz. Both Metz and Cologne had long been of importance to the Pippinids/Carolingians. A charter of 691 records how Pippin II gave a villa to the church of Metz 'where Lord Arnulf, our ancestor, rests in his body', and by 700 this church is referred to as St Arnulf's.[4] The cult of St Arnulf was the oldest of the Carolingian family cults; Charles Martel's nine-year-old son Jerome wrote out a 'Life of St Arnulf' as a school exercise. As for Cologne, it was a major stronghold of Pippin II's, and after his death became the stronghold of his widow Plectrudis, who attempted in vain to maintain the rights of their legitimate son against the ambitions of the bastard Charles Martel.

The reign of the Neustrian Clovis II (638–57) seems to have been remarkably peaceful, partly because of Erchinoald (who outlived his king by a year or more) and partly because of Clovis's forceful queen Balthild. An Anglo-Saxon slave in Erchinoald's household, she married the king probably in 648 and, even allowing for the exaggeration of the *Vita Sanctae Balthildis*, played an important role at court. She had close relations with the bishops (or with those whom her *Vita* calls 'the good bishops', like Eligius and Audoen), and under their influence and that of the by now fashionable Columbanian monastic ideas, she reformed nearly all the important monasteries of the kingdom. Monasteries received royal immunity, and the interference of outsiders, including bishops, was ended. She founded two monasteries her self: Chelles and Corbie, great centres of learning and manuscript production in the later Merovingian period. She may even have been instrumental in acquiring the *cappa* or cloak of St Martin for the palace relic collection: by the end of the century this was to be taken over by the Carolingians, to become a major relic, with a *capella* to house it and *capellani* to look after it (giving us our words 'chapel' and 'chaplain'). 'Thus, in the burial-places of the royal dead and in the home-base of the living king, direct contacts were made between the Merovingian family and the sources of supernatural power – contacts which superimposed new centripetal forces on a previously localised field.'[5] In doing this, Balthild was doing nothing unique. At just this time Frankish aristocrats all over northern Gaul were doing what Gallo-Roman senators in the south had done long before: enlisting the support of the supernatural for their families. But whereas the Gallo-Roman aristocracy had concentrated on gaining control of the *civitates*, by means of bishoprics, the Franks achieved their end by founding monasteries. By the end of the century the Carolingians for their part had founded a number of monasteries on their lands, including Nivelles, the foundation of Pippin I's wife Itta and the home of Pippin's daughter Gertrude, who joined Arnulf on the roll of Carolingian family saints.

The years of Balthild's regency for her son Chlothar III are confused ones for the historian. Sigibert III had died in Austrasia in 656, a year before his brother Clovis II. The mayor Grimoald, in the words of the eighth-century *Liber Historiae Francorum*, 'tonsured Sigibert's little son called Dagobert and sent him to Dido, Bishop of Poitiers, to be sent to Ireland, and Grimoald made his own son king'.[6] This passage raises numerous questions, few of which can be answered. Ireland was perhaps not such a strange choice for Dagobert's exile; by then it must have had a considerable reputation. The Frank Agilbert was at that time in Ireland for his education; he returned, by way of the bishopric of Wessex, to become Bishop of Paris. From later king-lists, and one charter, the name of Grimoald's son is known to be Childebert. Childebert is, of course, a typically Merovingian name; did he receive this after formal adoption into the Merovingian family, or does it betray the presence of Merovingian blood in the Pippinid line? Is it a brave but premature attempt by the Pippinids to secure the throne for themselves, or merely a legal fiction, designed by Grimoald to preserve his own position? The outcome is as puzzling as the event. On Childebert's death, in 662 or earlier, did the Neustrians under Balthild and the mayor Ebroin impose Clovis II's second son Childeric II on the Austrasians, or did Grimoald in fact negotiate with them and arrange the (near-incestuous) marriage between Childeric and his own ward Bilichild, Dagobert's sister?

Childeric II seems to have been a Merovingian with a mind of his own. When his brother Chlothar III died in Neustria, the Neustrian mayor Ebroin installed the third son of Clovis II and Balthild, Theuderic III, on the throne. Since he had already forced Balthild to retire into one of her own monasteries, he presumably felt that he now had a free hand. But Childeric II invaded, captured Ebroin and Theuderic, had them tonsured and packed off to the monastery of Luxeuil, and became king of a newly united Francia. Childeric 'stirred up a great deal of hate and scandal by oppressing the Franks greatly'.[7] Above all, he antagonised a certain Bodilo, who joined with other Frankish magnates to assassinate the king and his pregnant queen. His chief supporters fled back to Austrasia. Probably we see here a result of the hostility between Neustria and Austrasia that, since the time of Dagobert I or earlier, seems to have grown into real bitterness. The reasons for this are difficult to fathom. The linguistic division between Romance west and Germanic east may lie behind it, but the long political separation, bringing about a very real consciousness of different traditions and way of life, may have been more crucial.

On Childeric II's death, in 675, the Neustrians chose for their mayor Leudesius, son of the former mayor Erchinoald, who ruled in the name of King Theuderic III: as in Austrasia, there were signs that the Franks were beginning to regard the mayoralty as a hereditary office. One of his most significant supporters was Leudegar (better known to racegoers as the original St Leger), an Aquitanian who had been chosen as Bishop of Autun by Balthild, after two years of faction-fighting within the *civitas* over the bishopric. The former mayor Ebroin, however, 'having let his hair grow back . . . left the monastery of Luxeuil in military array':[8] he killed Leudesius, secured the person of Theuderic, and tortured and killed Leudegar, ensuring his posthumous reputation as a martyr. Many of Ebroin's enemies escaped into the by now virtually independent Aquitaine.

The *Liber Historiae Francorum*, the only narrative source for the period, is silent about contemporary Austrasia: our only evidence, surprisingly enough, comes from Eddius' *Life of Wilfrid of York*. After Childeric's death Wilfrid was approached by the Austrasians to arrange for the return of Dagobert II, exiled nearly twenty years earlier to Ireland. According to Eddius, the newly installed Dagobert offered Wilfrid the see of Strasbourg, but the Northumbrian refused. Four years later Wilfrid was returning from Rome, and heard that the king had been assissanated. An irate Frankish bishop told him that Dagobert had been a *dissipator urbium* (a destroyer of city walls? an attacker of episcopal independence?), who despised the counsels of his elders and, above all, who imposed heavy taxes. He met his death, Wilfrid was told, 'through a trick of the dukes and with the agreement of the bishops'.[9] The Austrasians made no attempt to choose another king. Instead their new mayor, Pippin II (the first to be descended from both Pippin I and Arnulf of Metz) negotiated unsuccessfully with the Neustrian mayors and, in 687, invaded Neustria, defeated its unpopular mayor Berchar at the battle of Tertry, and took charge of the hapless Theuderic. Theory declared that once more the Frankish realm was united under one Merovingian king; in political reality it was united for the first time under one mayor of the palace, or, as the *Liber Historiae Francorum* now calls Pippin, under one *princeps*. Effectively the Neustro-Burgundian palace lost its power, although Pippin did appoint a mayor, and indeed in 700 installed his own son Grimoald. Tertry in fact signified the beginning of the long predominance of Austrasia over Neustria, and of the effective rule of the Carolingians over the Frankish realm.

Tertry may also have helped to ensure that, in the last years of the seventh century and first few decades of the eighth, effective rule did not extend very far outside north-east Gaul. A residual loyalty to the Merovingian kings survived; but there was little or no loyalty to the Carolingian mayors. It is difficult to trace the moves towards independence in the various regions of Gaul, partly because of the serious deficiencies of the sources (Brittany is virtually a blank between the 640s and the 750s, and some other regions are not much better served), but also because of problems of definition. At what stage can a king or a mayor in north-east Gaul be said to have lost control of a particular region in the south or the west? Is it when he loses the ability to appoint counts or bishops in that area, or the ability to control and discipline them? Is it when he loses his ability to draw any revenue from taxation and customs, or to draw any revenue from his own private estates there? Clearly there are degrees of independence, difficult to establish in a type of régime which even at its height, in the sixth century, allowed considerable freedom of action to the local aristocracy. For Provence, for instance, we can do little more than note that Chadalric seems to have been appointed *patricius* in the name of Clovis III in 676, and that Bonitus was appointed prefect in Marseilles by Theuderic III, some time before 690. Both of them were outsiders, which makes the appointments the more interesting: they were not simple confirmations of existing power structures. But we do not know how effective they were in Provence. Later patricians, such as Antenor and Abbo, probably had no connections or relations with the north at all; the last patrician was Maurontus, who fell victim to the Frankish reconquest in 756–9. Marseilles seems to have been the principal seat of these men; perhaps their power was based partly on their share of the customs revenues of this town, over which Merovingian kings had fought in the sixth century. Further north, in Burgundy, there are still royal appointments to bishoprics in the late seventh century, but there are also a number of powerful bishoprics which, as we have already seen (p.60), were independent 'city-states': Lyons, Orleans, Auxerre. The tenth-century *Deeds of the Bishops of Auxerre* claimed, anachronistically, that Ainmar had extended his secular power over almost the whole of the 'duchy of Burgundy'.

The most important of all the independent powers that shared domination over Gaul, however, was undoubtedly the state of Aquitaine. After the brief experiment of the kingdom of Toulouse (629–32), the first man to have extraordinary powers within Aquitaine was Felix, appointed perhaps by Ebroin: 'a very noble and illustrious patrician from the town of Toulouse who had obtained the *principatum* over all the *civitates* up to the Pyrenees, as well as over the most wicked nation of the Basques'.[10] Thus, much later, wrote a cleric from Limoges, our only evidence for Felix. The same source tells how Felix's protegé Lupus became prince after Felix, and how he 'declared war against the king of the Franks and installed himself in a royal residence'. Lupus is attested elsewhere, in contexts which fully support the otherwise dubious testimony of the anonymous cleric. Julian, Bishop of Toledo, in his history of the rebellion of Paul against King Wamba, provides contemporary evidence for the invasion of Septimania by 'one of the dukes of Francia, Lupus by name';[11] the acts of the church council of St-Pierre-de-Granon (673–5) declared that the council met 'on the orders of the glorious prince Childeric . . . *mediante inlustri Lupone duce*', perhaps to be translated as 'under the chairmanship of Duke Lupus'.[12] The chairmanship of a council by a lay *vir inluster* (a title held elsewhere in Francia only by kings and mayors) is unique in Gaul, but has its parallels in Visigothic Spain. Equally interesting is the fact that the bishops declared that they were assembled to discuss the 'state of the Church and the stability of the kingdom', *cum provinciales Acutanis*: the first time that the inhabitants of Aquitaine had given themselves the name of Aquitani. The emergence of the independent Aquitaine must have been inseparably bound up with the development of a new 'national' consciousness. But the council of St-Pierre-de-Granon (unlike most earlier councils) had been able to assemble bishops from almost all the sees of Novempopulana, that is, from the province by then overrun by pagan Basques and already known as Vasconia or Gascony. The future of the new state of Aquitaine in fact seems to have depended upon the co-operation between Aquitanian and Basque. The rulers of Aquitaine depended on Basque soldiers just as the late Roman Emperors had relied on their Germans, to such an extent that in the eighth century their Frankish enemies at times referred to them all as 'Vascones'.

The next Aquitanian ruler appears in a later source, the *Miracula Austregiseli*, as active around the year 700: 'Eudo, prince of the province of Aquitaine', portrayed as a Roman fighting the *barbari* led by Pippin, prince of the Franks.[13] Whether Eudo was the direct successor of Lupus cannot be known. But it does seem likely that it was under Eudo that the control of the Aquitanian prince extended into the northern *civitates* of Aquitaine, until by the 720s at the latest Eudo ruled over the whole territory south and west of the Loire, excluding only the Touraine. For the first three decades of the eighth century, Eudo may well have been the strongest and most effective ruler in Gaul, the ruler of a prosperous people still mindful of its Roman past. By a mixture of military skill and diplomacy Eudo held the Saracens at bay after their conquest of Visigothic Septimania. Only in the course of the large-scale raid by Abd ar-Rahman in 732 did he feel obliged to call for help from his northern neighbours, giving the Carolingian mayor his first excuse to intervene south of the Loire, and starting the long series of wars which ended thirty-five years later in Frankish victory.

Not very much more is known about internal conditions in Francia around the turn of the century than in Aquitaine. Pippin II had two sons by his marriage with Plectrudis: Drogo and Grimoald. The former became Duke of Champagne, and is known to have intervened in Burgundy, to little effect. He died in 708. Grimoald, to whom Pippin resigned the title of Mayor, was assassinated by a pagan Frisian while on his way to the church of St Mabert's in Liège. His son, a small boy called Theudoald, succeeded him as mayor of the palace, which office he still held in 715 when his grandfather Pippin II died, in bed, at an advanced age. The widowed Plectrudis assumed power. This ironic situation, a puppet mayor of the palace in theory ruling in the name of a puppet Merovingian king (Dagobert III), might well have ended in the overthrow of the emergent Carolingian dynasty. Frankish opponents of the Carolingians elected their own mayor, Ragamfred, joined with the Frisians and swept into Austrasia. But there was a third contender for power: Pippin's illegitimate son, the first Carolus of the Carolingian dynasty, usually known by his later nickname of Charles Martel. The Neustrians (or at least that group of them who were behind Ragamfred) attempted to retain their legitimacy after the death of King Dagobert by finding another Merovingian: the Neustrian *Liber Historiae Francorum* contemptuously reported that 'a one-time cleric named Daniel, whose hair had grown back on his head, was established in the kingdom of the Franks, and they called him Chilperic'.[14] He and Ragamfred invaded Austrasia and successfully defeated Plectrudis, but were themselves defeated by Charles. Charles proceeded to gather Austrasian support behind him. He forced Plectrudis to yield Pippin's treasure to him, and found a Merovingian of his own, whom he set up as Chlothar IV in 718. But Charles's progress was slow. Chilperic and Ragamfred found an ally in Eudo of Aquitaine, and even after Eudo had surrendered to Charles the person of Chilperic (but not his treasure), Ragamfred survived. He seems to have maintained a state of his own in western Neustria, based on the city of Angers, until his death in 731.

Charles Martel, from the point of view of the history of Gaul, is the most important of the early Carolingians, laying, on initially shaky foundations, the basis for future Carolingian power. It is difficult to get close to him; historical traditions veered between uncritical adulation and, later, just as uncritical vituperation. In the earliest sources he appears as a great conqueror, whose incessant campaigns are described in words borrowed from descriptions of great Israelite generals; the derivation of his name Martel or 'hammer' from Maccabaeus would be appropriate, even if it is not at all certain that the coiners of the nickname knew that Maccabaeus meant hammer! He defeated the Arabs in Aquitaine at Tours, or Poitiers, in 732 or 733, thus earning himself a place in any volume of Decisive Battles of World History. In 734 he fought in Burgundy, and rewarded his followers with confiscated land; in 735 he campaigned in Aquitaine; in 736 in Burgundy; in 737 in Provence and in Arab Septimania; in 738 against the Saxons. By the time of his death in 741 he had established himself as the chief power in Gaul, and the undisputed ruler over the former Frankish territories in the north – undisputed even in the legal sense, indeed, for when the Merovingian king Theuderic IV died in 737, Charles did not even bother to look around the monasteries for another one.

The opposite pole of opinion on Charles can be seen over a century later, in the 850s, in the vision of Eucherius as written down by Hincmar of Rheims. Eucherius was a bishop of Orleans, exiled to Austrasia by Charles in 733, who, before his death, had been led by an angel to hell, where he found Charles burning. Eucherius told his vision to St Boniface of Mainz and Fulrad of St-Denis, archchaplain to the king, and they made an investigation. They went to Charles's tomb and opened it up; a serpent came out, and the interior was all blackened, as if by fire. There are a number of regrettable errors and inconsistencies in the tale: Eucherius died before Charles did, the archchaplaincy was a later institution, and so on. But in the ninth century vision and prophecy literature was a well-known and safe means of political criticism for churchmen. One of the most prolonged examples was Walahfrid Strabo's *Visio Wettini*, in which one of the denizens of Hell was Charlemagne himself, who stood for eternity rooted to the spot while a wild animal tore at his genitals: the angelic guide commented 'he sullied his good actions with shameful debauchery, thinking that his sins would be buried under the great quantity of his virtuous acts'.[15] Charles Martel's particular sin was as common as Charlemagne's among Carolingian rulers: the distribution of church land to his followers. In the conditions of the mid-ninth century this could appear as a heinous sin; in Charles Martel's time, when the local aristocrats against whom he fought frequently held bishoprics and monasteries in their own hand and regarded them as private property, the exile of bishops and sequestration of church property was the only way, not just to break the political power of the aristocracy, but also to bring about a reform of the Church on correct canonical lines. We must not assume that in the eighth century the clergy were necessarily against a little judicious secularisation. Hundreds of miles to the north, the venerable Bede was at this time complaining about how the abundance of church land in the hands of the lay aristocracy was weakening the Northumbrian kings and leaving the kingdom open to enemy attack.

Charles Martel did more than any Frankish ruler since Clovis to establish the political dominance of the Franks. His son Pippin III took what seems to us the logical step and had himself declared King of the Franks: King Pippin I. There is probably no reason to ask why Charles did not want to take that step himself: he concerned himself more with realities than titles. In the following generations even those who were, presumably, well aware that Pippin I was the first Carolingian king nevertheless used *rex* of Charles Martel, and other words normally restricted to royal rule. There are contemporary references of interest too. In a document of 739 a private individual uses the dating formula 'the twentieth year that our most illustrious Charles has governed the kingdoms of the Franks' when (there being no king in 739) it was more correct to use 'the third year after the death of King Theuderic'. There are even contemporary references to Charles as king, in the so-called Calendar of St Willibrord from the monastery of Echternach, and in the Continuation of Bede's Chronicle, which reports the death of *Carolus rex*. Both these sources are Anglo-Saxon in origin: to them, at least (to men, that is, so careless of the legal niceties as to call their own most powerful rulers *imperatores*) Charles appeared to be a king.[16]

We can learn more about the process by which the Carolingians emerged as kings from studying the words they used of themselves in their official enactments. The study of 'self-proclamations' has been used with great effect in recent years by German scholars of the Carolingian period. The primary title of the Carolingian mayors of the palace is, of course, *maior domus*. It was rarely used in non-official sources after 687, and not used by the mayors and kings themselves after the death of Charles Martel. An increasingly popular title was *princeps*. In the plural this word had on occasions been used in the Merovingian period of aristocrats or magnates as a group, but in the singular was reserved for the king or the emperor. Now in the eighth century it was used by Eudo of Aquitaine, perhaps in direct imitation of Roman precedents. It may be that the Carolingian mayors adopted the title in order to maintain their parity with the Aquitanian ruler. (Indeed, if some coins minted in Poitou and Limousin and bearing the letters ER indeed relate to Eudo Rex, then the Aquitanians anticipated the Carolingians in this respect too.)[17] The use of the word *princeps* later spread to other non-royal rulers, such as the Duke of the Thuringians. The Latin title of *dux* originally meant 'war-leader'; in the sixth century it was used of royal officials placed in military or civilian charge of a number of counts. The dukes, as royal appointments, were probably far more important in the Merovingian realm than the counts, who were often only local men with no court connections. But in the eighth century and thereafter *dux* was often, like *princeps*, used of non-royal rulers of peoples. When Pippin III called himself *dux et princeps Francorum*, therefore, he was not only claiming parity with such rulers as the princes of Aquitaine, but also saying that, although a Merovingian was king, he himself was *ruler* of the Franks. Another aspect of rank was the honorific, far more numerous in Latin than our Majesties and Excellencies, and just as specific. We find, for instance, that the eighth-century Mayors are called *inclitus* and *excellentissimus*, both normally royal honorifics. The path to the Carolingian kingdom was very carefully laid.

When Charles Martel died in 741, his two sons Carloman and

Pippin III succeeded: they seem to have acted swiftly to prevent their brother Grifo from sharing power. It is interesting to see how Carloman coped with rule without a king. Legislation in 742 was headed '*Ego Carlomannus, dux et princeps Francorum*', and dated, not 'six years after the death of Theuderic' or 'in the second year of my rule', but, for the very first time in Frankish history, by our familiar system of dating after the incarnation of Our Lord – AD. Carloman may well have learnt this useful dodge from the Anglo-Saxon Boniface, for it was already in use in England. The dating is followed by the phrase 'with the counsel of the servants of God and my nobles and my bishops who are in my kingdom'.[18] He avoided the mention of the king, but he talked of 'my kingdom'. In the following year, however, perhaps as a result of pressure from Grifo and his supporters, unhappy at the semi-regal position of the brothers, Carloman appointed a new Merovingian, Childeric III. Incarnation dating survived, but with the regnal year added. The elevation of Childeric III may also have been designed to strengthen Carloman's own position in the face of his brother Pippin III's ambitions. But Pippin now set about removing all rivals within Francia. In 747 Carloman retired to a monastery in Rome, presumably under pressure from Pippin, there to receive a stream of visits from discontented Frankish aristocrats. Grifo tried to get support against Pippin in Saxony and Bavaria; in 748 Pippin campaigned in Bavaria, captured Grifo and made his seven-year-old nephew Tassilo Duke of the Bavarians. Only then did Pippin send an embassy to Rome to ask Pope Zacharias 'whether or not it is good that there should be kings in Francia that have no kingly power'.[19] Zacharias, who badly needed Pippin's military support in Italy, declared that he who had the power should be king. In 751, said the Royal Frankish Annals, 'according to Frankish custom Pippin was elected king, and anointed by the hand of Archbishop Boniface of blessed memory and elevated by the Franks into the kingdom at the city of Soissons: Childeric, falsely called king, was tonsured and sent into a monastery'.[20]

7. The Carolingian Experiment

'IS there any harm in trying, as I have been instructed, to commemorate the deeds of our princes and nobles by writing them down? . . . If I cannot be useful to posterity in other ways, I will at least by this effort disperse the haze of error about these matters for those who come after us.'[1] Nithard, the son of Charlemagne's courtier Angilbert and his successor as Abbot of St-Riquier, was killed in a battle against the Vikings shortly after writing those words. His history of the conflict between his patron Charles the Bald and his royal brothers, particularly in the three years following the death of their father Louis the Pious, does indeed give us an insight into the relationships between the princes and their nobles, and above all into the problems created for the Frankish monarchy by the conflicts of loyalty which inevitably resulted from civil war. Nithard wrote in 843, when it was already clear that the Carolingian experiment to create a unified monarchy and Church administered by a united and loyal aristocracy had failed. For some aristocrats, local ambitions and interests proved more compelling than the public interest. Nithard, at the end of the century inaugurated by the deposition of the last Merovingian king, was aware of this. But, like earlier writers, he concentrates on the doings of the kings and of those aristocrats particularly involved with the affairs of the kingdom. For all the wealth of legislative and narrative material from the reigns of Pippin, Charlemagne and Louis the Pious, it is in fact very difficult to reach the world of the regional aristocracies, in whose hands, ultimately, the fate of the Empire lay. We know a good deal about the aspirations and endeavours of central government, almost nothing of how those aspirations were received (*if* they were received) by those whose business it was to implement them. But at least royal pronouncements do give us some clues as to royal policy towards the aristocracy, and some hints as to why that policy failed.

According to the Continuator of Fredegar's Chronicle, written under the auspices of none other than Pippin's uncle Childebrand, Pippin approached Pope Zacharias in 749 *una cum consilio et consensu omnium Francorum*, 'together with the advice and consent of all the Franks'.[2] He was then chosen king 'by all the Franks', was consecrated by the bishops (only the much later, and hence more unreliable, Royal Frankish Annals give the sole credit to St Boniface), and received the submission of the *principes*. *Consilio et consensu* was a standard formula, just as *consilio et auxilium* was later to be, the 'advice and assistance' promised by vassals to their lords. 'All the Franks' may refer to the Frankish army assembled in late spring for the annual campaign; in practice they were no doubt those Franks whose wealth and local importance made their consultation a necessity, in particular perhaps the bishops and important abbots. The *principes* are more difficult: are they simply the magnates, or are they the independent rulers of individual *regna* within the Frankish kingdom, such as Aquitaine, Thuringia or Bavaria? The latter seems more likely, but if so the submission they made to the new king was no doubt fairly token. How significant was 'the consent of all the Franks'? The history of the early Carolingian monarchy, not to mention the monarchy in the ninth and tenth centuries, suggests that it could be all-important. To take an early and extreme case reported by Einhard: in 755 Pope Stephen begged Pippin's help against the Lombards, which Pippin was able to provide, but only 'in the most difficult circumstances, for certain of the Frankish leaders (*primores*), whom Pippin was accustomed to consult, were so opposed to his wishes that they openly announced their determination to desert their king and return home'.[3]

A major factor in the general support given by the Frankish aristocracy, or by a sufficiently large section of it, to the early Carolingians must have been their continued success in war, which brought not only booty, but offices and lands in the conquered territories. The Austrasian aristocracy, the supporters of the dynasty since the days of Charles Martel or earlier, benefited the most: Austrasia was, in Poupardin's words 'une pépinière de fonctionnaires', a seedbed of officials.[4] The influence of some of these extensive Austrasian families reached out through the whole Empire, and lasted even into the tenth century. The Widones or Guidones, originating in the area around Trier, are a famous example. Wido or Guy, commander of the Breton March, fought successfully against the Bretons in 799; he seems to have had two sons, Lambert and Guy. The former succeeded his father as marquis and was also Count of Nantes and Angers, while the latter was Count of neighbouring Vannes. Lambert was exiled from Gaul in the aftermath of a revolt, and died in Italy. His son Lambert became Duke of Spoleto; this Lambert's son Guy had himself crowned king at Langres in 888, and fought for the kingship of Italy. Other members of the family remained behind to dispute the succession to counties in the Breton March, and in the tenth century ended up in Burgundy, in the region of Langres. Guy of Spoleto's rival for the kingship of Italy, Berengar, belonged to another great Austrasian family, the Unrochids. Unroch's sons were Eberhard, Marquis of Friuli, son-in-law of Louis the Pious and one of the most illustrious of ninth-century aristocrats, Berengar, Marquis of Toulouse, and Adalhard, Abbot of St-Bertin and St-Amand. The Unrochids may have been related to the Adalhard who was such an influential figure under Louis the Pious, and whose niece married Charles the Bald. Nithard was not one of his admirers. 'Charles' father [Louis] in his time had loved this Adalhard so much that he did anything in his whole empire that Adalhard wanted. Adalhard cared little for the public good and tried to please everyone. Again and again he advised Charles' father to distribute liberties and public property for private use and, since he knew how to manage it so that everyone got what he asked for, he ruined the kingdom altogether. This is how he was easily able at this time to coax the people to do what he wanted.'[5]

The Guidones and Unrochids are representative of the more prominent of those aristocratic families whose support the Carolingians won by their largesse. Not all were Austrasians, nor were the early Carolingians averse to maintaining the local aristocracies of conquered areas if they felt that their loyalty could be relied upon. Aristocratic conspiracies in Gaul were few, and the aristocracy appears to have caused little trouble for Pippin and Charlemagne. Ability to reward was important, but so too was force of personality. Charlemagne in particular, a man of great physical strength and energy, was just the person to dominate and control his aristocrats. He was careful not to distance himself from them; it is noteworthy that the Carolingians very frequently married into their own aristocratic families, unlike the Merovingians, who seem deliberately to have maintained their separate identity either by marrying into foreign royal houses or else allying themselves with low-born or even slave women. Like Dagobert, Charlemagne brought the sons of the great to his court for their education; he kept in touch with his aristocracy, not so much by travelling round (after 778 he never visited Aquitaine, between summer 791 and winter 794 he never even visited Gaul), as by summoning them to his court for regular councils and assemblies of the army. In later life, of course, his court settled at Aachen, a Roman spa resort which he had chosen, according to Einhard, because of its natural hot waters. He used to swim every day, and 'would invite not only his sons to bathe with him, but his *optimates* and friends as well, and occasionally even a crowd of his attendants and bodyguards, so that sometimes a hundred men or more would all be in the water together'.[6] Charlemagne's joviality and accessibility were two of his most important assets.

This is not the place to catalogue Carolingian triumphs outside Gaul, including north-eastern Spain, Saxony, Carinthia and Hungary and, perhaps most important of all, Italy, where in 774 Charlemagne became King of the Lombards. Until the late 760s, the campaigns within Gaul ran simultaneously, or alternated with campaigns elsewhere, year and year about. After Charles Martel had subjected Neustria, he turned his attention towards Burgundy and Provence, about whose conquest we are remarkably ill-informed. The last Provençal leader Maurontus, 'with base, craven collaboration'[7] as the Continuator of Fredegar put it, attempted to save his power with the help of the Saracens from Septimania. Charles and his brother Childebrand defeated Maurontus in 737 and 'restored' Provence to his rule. Through much of the 750s Pippin was engaged in the reduction of Septimania, during which he had to combat not only the Saracens but also the Goths, who, like the Provençals, disliked the thought of Frankish quite as much as Saracen domination. In the end, in 759, the Goths of Narbonne massacred their Muslim garrison and submitted to Pippin, but only after he had agreed to allow them their own law, and other privileges.

The most bitter enemies of the Carolingian mayors and kings, and also the most formidable, were the Aquitanians. Under Eudo's son Hunald until 745, under Hunald's son Waifar until 768, and finally under Hunald II, the Aquitanians held out against repeated Frankish invasions which, however much the Frankish chronicles might trumpet their successes, often did no more than penetrate a few miles into Aquitaine, to plunder and to besiege fortresses. Pippin campaigned against Waifar in 760, 761, 762, 763, 766, 767 and finally, in the year in which both he and Waifar died, in 768. In the years 764 and 765 Pippin stayed in Francia, unusually going on no campaign at all, but recouping his forces and occupying himself with diplomatic intrigues against Waifar and Tassilo of Bavaria. There were a few collaborators who aided the Franks, but on the whole the loyalty and the determination of the Aquitanians seems to have been exceptional: it certainly exceeded that of any other enemies of the Carolingians, save the pagan Saxons. The treasure won in the fertile province was prodigious; the devastation wrought there very considerable.

Before Pippin left Aquitaine after his final defeat of Waifar, he issued a capitulary for the Aquitanians (the oldest known Carolingian capitulary), in which he assured them that they could keep their Roman law. The rebellion of Hunald II after Pippin's death was short-lived; he was handed over to Charlemagne by Lupus, 'prince of the Gascons', as Frankish sources called him.[8] The Carolingians may have quelled the Aquitanians, but the Gascons/Basques, old allies of the Aquitanians, long remained independent of Frankish power. Indeed, in 778, they were responsible for one of Charlemagne's worst defeats, at Roncesvalles in the Pyrenees, while the Frankish army was returning from a campaign in Spain. No doubt incited by this, Charlemagne issued a capitulary at Herstal, designed to introduce reforms in Aquitaine. Perhaps the Aquitanians had revolted in sympathy with the Gascons; certainly nine Aquitanian counts were replaced, apparently all by Franks, and he nominated some abbots to Aquitanian abbacies and settled a number of Frankish warriors in the region, 'who are vulgarly called *vassals*', as Louis the Pious's anonymous biographer added.[9] The Gascons still retained considerable independence, but two counts were established on their borders to control them, at Bordeaux and at Fézansac. Segwin of Bordeaux (either one of the nine counts of 778 or his son) was removed by Louis the Pious in 816 'because of his boundless arrogance and wicked ways':[10] the Gascons, who by then regarded him as 'their duke', revolted, and had to be put down in two campaigns. It was not the only occasion on which one of the peoples subject to the Franks in Gaul took as their leaders an aristocratic family established in power by the Franks themselves.

The most independently minded of the *regna* which constituted Charlemagne's kingdom were given his sons as their kings: in 781 Pope Hadrian I anointed Pippin as king of Italy, and the three-year-old Louis king of Aquitaine. His eldest son by Queen Hildegard, Charles, was given charge of a *regnum* between the Seine and the Loire, an area often bestowed on eldest sons in the ninth century. It was not until 800 that Charles was made king, in the same ceremony in Rome in which his father became Emperor; it was the first time in which a crown appeared as a constituent element of a royal inauguration in western sources (although it is likely that the first European coronation was that of Pippin I in 751). He is referred to as *Carolus junior*; it was probably during his lifetime that his father was first called *Carolus magnus*, Charles the Elder, to distinguish him from his son. There was a still older son, the illegitimate Pippin the Hunchback. He was involved in one of the few conspiracies against Charlemagne, in 792, and was packed off to the monastery of Prüm. According to Notker, writing a century later, he advised his father, while digging the monastic garden, to dig up useless weeds so that useful vegetables might grow more freely. Charlemagne was delighted with the advice: 'he removed all these conspirators from the land of the living, and gave to his loyal supporters the room to grow and spread which had been occupied by these useless men'.[11] But Charlemagne's main problem was not the suppression of active rebellion; it was to ensure that his aristocracy ruled his kingdom justly and in obedience to his commands.

The basic structure of rule in Charlemagne's Gaul would have been fairly familiar to a Frank from the days of Gregory of Tours. The fundamental units were the counties, some of which (particularly in the south) had the same boundaries as the ancient *civitates*. Charlemagne gave a portion of the royal domain in the county to the count: this *comitatus* provided the revenue which supported the count, and was surrendered if the count was replaced. Many counts in the newly conquered areas were no doubt Franks, probably from Austrasia; but the bulk of Charlemagne's counts were drawn from the local aristocracy, and even the newcomers seem soon to have become well established in their own areas. By the end of Charlemagne's reign it was common for the emperor to allow the sons of counts to succeed their fathers; it was not long before the office came to be regarded as a hereditary right, and for the lands of the *comitatus* to become indistinguishable from the family estates of the count. The potential disadvantages of the system were no doubt recognised by Charlemagne and his advisers, and he did what he could to minimise them. He made sure (unlike his successors) that counts did not acquire additional counties in order to expand their power. He brought his counts frequently into his presence, at court or on campaign (and instituted the office of viscount (*vicecomes*) to act as deputy during the count's frequent absences). He appointed and kept close control of those officials, military commanders, who had control over a number of counties. In his reign they were often called *praefecti*; later they would be called *marchiones* (Anglicised either as marquis (Fr.) or margrave, from Gn. *Markgraf*), in charge above all of the marches, or frontier regions, such as those of Brittany and Spain; and later still writers would resurrect the Latin word *dux* or duke. Finally, Charlemagne instituted the *missi*, special emissaries sent out into the provinces with very considerable powers in order to root out corruption, injustice or disobedience. In 802 the system was reorganised, pairs of *missi* (one a senior ecclesiastic and the other an important layman) each being given a *missaticum*, a region over which they might exercise their duties of inspection and correction.

A more direct approach was to secure the loyalty of each count to his monarch by personal bonds, by means of the oath of fealty and the institution of vassalage. The two were connected as early as 757, when Tassilo III, Duke of the Bavarians, came to Pippin at Compiègne and 'commended himself into vassalage by his hands; he swore innumerable oaths, placing his hands upon the relics of saints, and promised fealty to King Pippin and his sons, the lords Charles and Carloman, to be their vassal with right mind and with steadfast devotion according to the law, as a vassal should be towards his lords'.[12] 'Commendation by hands', placing the hands together inside those of a superior (the origin of our modern gesture of prayer), was a peculiarly Frankish ceremony, which went right back into the Merovingian period; the Roman equivalent, which was to be found in the south, involved commendation into the *patrocinium* of another by means of a written document. The inferior was known to Franks as a *vassus* – originally a Celtic word, which in the Germanic glosses to the Salic law had to be translated: '*vassus, id est horogavo*'. *Vassus*, or its doublet *vassallus*, originally meant slave, and it long retained its subservient overtones; even in the case of Tassilo III it may be that a deliberate humiliation was forced upon the insubordinate duke. But by the late eighth century even the highest aristocracy within the kingdom had been brought into the system, and that system was becoming more legally defined. Thus in one capitulary Charlemagne laid down that a vassal was permitted to abandon his *senior* (his lord, or *seigneur*) if the latter had tried to reduce him to slavery, or to kill him, or if he had committed adultery with the vassal's wife or failed to defend him if he had been in a position to do so. By making all counts his vassals Charlemagne might hope to strengthen the obedience of his officials, by making it the obedience owed by a vassal to his lord. It could be further strengthened by an oath such as Tassilo III had taken, upon relics. Disloyalty would thus be not only perjury but also sacrilege. The system could be extended: the count's own officers, from the viscount down, became the count's vassals. And as an additional check upon the count, Charlemagne created other vassals throughout his kingdom, *vassi regales* or *vassi dominici*, 'the king's vassals'. These men were not under the direct authority of the count, and could act as royal agents or watchdogs in the provinces. These vassals may have been granted the right to collect royal dues and administer justice on their own estates, without the intermediary of the count; this, rather than the royal grant of lands, was their reward.

Vassals certainly expected a reward for their service; the early medieval mentality expected that any gift of goods or services would engender a counter-gift, and even felt that the gift was forfeit or invalid if the counter-gift was not forthcoming. In return for their promise of aid to their lord – particulary military aid – the lord would grant them a *beneficium*, a favour or benefit. This is a difficult word (Niermeyer finds forty-one different shades of meaning in his medieval Latin dictionary, mostly from Carolingian sources) which covers a wide range of possibilities. But in the context of vassalage, it came to mean in particular a grant of land, '*quod vulgo dicitur feodum*' (which is commonly called a fief), as an eleventh-century document puts it.[13] The benefice was granted of the king's or lord's free will, but was of course to his own advantage; only if his vassal had sufficient resources would he be of any use to his lord, particularly in a military context when he would be expected to provide men, horses and equipment. In northern Gaul the land itself was granted; in the south it seems that it was often the right to collect a certain revenue which was ceded. In both cases the grant was for life only, and could be revoked if the vassal did not fulfill his obligations. The Carolingian kings occasionally granted from their own estates, or from those confiscated from rebels or conquered from enemies, but could also prevail upon bishops or abbots to provide ecclesiastical land on which royal vassals could live. Since in theory the land was not alienated, and only temporarily tenanted by the vassal, this procedure was strictly not contrary to canon law. Such land, held *precaria verbo regis* (precarious tenure by order of the king), was subject to a second tithe; one tenth of all agricultural produce went to the church, as established in the eighth century, an extra tenth (called the *nona*, meaning the 'ninth tenth') went from the church land held by royal vassals.

Benefices, like the *comitatus* held by counts in virtue of their office, had a propensity to become hereditary and, within a couple of generations or less, to be regarded by their possessors as their legitimate property. As early as 806 Charlemagne complained that 'counts and other persons who hold benefices from us treat these as if they were their own allodial possessions'.[14] But it was difficult even for Charlemagne to act against his aristocracy. The anonymous biographer of Louis the Pious, known as the Astronomer, tells how Charlemagne once discovered that most of the royal estates in Aquitaine, his infant son's kingdom, had fallen into the hands of the Frankish counts who had been sent there after the conquest. 'Charles learned from Louis that a lord in name only may be treated as in want of everything, since all of the nobles, so careful of private matters, are with perverse course neglectful of public affairs, and public lands are thereby turned into private properties.' Charlemagne moved very discreetly to restore these lands to Louis, 'keenly desirous that affection for his son among the magnates suffer no diminution'.[15]

The theoretical advantage of vassalage as it was conceived in the eighth century was that it represented a personal bond between men, in particular between the king and those who governed his kingdom for him, not a distant, abstract, legal relationship. The bond dissolved on the death of either vassal or lord: if it was renewed by the son of one or the other, this was done in person. As the system became more institutionalised, or when the king was not sufficiently attentive to the personal element, as in Louis's infancy or Charlemagne's old age, its value weakened almost beyond recall. When Charlemagne's great-grandson Louis the Stammerer inherited the kingdom of West Francia in 877, he decided to revoke many benefices and to redistribute them to his own supporters, in theory a perfectly legal procedure, but politically quite impossible. The whole aristocracy rose in vociferous opposition, and the plan was abandoned.

There were various kinds of fealty or fidelity in Frankish practice, including that sworn by an antrustion or a vassal to his lord, and that sworn by ordinary subjects to their king. The general oath of loyalty was revived by Charlemagne; perhaps it would be more accurate to say that he extended the oath given by vassals to a much broader section of the population, in an attempt to strengthen his control. This seems to have happened after a conspiracy in Thuringia in 786; the conspirators apparently excused themselves from the charge of disloyalty on the grounds that they had never sworn an oath – an interesting sidelight on contemporary views of the relations between subject and king. A capitulary of 789 preserves a formula of oath, as taken by all free people, including serfs who held office or who were vassals and hence arm-bearing: 'I promise that I am and shall be faithful to my lord Charles the king, and his sons, all the days of my life, without deception and without deceit.'[16] In 802, as part of the long reassessment which Charlemagne seems to have made at Aachen after his coronation as emperor, a new and more positive element is added to the oath. All men over twelve were to take this oath, which contained 'not only, as many have thought until now, the profession of loyalty to our lord the Emperor throughout his life, and the undertaking not to bring any enemy into his kingdom for hostile reasons, nor to consent to or be silent about anyone's infidelity towards him', but also other elements: to do God's word, to honour imperial property and the church, to perform military service, to obey imperial commands, to do justice, and so on.[17] It was a new concept, but probably of little practical political importance. Certainly the swearing of oaths of loyalty continued throughout the ninth century, but one may legitimately doubt whether they, or indeed the whole structure of vassalage and fealty, served to preserve the huge Carolingian Empire. Was the collapse of the Empire inherent in the system, in that too much local power was given to the aristocracy without adequate safeguards? Or was it rather the crisis in the structure of leadership at the very top which enabled weaknesses to show themselves?

Historians, with their usual prejudice in favour of any type of centralised government, have tended to regard the collapse of the Carolingian Empire as a disaster – an echo of scholarly reaction to the fall of the Roman Empire. The Roman Empire, of course, had generally been conceived as a political unit; the Carolingian Empire (to use modern historical jargon, which itself distorts the issue) rarely was. Under the first emperor, Charlemagne, there were three subordinate kings. In 806 Charlemagne ruled for the succession in such a way that, if all his sons had survived, the title of Emperor and the unity of Empire would have disappeared on his death. The survival of the Empire was almost as accidental as its creation. Would the Empire have come into existence without the retirement of Pippin's brother Carloman in 747 and the death of Charlemagne's brother Carloman in 771, or have survived without the death of two of Charlemagne's sons in 810–11? Louis the Pious was the only surviving son, and his coronation as emperor at Aachen in the last year of Charlemagne's reign (without papal participation, this time) must have seemed to some a sign that the Empire was, literally, destined to survive. It must also have strengthened the determination of those who wished to see Empire as something much more than overlordship. A sign of the new approach can be seen in the titles used. Before his death Charlemagne had been styling himself 'Charles, most serene Augustus, crowned by God, great and pacific Emperor, governing the Roman Empire, and by the grace of God king of the Franks and the Lombards', and dating documents 'in the fourteenth year of our Empire, the forty-sixth of our reign over the Franks and the thirtieth of our reign in Italy'. Immediately Louis cut the title to 'Louis, by order of divine providence Emperor Augustus' and his dating clause to 'the first year of our Empire'. A number of clerics and imperial officials associated with Louis, some of them 'Romans' from Aquitaine, were inspired by the idea of a universal Empire, and offered suggestions whereby a measure of unification might be given to the miscellaneous institutions of the many provinces of the Empire; only Benedict of Aniane's plans for monastic uniformity came to anything like fruition.

Opposition towards the ideas of the 'imperialists' came not only from a large section of the aristocracy, who feared change and the loss of time-honoured privileges, but above all from Louis's younger sons, who justifiably feared disinheritance. In 817 the great men of the Empire came together, as usual, at Aachen; the record of their deliberations is preserved in the *Ordinatio Imperii*.[18] Louis announced here that his loyal subjects, 'by divine inspiration', had suggested a division of the realm on Louis's death, as was customary, but that Louis 'and men of sound judgement' felt that it was wrong that 'out of love or favour to our sons, the unity of the Empire preserved for us by God should be destroyed by men'. After three days of fasting and prayer the decision was reached to elect the eldest, Lothar, as emperor and to make Pippin king of Aquitaine and Louis the Younger king of Bavaria and the eastern realms. Lothar was to have a somewhat ill-defined supremacy over his two brothers; the Empire was to remain intact, but sub-kingdoms were to remain. This compromise neglected two problems in particular: what was to happen to Louis's nephew Bernard, ruling in Italy as successor to Pippin, and what would happen if Louis had another son.

The first problem was solved fairly rapidly. As soon as Bernard of Italy heard of the provisions of the *Ordinatio Imperii* he rebelled, along with a number of high dignitaries. He was brought to Gaul, and died three days after being blinded on Louis's orders. The ultimate outcome of this action was an event unprecedented in Frankish political history: at a general assembly of his subjects at Attigny in 822, Louis performed public confession and penance for what he had done to Bernard, and for his unjust exile of his cousins Adalard of Corbie and Wala. Louis the Pious was the first Frankish king to have absorbed the moral teaching of the Church; regrettably, mildness, a love of peace, and a penchant for forgiving enemies were among the worst qualifications for political success. His *Admonitio* of 822–3 expressed his own ideas concerning the Christian Empire: 'May peace, concord and unanimity reign over the whole Christian people, between bishops, abbots, counts and judges, and everywhere between rich and poor. . . . The Gospel says "Blessed are the peace-makers, for they shall be called the sons of God."'[19] For an aristocracy whose main hobby and chief means of enrichment was warfare, this was discouraging news! An idealist certainly, but Louis was not the weak and impractical ruler that is often portrayed. His difficulties were inherent in the attempt to reconcile the idea of Empire with the traditional Frankish methods of rule. Louis compromised, as he was bound to do, and inevitably lost some of those churchmen who had seen political unity as the necessary complement to the unity of the Church, both the result of God's will on earth. Some interpreted the *Ordinatio Imperii* as a document preserving the unity of Empire; others, understandably confused by its whole conception, referred to it as a 'partition'. But some of the imperialists came to see Louis as the betrayer of the ideal, and threw in their lot with the other crowned emperor, Lothar.

The second problem began with the birth on 13 June 823 of a son to Louis's second wife Judith: Charles, much later (naturally enough) known as 'the Bald'. Pushed by Judith and her powerful aristocratic relations, Louis had to spend much of the rest of his reign fighting to provide his new son with a place in the succession, against the opposition of his three sons by his first wife. Some of the consequences of these civil wars will be mentioned in the last chapter; it is enough here to say that Charles survived, eventually to win himself the western portion of Francia by the treaty of Verdun, 843. The civil wars, and the wars which continued after Verdun with Pippin II, Charles's nephew, who claimed Aquitaine in succession to Pippin I, as the *Ordinatio Imperii* had envisaged, irremediably weakened the system which Charlemagne had created. It was impossible to preserve vassalage and fealty when vassals found their benefices in rival kingdoms, or their lords being changed by political agreements. The mutual antagonism of kings did more than the greed or malice of aristocrats to dissolve the bonds holding their kingdoms together; the main concern of the aristocracy was to survive in a situation where there could be no general agreement as to where loyalty should lie.

The negotiations leading up to the Treaty of Verdun are known in some detail, thanks to Nithard's *History*. In 842, two of Louis the Pious's successors, Louis the German and Charles the Bald, divided the Empire between them, with the help of twenty-four commissioners (of whom Nithard was one). They left Italy to Lothar. But they were later forced to include Lothar in the partition, and agreed that 120 commissioners should meet to agree on the boundaries. They seem to have drawn up inventories of royal possessions – churches, the *comitatus* ceded to counts, estates in the possession of the kings and those granted out as benefices – in order to make sure that each of the part-kingdoms was roughly equal in terms of royal resources: one of these *descriptiones*, for what is now part of Switzerland, still survives.

The partition was finally agreed in August 843, at Verdun. It broke the political unity of Gaul, as well as of the Empire (see Map 5). The title of Emperor belonged to Lothar, who held the Middle Kingdom, which contained the imperial cities Aachen and Rome but possessed little linguistic, cultural or political coherence: it included Provence, much of Burgundy, and the traditional heartland of the Franks, the valleys of the Meuse and Moselle. In 855 on the death of Lothar it was itself partitioned: the imperial crown and Italy went to the eldest son, Louis; Lothar II received the northern part, from the North Sea to the Alps, a territory known after him as Lotharingia (of which modern Lorraine forms a part); Charles 'of Provence' received the rest, from the Alps to the Rhône. The partitions of 843 and 855 had laid down the boundaries within which the events of the later ninth and tenth centuries would unfold. Within this framework of areas of royal competence the aristocracy had already begun to build its own small empires.

8. The Fragmentation of Gaul

THE Carolingian dynasty survived the Treaty of Verdun by a century and a half. By the year 1000 they had been supplanted in West Francia by what came to be known as the Capetian dynasty; a non-Carolingian king ruled in the kingdom of Burgundy; and both monarchs were overshadowed not only by the kingdom of the Ottonians – Saxon rulers who now controlled the heartland of their traditional Frankish enemies, including Aachen itself – but even by the more powerful of their own subjects. The late ninth and tenth centuries are the age of the independent principalities, founded, as has recently been said, not 'by the "rebels" against royal power but by the "loyal", the men by whose help alone the king could suppress rebellion, who held the apparatus of power in their hands, legitimised by royal grant . . . the final, exteme form of the general principle that the ruler was dependent on those who were prepared to obey him'.[1] But by the year 1000 even the power of those princes was being whittled away by the lesser aristocracy, who, over large parts of Gaul, themselves took over many of the royal functions and began to rule their own small territories from the shelter of their castles.

It would be useful to begin looking at these changes from the point of view, not of the monarchy, but of one of the more important aristocratic families – not a typical family, if such exists, but an interesting one, that of St William of Gellone. William was from an Austrasian family related to the Carolingians (like so many of the important aristocratic dynasties in these centuries). In 789 he was appointed to the strategically crucial county of Toulouse, on the borders of the hostile territories of both Basques/Gascons and Spanish Muslims. His name survived in later tradition in two forms – as St William, one of the most influential of the early recruits to the new monasticism of Benedict of Aniane, and founder of the monastery of Gellone, in which he died as a monk, and as William of Orange, hero of medieval *chansons de geste* and victor over the Saracens. His son Bernard of Septimania was naturally a prominent magnate in the kingdom, sponsored by Louis the Pious at his baptism, and married in 824 in the palace at Aachen. Bernard's wife Dhuoda is in a sense the most remarkable member of that remarkable family; she was the author of a learned and pious handbook of conduct, the *Liber Manualis*, intended for her own son William. She began it 'in the second year after the death of the late Emperor Louis' (841) and finished it 'under the propitious reign of Christ and in the expectation of the king whom God shall designate'[2] – a cautious dating, paralleled in other documents from south-west Gaul at that time, when it was very difficult to know whether to be loyal to Charles the Bald or to Pippin of Aquitaine, both of whom claimed to be the legitimate king in Aquitaine. The Manual was in fact written just after Dhuoda's son William had been sent off to become Charles's vassal; Bernard was hedging his bets, for earlier he had been a loyal supporter of Pippin. The Manual is a unique insight into the education and intellectual interests of a ninth-century lady, but is important also for her remarks on the importance of fealty to the king, which have often been quoted. As Wallace-Hadrill has commented, it is even more interesting that she harps on the possibility of unfealty, of *infidelitas*: 'A great man's son needs such a warning at the outset of his career.'[3] But it is also worth pointing out that Dhuoda considered that a young man might have higher loyalties than those he owed as vassal to a king. 'Without doubt, in the eyes of men the royal or imperial dignity and power is all-important in this world. . . . But nevertheless, my son, this is my wish, that on the advice of My Lowness, and following God's word, you start first of all by not omitting to render throughout your life a special, faithful and sure homage to him whose son you are.'[4] Indeed, when Dhuoda refers to William's 'master and lord' she is normally referring to Bernard, and not Charles the Bald; Riché, in his modern edition, has spoken of her 'religion of paternity'.[5] No doubt many ninth-century aristocrats lived in that moral world.

Dhuoda's detestation of infidelity reads oddly in view of her husband's career. In the mid-820s he was an able commander on the Spanish March, like his father; in 829 he was made chamberlain of the palace at Aachen, the second position in the realm according to Nithard. He was highly unpopular at court, or among a certain faction at court, and malicious rumour associated his name with that of Queen Judith. He was disgraced and forced to flee to the southernmost frontier of the Empire, to Barcelona. He was reconciled with Louis in 831, but in 832 he and Pippin of Aquitaine were brought to Aachen to swear fealty; not long afterwards they were accused of breaking their oath, and Pippin was imprisoned. In 833, however, he fought on Louis's behalf in Burgundy, and was restored to the office of chamberlain. In 837 we find him again as *dux Septimaniae*; in the following year most of the aristocracy of Septimania came to Louis to complain about his tyranny, so presumably his power in that province was considerable. His stance at the battle of Fontenoy in 841, fought between the sons of Louis, is fairly typical of his career. He waited, with his Aquitanian contingents, three leagues from the battlefield; then, in Nithard's words, 'as soon as he heard of the victory of Charles, he sent his son William to him, telling him to render homage to the king, if the king was prepared to give him the benefices he had in Burgundy'.[6] Bernard's fence-sitting did not pay in the end; Charles did not trust him, above all because of his close association with Pippin, and in the course of his great expedition to Aquitaine in 844 he captured Bernard, tried him, and had him executed.

The family survived this disgrace, in the persons of two sons, one a loyal supporter of Pippin and the other of Charles. Shortly after Bernard's death the elder son William was made 'duke of Bordeaux' by Pippin; he was probably in charge of operations against the still fiercely independent Gascons. In 843 he distinguished himself by winning Ampurias and Barcelona; in 850 he was killed in Spain. The other son, Bernard, had an even more distinguished and long-lasting career – if it is possible to disentangle it: in the mid-ninth century there were anything up to eleven Bernards active in central and southern Gaul, and at least two of them are distinguished by being called 'Bernard son of Bernard' in the sources! Our Bernard son of Bernard is sometimes nicknamed *Plantapilosa*: Bernard Plantevelue, or Hairy-sole. From his father-in-law Bernard of Auvergne he inherited the countships of Auvergne and Velay. When Bernard 'the Calf', Count of Toulouse, was killed in 872, Charles the Bald gave Bernard Plantevelue (the murderer) the Toulousain, Limousin and Rouergue. And when Bernard of Gothia disappeared from the scene in 878/9, Bernard Plantevelue acquired Septimania, Berry, the Autunois and perhaps Poitou. Before his death he added the Mâconnais and Lyonnais to his extraordinary accumulation of counties. For the royal chancery, Bernard was a *marchio*, originally a man in charge of a frontier region, but by the later ninth century a man who held several counties and was the dominant figure in a particular region. In his own documents he often styled himself '*comes, dux et marchio*'. *Dux* was a word used of him also by annalists, for it had a more classical ring in Latin than *marchio*; it was avoided by West Frankish kings because it had connotations of ethnic rulership and hence of independence of the monarchy. Indeed, Bernard did dominate south-west Gaul far more directly and successfully than Charles the Bald himself. The office of *comes, dux et marchio* was inherited by his son William the Pious, although some of Bernard's southern counties passed to the son of the murdered Bernard of Toulouse, and William also lost the Lyonnais, Mâconnais and Berry. In 909 he begun to call himself '*Aquitanorum dux atque marchio*'. William the Pious, founder of the great monastery of Cluny, was thus the first 'Duke of the Aquitanians' in Carolingian times; not, of course, 'Duke of Aquitaine' as many historians anachronistically call him, any more than the *reges Francorum* were 'Kings of France'. His title depended upon his personal dominance within the region, and on his great collection of titles, and hence lands and privileges; it was not a 'duchy' in a territorial sense. Nor did it have any permanence. William was childless, and his lands split up on his death; only later in the tenth century did his title 'Duke of the Aquitanians' pass to the Counts of Poitou.

The family of William of Gellone created one of the first of the 'independent principalities' which, in the later ninth and throughout the tenth century, were to rival or eclipse the Carolingian kingdom of West Francia. The crucial period for the growth of these principalities was undoubtedly the reign of Charles the Bald (840–77). Charles was not the weak king that some historians have depicted; he was not an unworthy grandson of Charlemagne. But the problems which he faced were far greater than those which his grandfather knew. He could not expand his territory in order to win some support for himself; he had to cope with the ever-increasing virulence of Viking attacks; he had to deal with a well entrenched aristocracy. Initially he had to make concessions simply to survive, particularly during his attempts to win the loyalty of the Aquitanians. The wars in Aquitaine against his brother and his nephew, the two Pippins, created a situation in which some aristocratic families were able to accumulate considerable amounts of Carolingian lands, given away by both sides to would-be supporters. The problems of loyalty which these wars raised were likewise difficult to overcome. Charles himself responded to his occasionally desperate position by attacks on the aristocracy which could not have helped his popularity nor encouraged loyalty in his vassals: a number of distinguished aristocrats were executed at his commands. Charles obviously did have trouble controlling his counts. We find counts persecuting *vassi regales*, or persuading them to become their vassals as well as the king's, and counts who usurp royal privileges. Thus Fredelon of Toulouse issues diplomas imitating those of the king, with mention of a chancellor, a fisc, and so on. Counts make war on others on their own account, and depose them and annex their counties. Rebellious counts are ordered to be removed by the king, and yet continue to function; it took Charles five years to get rid of Gerald of Berry. Charlemagne had maintained his control over his officials by means of the *missi*, sent from the palace each year to check upon local affairs; under his grandson *missi* were appointed by the local aristocrats themselves, and no longer served as a centralising element.

Charles the Bald seems to have evolved his own policy for dealing with the aristocracy, a policy which was to have important consequences, as we have seen in the case of Bernard Plantevelue: in order better to orchestrate his defences against the Vikings and his own aristocracy, he deliberately reduced the number of effectual military authorities in his kingdom. He drastically reduced the number of counts, giving large blocks of counties to individual aristocrats, to Bernard Plantevelue, to his own brother-in-law Boso, to Hugh the Abbot (Queen Judith's brother and lay-abbot of St-Germain), or to Baldwin of Flanders. Charles's judgement in the short term was probably correct; these men were loyal to him, and useful. But they were loyal to him personally, and not necessarily to the concept of the Carolingian kingdom. From these men, and others like them, were descended most of the great independent noble dynasties of eleventh-century France, including the royal successors of the Carolingians, the Capetians.

The earliest ancestor of the Capetians about whom anything is known was Robert the Strong, who appears first in 852 as a *vir illuster* (and hence a count) and as lay-abbot of Marmoutier, St Martin's monastery across the Loire from Tours. In 856 Charles made an agreement with the ruler of Brittany, Erispoë: Charles's son Louis was to marry Erispoë's daughter. Charles gave Louis western Neustria, bordered by the Seine, the Loire, Brittany and the Channel, as his kingdom. Presumably this involved a considerable restriction on the powers of the local counts; Robert the Strong therefore led a rebellion against Charles. When Robert submitted he was made Marquis of the Breton marches, and when Louis the Stammerer again became king of western Neustria in 865 Robert was given substantial power in Burgundy as compensation. Louis proved in fact to be so incompetent in the war against the Vikings that in the following year Charles made him exchange his position with Robert; shortly afterwards Robert was killed in a battle against the Vikings. His sons were too young to succeed him; Hugh the Abbot became their guardian and took over Robert's counties. But the two sons were later able to build upon their father's prestige and positions; both ended their lives as kings of West Francia.

Charles was perfectly conscious of his weak position: in the assembly held at Coulaines shortly after the Treaty of Verdun he declared that 'it is clear that divine grace has abandoned us'.[7] He asked for the assistance and co-operation of the great churchmen and lay aristocrats, and promised to protect the Church, to leave his *fideles* with their honours and benefices, and to treat all justly. Mme Magnou-Nortier has recently argued that these agreements are the origin of contractual monarchy among the Franks, and points to the use of the word *convenientia* to refer to the agreement between king and magnates: it is used in Carolingian documents, particularly in the lands of Roman law in the south, to mean an agreement between equals in law.[8] It is in Charles's reign also that reciprocal oaths made by king and *fideles* play a much larger part in coronation ceremonies. Coronations themselves seem to have been consciously used by Charles as instruments of propaganda, reinforcing the ties between monarchy and subjects, and pointing up his own special position. The elaboration of the ceremony and the increased importance of anointing grew with successive ceremonies: his coronation as king of Aquitaine in 848, of Lorraine in 869, and as emperor in 876. The ceremony was even extended to women in 856 when Charles's daughter Judith was crowned queen. Nor was the lesson that such ceremonies could make kings lost on others in Gaul: according to later tradition the first non-Carolingian king was crowned and anointed in the mid-ninth century – Nominoë of Brittany. Certainly Bretons regarded their rulers as kings later that century.

Charles's inability to deal with the combined problems of the Aquitanians, the Bretons and the Vikings in the first half of his reign did not encourage loyalty from his own aristocracy. When his brother Louis the German invaded in 858, most of Charles's lay aristocracy deserted him, and he would have lost his kingdom had it not been for the support of the clergy, above all of Hincmar of Rheims. The only important cleric to declare himself for Louis was Wenilo or Ganelon, Archbishop of Sens, whose name reappears as that of the arch-villain in the first surviving French epic, the *Chanson de Roland*. Charles's fortunes recovered in the 860s, with the success of his defensive measures against the Vikings beginning to have effect, and with the disappearance of Pippin II of Aquitaine. His ambitions grew. Lotharingia was the centre of his attentions in the 860s, in the years of the struggle which Lothar II waged with the Church in his efforts to divorce his infertile wife. He was unsuccessful, and died without any children regarded as legitimate by the Church. His brother the Emperor Louis II, who had already taken over the kingdom of Provence on the death of his brother Charles, had his eyes on Lotharingia, which would have given him the whole Middle Kingdom possessed by Lothar I. Before he could act, Charles the Bald and Louis the German had divided Lotharingia between themselves. Both had ambitions south of the Alps too. In 871, when a rumour ran north that Louis II had died in Italy, both started south; when Louis II actually died in 875, it was Charles to whom the Pope offered the imperial crown, and Louis the German, already suffering his final illness, had to content himself with an invasion of West Francia. Charles the Bald held both Italy and West Francia – and neither of them securely – for shortly over a year, before dying himself at the age of fifty-two. He was the last king based in Gaul to be emperor.

The eleven years following Charles's death in 877 are confused, but of great significance for the future of the Carolingian dynasty in West Francia. The prestige of the Carolingian monarchy reached its lowest point ever. Hincmar of Rheims declared publicly to the king, 'you have so many partners and equals in the kingdom that you reign more in name than in reality'.[9] As we have seen, Louis the Stammerer's first act was to try to redistribute the benefices of his kingdom; he merely proved to himself his impotence when faced with an aristocracy united in opposition. One of the most important of the magnates, Bernard of Gothia, refused to recognise Louis's authority, although he did not go so far as to declare himself king. Louis rid himself of this threat with the help of Bernard Plantevelue and Boso, who themselves picked up the counties that Bernard of Gothia had accumulated. Louis died in 879; the magnates decided that his two children by his first wife should succeed, even though their legitimacy was in doubt, in order to exclude Louis the German. Louis III became king of the northern part of West Francia, and Carloman of the south. But in reality the great magnates ruled the kingdom; Hugh the Abbot was effectively regent for Louis III. The Annals of St Vaast for 884 record that 'since the king was young, all the *principes* gathered at the palace of Compiègne to discuss what had to be done'.[10] The Carolingian kings were in the position in which a number of Merovingians had been in the seventh century, a position which the earliest Carolingians had exploited so well. One magnate, at least, was not prepared to accept this situation: Boso, Count of Troyes in 870, Count of Vienne in 871, one of the leading counsellors of Charles the Bald and Louis the Stammerer. He was virtually a Carolingian himself: his aunt had married Lothar II, his sister had married Charles the Bald, and he himself had married the daughter of Emperor Louis II. When Charles the Bald had died, Pope John VIII had even offered him the imperial crown. Presumably these links by marriage led Boso to feel that he had some right to a kingdom of his own, to become the first Frankish king since the days of Clovis who was not either a Merovingian or a Carolingian. He was probably already thinking of taking the step in July 879, three months after Louis II's death, when he styled himself by a unique formula, almost a parody of the royal style: 'Ego Boso, Dei gratia id quod sum', 'I Boso, by the grace of God what I am, and my beloved wife Ermengarda, daughter of an Emperor'.[11] Three months later, at Mantaille, a Carolingian palace between Vienne and Valence, he was chosen and crowned king, with the assistance of twenty-one southern bishops. He proclaimed himself Louis the Stammerer's heir, but in fact his kingdom seems to have been a revival of that of Charles of Provence: it stood outside the frontiers of West Francia. Boso himself held power for only three years, but his dynasty survived, his son Louis the Blind becoming king of Provence in 890.

The precedent of a non-Carolingian king was to be followed not long afterwards in West Francia. Louis III died in 882, and Carloman in 884. Charles III, 'the Fat', king of East Francia, was recognised as king by the West Frankish magnates, who thus ignored the claims of Louis the Stammerer's posthumous son Charles the Simple, then five years old. Charles the Fat died in 888. 'Then', wrote the chronicler Regino of Prüm, 'the kingdoms which had been subject to Charles split up into fragments, breaking the bond which united them, and without waiting for their natural lord, each one sought to create a king of its own, drawn from within itself; which thing was the cause of long wars, not that there were lacking Frankish persons worthy of Empire by their noble birth, their courage and their wisdom, but because their equality in origin, dignity and power was a fresh cause for discord: none of them in fact was sufficiently raised above the rest to make them willing to submit to his authority.'[12] The *Annals of Fulda* tell the story in more detail, if with less insight: 'Many little kings [*reguli*] arose in Europe or in the kingdom of Charles, its progenitor. For Berengar, the son of Eberhard [of Friuli] made himself king in Italy; Rudolf, the son of Conrad, began to rule as king in Upper Burgundy; Louis the son of Boso and Wido [Guy] the son of Lambert set themselves up as kings in Provence and Burgundy; Odo, son of Robert [the Strong] usurped the kingdom up to the Loire and Aquitaine, and there [in Aquitaine] Rannulf declared himself king.'[13] The *Annals of Fulda* are the only source to mention the ambitions of Rannulf II Count of Poitou, who was descended from Louis the Pious; it could be a misunderstanding of an attempt made by Rannulf to champion the obvious Carolingian candidate, the young Charles, who was at that time at his court in Poitou. At any rate, Rannulf soon abandoned his designs and recognised Odo as king of West Francia in 889. Wido, who had been crowned at Langres, in West Francia, returned to Italy to contest the kingship with Berengar. Had either Rannulf or Wido pursued their claim the future history of France might have been very different. As it was, Odo (Fr. Eudes) was the only king in Charles the Bald's former kingdom of West Francia. But there were now other kings in Gaul, of non-Carolingian stock. Rudolf, of the same Welf family to which Louis the Pious's wife Judith had belonged, was crowned king of Upper Burgundy in the old Burgundian royal church of St-Maurice-d'Agaune; Louis of Provence came to power in his father Boso's kingdom, with the help of Boso's brother Richard the Justiciar. Both men founded dynasties which outlived the Carolingian dynasty of West Francia.

In the past the reign of Odo (888–98), the first Robertian king, has been seen as a watershed in French history. Carolingian methods of government, like *missi* and capitularies, ceased to be employed, and royal power no longer effectively extended beyond northern Gaul. Odo, war-hero, fresh from his success in defending Paris against the Vikings in 885–6, should have been the saviour of the monarchy rather than the man who presided over its demise. And indeed it is now recognised that he was a very active king, preserving as best he could what had survived of the Carolingian system during the short reigns of his ineffective predecessors. He defeated the Vikings again; he spent a year touring the Aquitanian parts of his kingdom (and was one of the last kings to visit Aquitaine to defend his interests for three centuries); he was active in defending his interests in the north; and he was not nearly so prodigal with royal rights and estates as his immediate predecessors. Yet his real power was fairly narrowly confined. South of the Loire, in the West Frankish part of Burgundy, and in the further parts of northern Gaul, he had little direct authority. Oddly enough, in the furthest-flung areas of his kingdom, in Septimania and the Spanish March, he was able to intervene effectively: this was a phenomenon to be found in the reign of his successor Charles III, and in the tenth century also, and has much more to do with local conditions than with royal power. These interventions were always at the request of the inhabitants, either counts wishing for royal endorsement of their position or, more frequently, on the initiative of churches, who hoped that royal protection would save them from lay encroachment. An example is to be found in the Bizac case. This estate was given to a Nîmes monastery, but taken away again by the donor's son, who only restored it after being condemned twice in the local tribunals. Then the estate was occupied by someone else, who claimed to have been granted it by King Odo. The Bishop of Nîmes travelled northwards to find Odo, and persuaded him to give an order to the count to restore Bizac to the Church: the estate was recovered in 892. The Church in the far south continued to look to the king; and the local officials, in this area in which ideas from Roman law still flourished, were still prepared to regard themselves as officials, and to be seen to obey the king when it suited them. As Dhondt has pointed out, the king was never called upon to intervene in Burgundy, where the king was a much more real and plausible political force, but where the church was already effectively in lay hands.[14] In Poitou, much nearer home than Septimania, Odo had little influence; he endeavoured to appoint his own count on the death of Rannulf II, and failed totally.

The other powers in West Francia under Odo were the princes, mostly men linked by blood or by marriage to the Carolingian line. We have already seen how Bernard Plantevelue and William the Pious had established themselves as rulers in Aquitaine. In Burgundy Richard of Autun, brother of Boso, king in Provence, had won a predominance for himself; by his reorganisation of the region he earned the later nickname of 'the Justiciar'. Before his death in 921 he was being called *princeps* and *dux Burgundionum*, the latter presumably in imitation of William the Pious, *dux Aquitanorum*. In the north-eastern corner of the kingdom, a new power was emerging in Flanders, under the son of Baldwin I. Baldwin had established himself by astutely eloping with Charles the Bald's daughter Judith, who had formerly been married, first, to King Aethelwulf of the West Saxons and then to

Aethelwulf's son Aethelbald. He was pardoned, and given counties in Flanders. He died shortly before the great Viking invasion of the Low Countries, which proved the making of his house. Baldwin II was able to move into the vacuum created by the Viking devastation, and began ruthlessly to add territories to his new state: in the process he assassinated both Herbert I of Vermandois and Fulk, Archbishop of Rheims. His son Arnulf (918–65), given a Carolingian name in virtue of his descent from Judith, won equality with the rulers of Aquitaine and Burgundy by being granted the title of *marchio* in royal diplomas.

In the territories of men like William, Richard or Baldwin, Odo and his successors had only nominal authority. The local counts looked to the *marchio* or *dux*, and not to the king; the *vassi regales* became his vassals, and no doubt those royal estates not already granted to him soon became his, as well as control over bishoprics and abbeys. The princes were well aware of their role within the kingdom, and of the legal suzerainty of the king; their not infrequent contacts with the king and presence at court in the tenth century contrasts noticeably with the way in which in the eleventh century the Capetian monarchy was virtually ignored over much of France, particularly the south. The princes were partners of the king in his kingdom, and Odo had the political sense to realise this. In the year of his greatest test, in 893, when a number of northern magnates, including Fulk of Rheims, had Charles the Simple crowned at Rheims, Odo's first move was to assure himself of the support of William of Aquitaine and Richard of Burgundy. He then moved against Charles's supporters, defeated them, and chose Charles as his successor. When Odo died in 898 the succession was smoother than any since the death of Charlemagne, and chroniclers who had been using words like 'usurpation' of Odo's rule felt that the situation had returned to normal.

Charles III has been unfortunate enough to be remembered as 'the Simple'. As the Chronicle of St Benignus of Dijon put it, 'During his life he was called *simplex* because of his good nature; he would better have been called 'the Saint', because he had been called to a better life after having been plunged unjustly into a long captivity by those who had become unfaithful and forgotten their oaths to him.'[15] *Simplex* was the opposite of *duplex*: it meant 'honest' or 'straight-forward'. Misinterpretation of his nickname has helped some historians to underestimate Charles as a ruler. He is better known for his concessions than for his gains for the monarchy; in particular he gave control over much of the area west of the Seine to Robert, Odo's younger brother, and, more famously, gave a number of counties near Rouen to Rollo, or Hrólfr, a Viking chieftain. This is perhaps not the shortsighted move that it appears to be at first sight. Breton expansion westwards had effectively withdrawn much of the Channel coast from Frankish control; the disappearance of the bishops of Avranches in the late ninth century may have been the result of Breton and not Viking attacks. By creating a buffer-state led by a distinguished war-leader, and by bringing him within the Frankish structure with an oath of loyalty and the title of count of Rouen, Charles could hope to prevent further Breton incursions. Indeed Viking/Norman aggression was initially at the expense of the Bretons and not the king, and great aristocrats such as Robert and his son Hugh the Great tried to win Norman assistance against the king in vain.

Charles was not unsuccessful in his eastern policy either. The last Carolingian monarch in East Francia, Louis the Child, died in 911, and Conrad of Franconia was elected by the nobles to rule in his place. Charles the Simple could claim to be the legitimate heir of Louis, and although the magnates in East Francia ignored him, those in Lotharingia were won over to Charles's allegiance. He recognised Reginar as *marchio* in Lotharingia – a title otherwise used by him only of William the Pious. The Lotharingian alliance was important for Charles, and ultimately fatal. He was provided with a good deal of support, which he encouraged by a Lotharingian marriage, but, less happily, he chose a Lotharingian called Hagano as his chief adviser. The chroniclers stress Hagano's low birth as a reason for the hostility of the magnates, but it was also Charles's willingness to upset old privileges in Hagano's favour which determined their attitude. For instance, Charles tried to replace Rothild, Abbess of the Carolingian house of Chelles, by Hagano; Robert's son Hugh, who was Rothild's son-in-law, raised a revolt. Most of the northern magnates abandoned Charles; Robert was elected king, and crowned in 922 by the same Archbishop Walter of Sens who had crowned Robert's brother Odo in 888. In the following year Robert met the forces of Charles on the battlefield, and was killed. But Charles failed to win back the support of the magnates. Ralph of Burgundy (Fr. Raoul, Gn Rudolf), son of Richard the Justiciar and son-in-law of King Robert, was crowned by Walter of Sens, and Charles was captured and imprisoned by Ralph's kinsman Herbert II of Vermandois. Ralph's reign was tarnished by this perfidy, in the eyes of posterity, and in the eyes of some contemporaries. William the Pious's nephew Acfred, Duke of the Aquitanians, dated a document to 'the fifth year since the faithless Franks degraded their king Charles and illegally elected Ralph', and after Charles's death in prison men south of the Loire began to date by the number of years since his death, sometimes adding 'in the reign of God' or 'of Christ'.[16] Loyalty to the Carolingian dynasty in the south remained strong. To them the king was not a political figure, but a legal sovereign: legitimacy was more important than political effectiveness.

Ralph, not even a Robertian, was the first non-Carolingian king in West Francia whose estates and interests were not in Francia proper, but in Burgundy. Because of this, presumably, Ralph seems to have been little interested in protecting royal interests in the north. Lotharingia broke away from West Francia; in 925 Gilbert, son of Reginar, recognised the Saxon king of Germany, Henry I, and was in turn recognised as Duke of Lotharingia. The power of the great magnates in West Francia – the Counts of Flanders and Vermandois, the rulers of Brittany and Normandy, and Robert's heir Hugh – extended over most of northern Gaul. Hugh, known as 'the Great' although like Charlemagne he was probably called *Hugo Magnus* to distinguish him from his son Hugh the Younger (who, since the twelfth century, has been better known as Hugh Capet), controlled most of Neustria, including the city of Paris and the former royal monastery of St-Denis. But the dominant figure in the north in the 920s and 930s was Herbert II of Vermandois. His ancestry no doubt helped him, particularly during the reign of a non-Carolingian: he was directly descended from Charlemagne, through Charlemagne's grandson Bernard of Italy. After Bernard's blinding by Louis the Pious, his son Pippin had continued to hold a number of counties in north-east Gaul, which were inherited by Herbert I and then Herbert II. Herbert II's greatest coup, apart from his capture of Charles the Simple, was the election of his son Hugh as archbishop of Rheims. Since Hugh was only five years old at the time, the great revenue and numerous vassals of the archbishopric were in Herbert II's hands. By the time of Ralph's death in 936, Herbert had amassed a large collection of counties, and even held the royal stronghold of Laon; other counts in the region seem to have recognised his authority rather than the king's. Altogether his 'state' stretched from Auxerre in the south to Artois in the north, and he controlled bishoprics and abbeys as well as counties. Like the collection of counties assembled by Bernard Plantevelue earlier, Herbert's empire did not survive his death in 943; the various counties were divided among his sons. But in 936 Herbert II was at the height of his power, and an obvious candidate for the kingship, together with Ralph's brother Hugh the Black of Burgundy. It was probably to forestall their claims, and in the knowledge that he himself had no chance, that the Robertian Hugh the Great urged on the magnates who attended Ralph's funeral the acceptance of Louis as king, the son of Charles the Simple and Eadgifu. Ambassadors were sent to England, where Louis was in exile, and they found him at the court of Athelstan, then at York, and brought him back to Francia: hence Louis IV's usual soubriquet 'd'Outremer', 'from beyond the sea'.

For another fifty years, therefore, a Carolingian king ruled in Gaul, seldom venturing far from the Paris region, and frequently having to rescue himself by alliance with the Robertians or with the new dynasty in Germany, the Ottonians. The final transfer of power to the Robertian, or Capetian, dynasty in 987, when Louis V died without a direct heir, often seems inevitable. During these fifty years the Robertians had been establishing an impregnable position for themselves in northern Gaul. The assassination of William Longsword of Normandy in 942 by Arnulf of Flanders plunged his province into a state of disarray from which it was hardly to emerge until the eleventh century; the death of Herbert II of Vermandois in 943 broke up that particular power-block; the death of Hugh the Black, last descendant of Richard the Justiciar, led to a weakening of Burgundy, which finally fell into Robertian hands; the death of Arnulf of Flanders in 965 put a temporary end to the Flemish expansion. Hugh the Great's son Hugh Capet emerged without rivals as the dominant figure in northern Gaul. His position was confirmed by the king with a title inherited from Hugh the Great. In 943, after the deaths of William Longsword and Herbert II, Louis IV had conferred upon Hugh the Great the title of *dux Francorum*. The title, and whatever power might have gone with it, was presumably in return for Hugh's promise not to gain advantage for himself in Normandy or the Vermandois: it was the king, if anybody, who stood to gain from the situation. What precisely was meant by 'Duke of the Franks' is a much-discussed problem. But probably Louis IV was putting Hugh on the same level as contemporaries such as the Dukes of the Saxons or the Lotharingians, leaders of peoples. These ducal titles were granted very sparingly by the Carolingian chancery, being denied, for instance, to the rulers of the Aquitanians, the Bretons or the Normans. Constitutionally speaking, therefore, Louis IV was king of all West Francia, and under him were various provincial or ethnic rulers, including the ruler of the Franks, the *dux Francorum*. The king retained his sovereignty and his royal lands, but the duke was intermediary between him and his counts. And indeed in the decades after 942 we can see the two Hughs extending their authority over the counts of northern Gaul, from the borders of Brittany to those of Flanders: a number of counties were administered directly by the dukes or their viscounts, and in other cases the existing counts were vassals of the Robertians. Even the Breton counts of Nantes and Rennes, being vassals of the duke's vassals (the counts of Anjou and Blois) were drawn into the Robertian structure.

Despite these developments, it would be wrong to imagine that the last Carolingian kings were as impotent as the Merovingian kings they had once dominated and deposed. Louis IV (936–54) and his son Lothar (954–86) were competent and energetic rulers, who did what they could to rebuild the monarchy from the weak position to which Ralph had reduced it. Louis IV recovered lost royal estates, and administered them with care. Only one donation of land is known from Lothar's long reign, and that in Anjou; he did not even allow his younger son Charles any estates. To conserve their resources the last Carolingians abandoned the principle of partition among the heirs in favour of that of primogeniture. They preserved some ambitions to restore some of their old authority in northern Gaul, Louis in Normandy and Lotharingia, and Lothar in Flanders and the Auvergne – his son Louis was crowned king of Aquitaine in 981. But they had rather more success nearer home. Laon and Rheims were recovered from the sons of Herbert II of Vermandois, and the kings regained control of a number of counties, bishoprics and abbeys, particularly in the area north-east of Paris: rather than bestowing all these counties on potentially disloyal counts, in at least two cases (Rheims and Langres) they handed over comital control to the bishops, setting up small but important ecclesiastical principalities loyal to the monarchy. Occasionally Louis and Lothar achieved these limited successes with the help of the Robertians or the Lotharingians, but their most important allies were undoubtedly the Ottonian rulers of Germany. The marriage of Louis IV to Gerberga, Gilbert of Lorraine's widow and Otto I's sister, was one manifestation of this alliance, and an excuse for further pleas for help. Gerberga herself several times acted as Louis's ambassador in this respect. In 942 Otto was brought in to persuade Hugh the Great and Herbert II to become reconciled with the king; in 946 Louis and Otto joined to drive Herbert's son Hugh from the see of Rheims; in 948 a council held at Ingelheim, in the presence of Louis, Otto and a papal legate, excommunicated Hugh of Vermandois. In the 950s and 960s an Ottonian cleric, Bruno Archbishop of Cologne, played an important role in both French and German royal affairs: he was in a unique position to do so, as uncle to Otto II, Lothar and Hugh Capet. It was thanks to Bruno's influence that a Lotharingian, Odalric, obtained the see of Rheims, a crucial position in Lothar's kingdom. Odalric's successor was a Lotharingian too: Adalbero, nephew of Adalbero of Metz, a leading supporter of Otto II.

The alliance with the Ottonians ended in the 970s; one direct result was the end of the Carolingian dynasty. Lothar quarrelled with his brother Charles; Otto II made Charles Duke of Lower Lotharingia. The following year, 978, Lothar invaded Lotharingia, to assert his claim over the territory and, according to the contemporary Rheims historian Richer, because he was annoyed that Otto should take up residence in the Carolingian imperial capital of Aachen. Lothar achieved remarkable success, nearly capturing Otto, and entering Aachen. 'The bronze eagle in the attitude of flight which Charlemagne had fixed on the roof of the palace was turned again to face the east [and the traditional enemies of the Carolingians, the Saxons]. The Germans had turned it towards the west, as a symbolic indication that their cavalry could defeat the Gauls whenever they wished.'[17] Otto retaliated by invading West Francia, taking Laon and attacking Paris. A peace was agreed in 980, but Lothar took advantage of Otto's death in 983 to invade again. He captured Verdun, and later the person of Godfrey, Count of Verdun, brother of Adalbero, Archbishop of Rheims. When Lothar died, and Louis V shortly after him, and the magnates met in 987 to decide whether to offer the crown to Charles of Lotharingia or to Hugh Capet, Adalbero was the first Capetian's most eloquent supporter.

Hugh Capet was crowned at Noyon in 987, according to Richer with the acclamation of 'the Gauls [West Franks], the Bretons, the Danes [Normans], the Aquitanians, the Goths, the Spaniards and the Gascons'.[18] These are the various peoples of West Francia whose acclamation was theoretically necessary for the royal inauguration. In fact, of course, it was a purely northern affair. Hugh was supported by Richard of Normandy, and his own brother Henry of Burgundy; after the coronation of his son Robert ('the Pious') in the same year, and his marriage to the widow of Arnulf II of Flanders, the support of the new Flemish Count Baldwin IV was assured. Hugh's position was finally secured when Adalbero of Laon invited Charles of Lotharingia and the new Archbishop of Rheims, Arnulf, son of King Lothar, to dinner, and had them arrested; the key towns of Laon and Rheims were restored to Hugh, and the last Carolingian threats to his power removed. The great princes of the south, above all William Ironarm, Count of Poitou and Duke of the Aquitanians, and William Taillefer, Count of Toulouse, seem to have been happy enough to accept Hugh's rule, in so far as it was relevant to them at all. Only a glimmer of Carolingian loyalism flickered in the south, becoming visible, for instance, in a charter of Roger of Béziers, which in 1035 was dated according to the regnal year of Louis, son of Charles of Lotharingia.

Gaul around the Year 1000

THE two hundred years since the coronation of Charlemagne had seen startling political changes. The royal successor to the most powerful western ruler since the fourth century controlled a territory some 200 kilometres long from north to south, stretching from Orleans to Senlis, and less than 100 kilometres broad. Even within this territory there were independent and hostile castellans, such as Montlhéry and Montmorency. Most of the territory had been granted out as benefices to the royal vassals, and the king had to augment his meagre income by revenue from vacant bishoprics, and to live by begging hospitality from monasteries and others. The kingdom only survived because it was a kingdom, because it possessed enough residual prestige among the major powers in northern Gaul, lay and ecclesiastical. But the personal bonds which had enabled the Carolingian kings to act effectively until the very end were weakening rapidly. Under Louis IV most of the princes in the kingdom were his *fideles*, that is, they had come to his court and sworn homage and agreed to act as his vassal. Under Robert the Pious (996–1031) only the counts in the vicinity of the Île-de-France were royal vassals: men like the Counts of Blois or Soissons. The southern princes never visited the court, and the royal chancery did not refer to them as *fideles*, but as 'friends' or 'companions in our rule'. It was more awkward for the northern princes. In the second decade of the eleventh century Dudo of St-Quentin wrote a history of the Norman duchy which endeavoured to explain the relationship between the king and the Norman ruler. In 911 Charles the Simple had made an agreement with Rollo that he should administer some *pagi* in the region of Rouen; this was not a benefice, but an allod.

Subsequent dukes (Dudo used the word anachronistically) held the duchy by hereditary right. Dudo admitted that after the assassination of William Longsword in 943 the Norman magnates had become royal vassals, but said that their oaths had stressed their primary duty to the duke. The relationship between duke and king was one of friendship and concord, not involving the *servitium*, military or otherwise, which a vassal owed to his lord. Two famous writings of the jurist Fulbert of Chartres from the early eleventh century show a similar reinterpretation: the relationship between lord and vassal was not the same as that between king and prince. When William V asked Fulbert whether Hugh of Lusignan was justified in breaking his oath of fidelity, Fulbert replied that a vassal must be worthy of his benefice, and give his lord *auxilium et consilium.* He who denied his oath should suffer not only the loss of his benefice, but also the loss of his hand, the punishment for perjury. But a different note is struck in a letter, apparently written by Fulbert, from Odo II of Blois (996–1037) to King Robert, around 1023. Odo II was one of the more colourful figures in that century of adventurers, throwing himself into a number of futile causes and ending his life on the battlefield in the course of an attempt to gain Aachen and the imperial throne. He had inherited the counties of Blois, Chartres and Tours, and in 1023 had just inherited those of Champagne and Troyes, which put him in a very powerful position that pressed closely upon the royal lands from both east and west. Robert had quarrelled with Odo, and wished to deprive him of his honours; apparently he conceded that there was a distinction between the benefices recently confirmed in 1021 and those which Odo had inherited from his father: to demand the forfeiture of those would be impossible, even if they had originally been granted by the king. Fulbert, in Odo's name, denied the distinction.

> If the nature of the fief [Troyes] which you have given me be considered, it is certain that it forms part, not of your fisc, but of the property which, with your favour, comes to me from my ancestors by hereditary right; if the value of my services be considered, you know how, as long as I was in favour with you, I served you at your court, in the host and on foreign soil. And if, since you have turned away your favour from me and have attempted to take from me the fief which you gave me, I have committed towards you, in defence of myself and of my fief, acts which displeased you, I have done so when harassed by insults and compelled by necessity.[19]

If a king withdrew his favour and broke the concord between himself and his magnate, then the magnate was entitled to defend himself. Fulbert concluded with a neat pun: 'I would rather die with honours than die without honour.'[20]

Who are those who share power and authority in Gaul with the king of West Francia around the year 1000? First in dignity, of course, was the twenty-year-old Emperor, Otto III, who in the very year 1000 had gone to Aachen to open up the tomb of Charlemagne: his predecessor was sitting in a chair, crowned, and holding a golden sceptre. Two years later, Otto III was himself buried at Aachen. The imperial town was in Lower (northern) Lotharingia: the duchy had been divided into two in 959, and its dukes remained under the control of the German kings and under the watchful eyes of their bishops. Under the close protection, and domination, of the German kings were the kings of Burgundy. Rudolf III, great-grandson of the Rudolf who had been crowned in 888, reigned from 993 to 1032 over a greatly enlarged kingdom: in the mid-tenth century, after the death of Louis the Blind, the kingdom of Provence had been joined to that of Burgundy. A German chronicler, Thietmar, described Rudolf's rule in sarcastic terms: 'There is no other king who is like him. He possesses only the title and the crown, and he gives bishoprics to those who are chosen by his magnates. He possesses very little for his own use; he lives at the expense of bishops, and cannot defend those around him who are oppressed in any way. Such people have to put their hands in those of the magnates and serve them as if they were their king, and thus obtain some peace.'[21] On the death of Rudolf III, 'the Sluggard', in 1032, the kingdom was incorporated into the Empire.

The most important of the magnates within Rudolf's kingdom, and among the more independent, were the Counts of Provence. Around the year 1000 the office seems to have been shared by Roubaud II and his brother William, later called 'the Liberator' because of his victory over the Saracen pirate stronghold at La-Garde-Freinet. Their importance within Gaul can be seen by their marriage alliances: William married Adelaide of Anjou, widow of King Louis V, and their daughter married King Robert the Pious. The frontier between the kingdoms of West Francia and Burgundy, measured in terms of men's loyalties and not a physical boundary, was not at all precise, despite the Treaty of Verdun. The Count of Vienne, Charles-Constantine, gave homage to Louis IV in 951; the Bishop of Uzès at the same time dated documents according to Louis's reign. The county of Mâcon was north of the border between French Burgundy and the kingdom of Burgundy, but its inhabitants ignored the fact. The estates of individual churches, magnates and peasants were to be found on both sides of the 'frontier', and charters can be dated by the regnal years of either the Frankish or the Burgundian king. Neither king played any role in the life of the county of Mâcon. The last royal property there had been alienated in 950, at the request of the count, and it was he who exercised all the rights that had, in Charlemagne's day, been regarded as those of the king. Only the church still looked to the king; he was informed of episcopal elections and was called upon to confirm immunities granted by his predecessors.

Another magnate whose power crossed the borders between kingdoms was the Count of Toulouse, William III Taillefer (961–1037). His power was considerable, and rested not on bonds of vassalage, as in the north, but rather on his position as representative of the king, backed up by the wealth deriving from his considerable estates. The count was still a respected authority, who could control the viscounts placed in the various cities within his territory and maintain much of the early Carolingian structure of government. Of his southern neighbours little can be said here: the Count of Barcelona, who acknowledged the sovereignty of the kings of West Francia, is outside the scope of this book, and very little is known about the rulers of Gascony, Bernard William (996–1009), son of William Sanchez, and his brother Sancho William (1009–31), '*totius Gasconiae princeps et dux*', the last members of a dynasty which originated with Aznar Sanchez in the days of Louis the Pious and may even have been linked to the dynasty of the pre-Carolingian princes of Aquitaine. In the year 1000 the prince of Aquitaine, or Duke of the Aquitanians, the northern neighbour of the Count of Toulouse, was William V, 'the Great' (995–1030), probably the most successful ruler of his time in Gaul. Descendant of Rannulf, Count of Poitou, whose family had held the county since the days of Charles the Bald and whose grandfather William III, 'Towhead', had first described himself as holding the duchy of Aquitaine in 959, William the Great hardly ever referred to himself as *comes*, but as 'Duke of the Aquitanians', 'Duke of the region of Aquitaine', and even 'monarch of all Aquitaine'.[22] Adhemar of Chabannes, writing his Chronicle in Angoulême during the lifetime of the duke, said indeed that he was thought rather to be king than duke: 'most glorious and most powerful, amiable to all, great in counsel, conspicuous in his prudence, most generous in his giving, defender of the poor, father of the monks, builder and lover of churches, and especially of the holy church of Rome. It was his custom from his youth to hasten to the threshold of the Apostles in Rome almost every year, and in that year in which he did not go to Rome he went by way of recompense to Santiago in Galicia.'[23] Adhemar described proudly how his friend the Emperor Henry III would send William gifts, as did kings such as Alfonso of Spain, Sancho of Navarre, and Canute, king of the Danes and the English. William was one of the few rulers of his time who managed to hold together a considerable territory, stretching from the Loire to the Garonne, maintaining the loyalty of his vassals, such as the Count of Angoulême or the Viscount of Limoges, and even being able to influence the election of bishops throughout his duchy. Nor was William V presiding over the last flowering of Aquitaine during a period in which political fragmentation was normal elsewhere; his successors, by shrewd marriages and careful administration, preserved his duchy, and even extended it, into Gascony and the Toulousain.

Few lords north of the Loire could match William's power. In Brittany, in so far as it is possible to know what was happening, there seems to have been a breakdown of the considerable unity of the ninth century. Bretons no longer recognised a king. The Counts of Nantes, all-powerful in the early tenth century, ceded to the Counts of Rennes, who took the ducal title. Both counties increasingly fell under the influence of their neighbours, the Counts of Blois and the Dukes of Normandy, and the network of vassal relationships extended into Brittany. The Normans kept the formerly aggressive Bretons within more restricted boundaries; but Breton territory was also lost to a dynamic new power, Anjou.

The first well-known member of the dynasty of counts was Fulk the Red, to be found in the entourage of Odo and Robert at the end of the ninth century: he came from a family that had included Adalard, Louis the Pious's seneschal and lay-abbot of St Martin's of Tours, and Raino, Bishop of Angers. Fulk himself married into the family of Lambert, Marquis of the Breton Marches and progenitor of the Marquises of Spoleto in Italy. The family which became so powerful in north-western Gaul in the eleventh century, and which eventually fathered Henry II of England, had thus been important in the area since the days of Charlemagne; this was true in the case of many of the great families of the late tenth century, including probably the neighbours of the Angevin Counts, the Thibauds (or Theudebalds) of

Blois, represented as we have seen around the year 1000 by Odo II. Even more colourful than Odo II was his contemporary Fulk Nerra of Anjou (987–1040), to whom Sir Richard Southern devotes a few memorable pages in his *Making of the Middle Ages*.[24] Brutal, courageous, unscrupulous, pious – three times atoning for his sins on that most heroic of pilgrimages, to Jerusalem, the last when he was nearly seventy – he epitomises the contradictions of the eleventh century. To the north of Fulk Nerra was Normandy, under Richard II (996–1026). In the tenth century the territory of Normandy was controlled by a count and his subordinates; Richard II, the Duke, appointed a number of counts in militarily important areas: at Avranches, to guard the Breton frontier, at Ivry, by the county of Blois-Chartres, and at Eu, near the frontier with Flanders. The counts were not drawn from the ranks of the local aristocrats, but were all his own relations. In part that gave Normandy its considerable political unity, but the landed wealth of the duke himself, and his absolute control over the bishoprics and abbeys in the duchy, were also important elements. The aristocratic civil wars during the minority of William the Bastard in the 1040s only temporarily halted the growth of ducal power. By then Normandy had a rival on the Channel coast: the county of Flanders. Flanders lost some of its predominance in the north-east during a succession crisis following the death of Arnulf the Great in 965, but recovered its position under Counts Baldwin IV (988–1035) and Baldwin V (1035–67). Profits from Flanders's growing trade and industry, as well as from her rich agricultural lands, to which the counts added by draining projects, helped make the Baldwins among the richest and most powerful of the northern rulers.

The princes at whom we have been glancing had most of the powers of the early Carolingian kings, and most of the problems. They too had to contend with their aristocracy; the small scale of their states, which made communications and control easier, was offset by the limited nature of their resources. Already by the year 1000 the power of some princes over the various counties or viscounties within their territory had diminished as thoroughly as had that of the kings over their kingdoms. A good example is that of the only such territory not as yet mentioned: Burgundy. Burgundy was Capetian territory, under Hugh Capet's brother Odo (956–65) and then his brother Henry (965–1002). He was called Henricus Magnus, to distinguish him from his great-nephew, King Henry I, and he called himself 'Duke of the Burgundians' or 'Duke of Burgundy' – his wife is the first ever to use the title *ducatrix*, duchess.[25] He possessed few domains, and little authority over 'his' counts. One of these was the Count of Mâcon; a study of the Mâconnais may serve as an introduction to the political and social changes of the years on either side of 1000, as it has done for all medieval historians since the publication of Georges Duby's classic study of the region in 1953.[26] The Counts of Mâcon in the last years of the Carolingian monarchy were descendants of the men who ruled on behalf of William the Pious of Aquitaine, who had held the Mâconnais and who founded his monastery of Cluny there in 910. Count Alberic, in 980, administered the county much as any Carolingian count would have done. He had the monopoly of minting coins; in the name of the king he could raise an army from the free men of the county; in the name of the king he administered justice at the *mallus*, the public law-court, in Mâcon, with the help of the lesser aristocracy of the county. He commanded respect partly through exercise of a power legitimised by the king, partly through habit, and partly through his status as the major landowner in the area. His officials, the *vicarii*, held law-courts in the countryside, advised by *scabini*, lawmen, as decreed by the royal capitularies of a century earlier. The countryside was defended by castles, originally built at royal or comital orders, and in 980 commanded by castellans who were *fideles* of the count and frequently attended at his court. The count acted as *advocatus* for the lands and men of the three great ecclesiastical immunities in the county (the cathedral church of Mâcon and the monasteries of Cluny and Tournus) and received a share of certain revenues of the these churches, such as tolls or market-dues. In short, the count alone exercised regalian rights within the county; all free men within the county were his subjects, and he alone was accorded the title *dominus*.

The rapid changes which destroyed this pre-eminence within a few decades are not easy to explain, even with the wealth of charter evidence the historian of the Mâconnais has at his disposal. Clearly a change in the pattern of landholding, for which the charters are eminently suitable evidence, was an important factor. In the mid-tenth century the count was by far the most important landholder, followed by a handful of other aristocratic families. The Church was relatively unimportant. Most of the land was allodial land, held without any obligations to a superior save those due from a subject to his king or the royal representative. Some had no doubt once been granted by the king or another as benefices; many, even the count's *comitatus*, were by then regarded as allodial. But a social position based upon the possession of land was far from secure. When parents died, the land was divided up among all the children: even though celibacy, or at least bachelordom, outside the Church was common (putting sons or daughters into the Church did not help, because monasteries expected gifts and secular priests could share in the partition), it could not prevent the fragmentation of a family's estates. The *fraternitia* (Fr. *frérêche*), whereby a group of brothers continue to work together to hold the family estates together, only held up the process for a generation. Moreover, the donation of lands to the church was becoming an increasingly common manifestation of lay piety, even at the lower social levels. In these ways allodial estates were diminished and fragmented; land held in benefice or by other forms of tenure was much more likely to survive, being inalienable without the permission of the lord, and not being subject to partible inheritance. Lay families, even at the highest levels, became impoverished, and descendants of aristocratic families became indistinguishable from the richer peasants. 'The ultimate reason for the great movements of men in the eleventh century, the knightly expeditions, the formation of a merchant class, the conquest of forests, is perhaps less a sudden demographic expansion, which remains to be proved, and rather the dissolution of allodial fortunes, which uprooted the rural population.'[27]

Political events also precipitated change. In 982 the widow of Count Alberic of Mâcon married Odo-William, who became count after the death of her children. He was the son of a dethroned king of Italy, a man used to politics on a large scale, who soon lost interest in the county of Mâcon. The count's castellans gradually ceased to come to court, gave up their customary obligations, and began to rule their districts in their own right. The count's court, having ceased to attract the great men of the county, lost its prestige and its attraction for lesser men. The castles became the centres of political life; their commanders raised armies, collected taxes, and administered justice, even carrying out the death penalty for serious crimes, instead of the fine which in earlier centuries had been customary for free men. The great churches of the Mâconnais claimed their independence from the count, interpreting their immunity strictly so as to exclude his influence. They held their own legal tribunals; even the fortified religious quarter outside the *castrum* of Mâcon, the centre of comital power, had its own tribunal. Relationships between men modified, in this new political situation. Formerly men who wished for protection or support commended themselves to aristocrats and became their vassals;

sometimes they even surrendered to their lord their own allods. By the first few decades of the eleventh century the situation had been reversed. Castellans and others who wished to survive in the increasingly violent Mâconnais countryside had to find supporters for themselves, and had to buy vassals by promising them benefices. It was above all military support that castellans and other lords required; by the later eleventh century a new class of *milites*, or knights, had come into existence.

Naturally the model created by Duby from the rich Mâconnais material cannot be applied everywhere. In some parts of Gaul similar developments were occurring, but at a quicker or slower rate than in the Mâconnais; in other areas developments were quite different. But there are a few constants. Castle building, for instance, was proceeding at a rapid pace in the decades on either side of 1000 over most of Gaul: the acceleration in the region of the Loire or in Provence clearly occurs after the disappearance of Viking or Saracen threats. In the ninth or early tenth century castle-building had been the prerogative of the king, and then of the prince. By the eleventh century a few princes, such as those in Normandy or Flanders, were in a position to destroy a castle (in most cases a flimsy wooden construction atop an earthen mound) erected by a vassal against their orders; someone like the Count of Toulouse was able to maintain direct control over sixty of the eighty castles in his territory; but an ineffective prince or count might authorise the building of a castle by a vassal to save face. Castles were not new, of course. Gallo-Roman senators had built them in the sixth century, and Aquitanian aristocrats in the eighth. Many fortifications went up in the years of Viking and Saracen attacks. But formerly castles had been fortified residences, military strongholds, or refuges for the population; increasingly they were becoming centres of government, or, if that is too dignified a word for the often brutal realities of domination by castellans, of protection rackets.

The roots of lordship by local aristocrats, which was to replace kingship as a method of government even where princely and comital power remained strong, used to be sought in the extension of the rights of landowners over their tenants. Even in Roman times great landowners seem to have had powers of jurisdiction over their tenants. Historians for a long time approached medieval society through the study of northern French and Belgian documents, which revealed that the bulk of peasants were tenants and tied to the land and to their lord by various legal obligations; the purpose of the polyptychs being to list those obligations, it is hardly surprising that the burdens of the peasants seemed so considerable. Naturally these historians concluded that it was as landowners that the greater and lesser aristocracy assumed the right to administer justice, levy fines, call out on militia service and so on. But if one looks further afield, this appears to have been a mistaken hypothesis. In the Mâconnais, for instance, in the transition zone between north and south, there were many free peasants, some probably belonging to formerly aristocratic lineages, living on their own allodial land; their obedience to counts or their subordinates was not based on landowners' rights. Further south, in Languedoc, the peasant living on allodial land was even more common; he might also be a tenant, but if so he made rental payments in money and did not owe any labour services. It is clear that the aristocracy ruled in all cases not as landlords but as agents, legitimate or otherwise, of royal power. The *bannus*, the right to command, was derived from the royal *bannus*; hence the authority of the castellan, acting as the delegate of the count, and hence the authority of the bishop or abbot, acting as lord of his immunity, granted in earlier times by the king.

The institution of the immunity, over much of Gaul, contributed not only to the extension of ecclesiastical lordship, but of lay lordship also. In the north, the *advocatus*, the lay aristocrat originally appointed by the king to act as legal representative of the ecclesiastical immunity, came to take over the lordship of part or the whole of the immunity. In the south (as in the Mâconnais) the *advocatus* was normally the count; and there other lay aristocrats frequently agreed a *comenda* or (in the south-east) a *salvamentum* with a church or a monastery, by which they took over the lordship of portions, particularly outlying portions, of the ecclesiastical estates. Lay aristocrats could, of course, extend their lordship through the Church very much more directly, by taking over abbacies and bishoprics, or by keeping close control over monasteries founded by their ancestors. Unlike allods, ecclesiastical estates were not subject to fragmentation through partible inheritance; they could thus be a very valuable addition to a lord's collection of estates and privileges. But, by the tenth century, the extension of lay power over the Church was bitterly resented by many churchmen, who had over the previous centuries evolved theories of authority which exalted the role of the clergy within the community. With the political fragmentation of Gaul, it was churchmen, rather than the king, who clung to ideals of political unity and who formulated these new theories which, in the eleventh century, in the age of Pope Gregory VII and Church reform, would sweep across Europe.

9. Bishops and Councils

THE Merovingian bishop could possess considerable authority within his *civitas*, because of his social position and spiritual power; the Carolingian bishop might hold the lordship of his see. But Carolingian bishops, acting together, won for themselves a powerful position on a national scale, far exceeding that wielded by their Merovingian predecessors. The move of the bishop from the local to the national stage was one of the most significant developments of our period, not only for the history of the church, but also for the political future of France. In this final chapter we need to look briefly at the changing position of the episcopate, and at its implications for the future.

Although autonomous in day-to-day matters, the Merovingian bishop was a member of a larger structure, a structure determined by that of the Roman state. The bishoprics were, in the late Roman period, grouped into a number of ecclesiastical provinces, corresponding to the imperial provinces. The bishop whose see was the provincial capital had, as metropolitan, certain powers and obligations which were enforcd with varying degrees of success by sixth-century councils. The metropolitan had to consecrate bishops in his province, and to adjudicate in disputes between bishops; his bishops had to attend the regular synods he called, and follow the liturgical practices he laid down. But the metropolitan system was clearly weakening in the sixth century, and the actions of kings did not help matters. Partitions of kingdoms split up provinces; kings called councils made up of bishops from their own *Teilreiche*, regardless of ecclesiastical provinces; and they insisted on their own rights to nominate bishops and settle disputes. It is significant that when a metropolitan actually did object to a violation of his privileges, when Leontius of Bordeaux expelled the Bishop of Saintes (the royal nominee) from his see, he was fined 1000 solidi by King Charibert, and Gregory of Tours (a metropolitan himself) commented, 'In this way the insult done to the king was avenged.'[1]

The corporate spirit of the Merovingian episcopate was thus not strong; drawn as they were mostly from either the local aristocracy or the local clergy, their interests were often narrowly parochial – concerned, that is, with their own *parochia*, or diocese. The legislation of Merovingian councils was solely ecclesiastical: they concerned themselves with clerical and monastic discipline, public morality, the administration of charity and the like. The implications of this were often far-reaching as far as public welfare was concerned: as Professor Ullmann has put it in a masterly article, it was 'the translation of one of the all-pervading Christian virtues, charity, into a social–legislative norm'.[2] But it was quite separate from secular matters: when kings such as Guntram or Childebert II issued legislation there seems to have been no role for the episcopate, unless the magnates who gave advice and consent included those bishops who happened to be at court. Sixth-century kings were, of course, well able to provide themselves with literate and legally trained laymen, still conversant with the aims and methods of late Roman administration as well as the new Germanic legal ideas. However, there was a foretaste of the mixed councils of the Carolingian period in 613. Chlothar II assembled nearly eighty bishops at Paris, for the largest of all Merovingian councils. The bishops deliberated on the state of the Church and then, eight days later, joined with the lay magnates to produce a combined set of secular and ecclesiastical reforms.

As we have seen, there was a collapse of ecclesiastical discipline in the late seventh and early eighth centuries, with a cessation of synods and councils, and in some sees a break in the apostolic succession of bishops. The situation began to be remedied with the first of the Carolingian councils, the 'German Council' of 742 called by Carloman in Austrasia, and the Council of Soissons in the following year called by his brother Pippin in Neustria. The councils were not concerned with the Church alone: Carloman declared that he wanted episcopal advice for establishing the 'law of God and the religion of the church' for his *populus Dei*. The programme of reform for the next century was already there in embryo: the regeneration of the Frankish people, the 'people of God', in the light of Biblical and canonical teaching. It was under Charlemagne, a genuinely pious ruler mindful of his religious obligations, that this programme was most clearly expressed. The reforming legislation was partly the result of councils of bishops, called by the king; but a large part was the result of the deliberation of assemblies of both lay and clerical magnates (bishops and abbots), given the force of law by the word of the king, and sent out to counts and bishops for dissemination in the provinces in the form of capitularies. The most comprehensive statements can be found in the *Admonitio Generalis* of 789 and the General Capitulary for the *missi* of 802. The latter, which we have already seen (p.166) as introducing a new positive form of oath of loyalty to the emperor, laid down a series of provisions to ensure that 'all men should live a good and just life in accordance with God's commands, and should with one mind remain and abide each in his appointed place or profession: the clergy should live a life in full accord with the canons without concern for base gain, the monastic orders should keep their life under diligent control, the laity and secular people should make proper use of their laws, refraining from ill-will and deceit, and all should live together in perfect love and peace'.[3] These Utopian aims were issued as a royal command, but clearly the influence of the palace clergy and the bishops in their formulation was considerable. The new and positively Christian tenor of the legislation was the result of the new generation of well educated and often idealistic clergy which Charlemagne had called forth. That clergy inevitably saw itself as an élite, and a corporate spirit built up, giving them an outlook on life and goals which distinguished them from the lay aristocracy and, eventually, from the king as well. Methods of recruitment helped the process. By the ninth century the old Merovingian custom of rewarding lay bureaucrats or loyal counts with a bishopric was unknown; most bishops had been dedicated to the clergy from an early age, and many were appointed to the episcopate from the monastery, often bringing to their office a more rigorous and idealistic attitude.

A new trend emerged in the last year of Charlemagne's life, with the reforming councils of 813, held at Arles, Chalon, Mainz, Rheims and Tours. Charlemagne did not attend; the bishops took the lead in forming a programme of government, with the help of the lay aristocracy. As Dr McKitterick has pointed out,[4] the influence of the Church can be seen in the unaccustomed emphasis placed upon written texts. Before the synod of Mainz, for instance, the rule of Benedict was read out to the monks, New Testament texts and Gregory the Great's 'Pastoral Care' to the priests and bishops, and the secular laws to the counts and judges: these are obviously the texts which were intended to inspire the legislation. The initiative remained with the clergy under Louis the Pious, who was even more imbued with religious ideals than his father. The tenor of the new reign was exemplified not so much in the reforming synods of 816–819 as in the extraordinary scenes at the assembly of Attigny in 821, when Louis led his magnates in a public confession and penance, he for his murder of Bernard of Italy and the exile of his cousins Adalard and Wala, and the bishops for negligence of their duties. Not since Theodosius the Great in 390 had a monarch so humiliated himself at the Church's behest, a parallel of which Louis's bishops were well aware. It was not a close parallel, for Louis was not expiating his crime alone: he was intending to lead his whole people to repentance, including his bishops. But, contrite as they were, the bishops yet blamed Louis in part for their negligence, in not allowing them sufficient freedom of action. Agobard of Lyons later claimed that at Attigny he had led an attack on laymen who appropriated church land: this was to be the constant complaint of ninth-century councils, and the area in which the aims of the bishops collided with the *necessitas regni*, the political demands made upon the king.

A further step towards episcopal independence came in 829 when, as in 813, a series of reforming councils were summoned, at Paris, Mainz, Lyons and Toulouse, but this time without lay participation. The bishops were asked to set down 'what divine authority teaches' for the benefit of king and subjects: they were being asked to draw up a legislative programme themselves. Only the decisions of the Council of Paris now survive: they were drawn up by the learned Bishop of Orleans, Jonas, and included a lengthy introduction which was later redrafted by Jonas as his treatise *On the Institution of Kingship*, 'one of the first written in Europe on a purely political theme'.[5] The bishops at Paris came up with few new ideas, but the context in which they were set made them revolutionary. Louis was told that he did not wield power because of his ancestors, but from God. The bishops called themselves the 'vicars of the Apostles and the lights of the Word', and recalled the words of both the Prophet Haggai ('Ask now the priests concerning the law') and of Pope Gelasius (who placed the *auctoritas* of the clergy above the *potestas*, the power of command, of kings and princes). The bishops insisted on the separation of the lay and clerical estates, and complained about the enforced involvement of clergy in royal administration. Wala, Abbot of Corbie and Charlemagne's cousin, had expressed himself in similar terms at Aachen the previous winter; when Louis effectively rejected the programme put forward by the councils of 829, Wala led the coup d'état, on behalf of the co-Emperor Lothar, the symbol of that unity of Church and state which the bishops had so emphasised at Paris. The revolution did not last long. By the winter of 830 Louis had packed Lothar off to Italy once more, and divided the Empire north of the Alps among his three other sons. But it heralded a decade of political disturbance during which the episcopate grew still more confidant and independent.

In 833 Lothar joined with his brothers Pippin of Aquitaine and Louis the German in an attempt to exclude Charles the Bald from the inheritance. They met the army of the Emperor Louis in June, near Colmar, at the 'Field of Lies'. Louis's army deserted him, and he was imprisoned. In October the bishops met at Soissons, under the chairmanship of Archbishop Ebbo of Rheims (the son of Louis's wet-nurse): Louis was declared to have offended God and scandalised the holy Church, to have forced his people into civil war, and to have forfeited his imperial power 'by a just judgement of God'. Louis was brought into the church of St Medard, and there did penance for his sins. The bishops had declared the word of God, and Lothar began to reign as emperor 'by order of divine providence'. The bishops had made it clear, as they themselves said, 'how great the strength and power and the office of the bishops is, and what sort of damning punishment awaits him who is unwilling to obey sacerdotal admonitions'.[6] When Louis regained power the bishops again played the major role: he was first restored to communion, then given back his sword and royal garments, and then assured at a synod in 835 that the measures imposed upon him in 833 were uncanonical. Finally, in 836, he was recrowned, by the bishops, and he began to use the formula 'Emperor by the grace which God has restored'.[7]

The reign of Charles the Bald saw a further development in episcopal authority, thanks in particular to the leading churchman of the day, Hincmar, Archbishop of Rheims from 845 to 882. It was Hincmar who united coronation and unction (anointing with holy oil) as the constituent parts of a royal inauguration, when Charles became king of Aquitaine in 848. Ten years later, when Louis the German invaded the West Frankish kingdom, Hincmar, speaking on behalf of the bishops (now elevated to the rank of 'vicars of Christ', a title not yet monopolised by the papacy), told Louis that Charles had to be obeyed because he was the Lord's anointed – *Christus Dei*: Louis the German, who had not gone through the ceremony of unction, was not. The king was set apart from his people by that ceremony – but so, for other reasons, were the bishops. 'We bishops, consecrated as we are to God, are not like ordinary men such as lay people who can enter into the relationship of a vassal or who can take an oath, which is forbidden to us by evangelical, apostolic and canonical authority . . . . We do not fight for a terrestrial king, but on behalf of the celestial Ruler for our own well-being as well as for that of the terrestrial king and of the whole people entrusted to us.'[8] Hincmar crowned and anointed

Charles as King of Lotharingia at Metz in 869, and his son Louis II at Compiègne in 877, developing a liturgy that was to be a model for later English as well as French coronation ceremonies. Royal inaugurations thus became ecclesiastical occasions, in the hands of the national episcopate, and not (as with imperial inaugurations) the Papacy. If bishops could make kings, could they unmake them? An unjust king was of course chosen by God to punish the sins of his people. But bishops could declare, as they did in 833, that the king had lost God's favour and was hence unworthy to rule. And Hincmar seems to have believed that, since an unjust king increased still further the social disorders of his people, and hence their sins, it was the obligation of clerics to remonstrate with the king and, if necessary, to excommunicate him. The lines of clerical thinking in the eleventh century were already laid down: above all, the supremacy of clerical authority over lay, and the separation of clerical from secular affairs.

One of the practical implications of this separation which exercised bishops and abbots most in the Carolingian age was the question of lay control of church property. The reforming councils of the 740s recognised the ultimate rights of the church over the land that had been expropriated by the Carolingians and their aristocracy, but decreed that individual monasteries and bishoprics should only possess enough of this land for their own needs. There was a *divisio*: the surplus continued to be held by laymen, theoretically as a benefice from the Carolingians, on payment of a rent to the appropriate church (see above, p.164) Although Pippin and Charlemagne did return considerable quantities of land to the Church (thus, forty-seven named and many un-named estates were restored to the monks of St-Denis in 750–1, and others by Charlemagne in 775), much land still remained in lay hands when Louis came to the throne. By then *divisio*, a reforming measure but very much of a compromise, was being seen by the church as an abuse, an unjustified extension of lay power over church land. *Divisio* was in fact abandoned as a principle by Louis in 819, thus allowing once more the free accumulation of lands by individual churches, but the land still in lay hands was not restored.

Bishops and abbots employed a number of means in their attempts to gain complete control of their lands. They complained vigorously at church councils. They evolved new theories of royal power over land: in Hincmar's letter to Louis the German in 858 he claimed that the king had complete control over the benefices of laymen, but that he had rights over church land only in so far as he assisted in the administration of ecclesiastical affairs. They endlessly petitioned the king for the restoration of individual properties, as Lupus, Abbot of Ferrières, did with regard to St-Josse. They retailed heavenly visions, as Hincmar did, of the appalling tortures in Hell awaiting those who expropriated church lands. And they resorted to forgery, sometimes on a grandiose scale. One ingenious forger or group of forgers compiled a history of the bishops of Le Mans up to 832 and a biography of Bishop Aldric, which together included copies of eighty-six charters, many of them total fabrications, in an effort to have some lands restored to the bishopric, notably the monastery of St-Calais. In these histories many of the new ninth-century ideas on ecclesiastical independence, landowning, and episcopal organisation, were placed far back in the past, to the confusion of some modern historians. The forgeries were used in a case at Charles the Bald's palace of Verberie in 863 to decide upon the ownership of St-Calais. To the consternation of the monks, the judges decided that it was royal property. In Goffart's words, this decision marks 'a stage in the process by which the Carolingian Church lost the public character its earlier leaders had striven for, and . . . announce[s] the advent of the French *Eigenkirche*, divided like the country itself among a multitude of lords'.[9]

The Le Mans forger, like most medieval forgers, was doing no more than supplying the written evidence for a truth of which he was sincerely convinced. The lack of such evidence was usually matched by the lack of any written evidence which could disprove the forger's case. The inadequacy of Carolingian archives, even at the royal palace, was amply demonstrated when Louis the Pious asked Ansegis to compile a collection of royal capitularies: he was able to find only twenty-six of the ninety or so royal capitularies issued between 768 and 827.[10] The same problem was faced by anyone who was dubious in the face of the greatest of all ninth-century forgeries, the 'Pseudo-Isidorian Forgeries'. These included the capitularies of 'Benedict Levita', a series of Spanish canons, the *capitula Angilramni* attributed to Angilramn of Metz, and, above all, a series of papal decretals and conciliar decisions attributed to 'Isidore Mercator'. These forgeries were possibly produced in the province of Rheims, probably in the years between 847 and 852, when they appear to have been quoted by Hincmar. 'Isidore Mercator', or Pseudo-Isidore, was clearly an exceptionally well-read person, drawing on an immense number of writers. His technique was to piece together sentences and phrases from writers of the correct period, to give his forgeries the aura of authenticity:

he also incorporated entirely genuine material, and earlier forgeries generally accepted as genuine by his day, such as the famous eighth-century papal forgery, the 'Donation of Constantine', by which the Emperor purportedly handed over to Pope Sylvester considerable secular power within the Western Empire.

The authority of the bishops was Pseudo-Isidore's main theme. 'In the bishops you should venerate God, and love them as your own souls.' 'You [bishops] are given us as gods by God.'[11] Bishops alone can try clerics, themselves the 'chosen people of the Lord'. Bishops can only be tried in a synod, and seventy-two witnesses of good reputation are needed to condemn one: the condemnation is not valid until confirmed by the Pope. Only a pope can call a synod of bishops. Such powers, of course, had never been claimed by the Papacy; yet the forgeries were brought to Rome within fifteen years, and Pope Nicholas I was already citing them in a letter to the Frankish bishops in 865. The concern of the forger was largely with the independence of bishops; he rarely ventured into secular affairs, save to say that any Christian could appeal to a church court. 'Benedict Levita' was rather different. His compilation was of royal capitularies, those, he says, omitted by Ansegis from his compilation: later on he and Ansegis were often copied together into the same manuscript. Benedict exalted episcopal and papal authority, but extended that authority over secular matters. 'The law of Empires is not above the law of God, but under it.'[12] Secular laws contrary to ecclesiastical ones are invalid; capitularies are only valid if confirmed by either the Pope or the bishops. Anyone who took property given to the Church, and hence to God, was guilty of sacrilege and liable to punishment by excommunication, and by loss of all dignities: he was then handed over to the secular courts. Kings were not exempted.

The revolutionary programme contained in the Pseudo-Isidorian forgeries was naturally not accepted by all. When they were used by Bishop Hincmar of Laon in his dispute with his uncle Hincmar of Rheims, the Archbishop accused him of using falsified canons. The question in dispute here was that of the rights of the metropolitan over his suffragan bishops. The metropolitan structure had been revived in the eighth century; the title of archbishop, which at first had been purely honorary and conferred on such men as Boniface of Mainz and Angilramn of Metz, was in the ninth century used by all metropolitans. Most of them had the privilege of wearing on certain occasions the *pallium* sent from Rome: a woollen stole which had rested overnight on the tomb of St Peter and was thus an important relic. According to Hincmar of Rheims, metropolitans could appoint bishops, convene synods, and punish suffragan bishops for transgressing the canons: all these were denied the metropolitan by Pseudo-Isidore, who allowed no intermediary between the bishop and the Pope. For Hincmar a bishop could not appeal to Rome until after a provincial synod had declared on the matter, and even then all a pope could do was enquire into the case and refer it to the synod of a neighbouring province. Hincmar defended himself against the accusation of ignoring the primacy of the Papacy: but for him primacy did not mean monarchy. In particular papal decretals could not overturn the decisions of councils: Hincmar accused his nephew of citing decretals which did just that. Although in the case of Hincmar of Laon the Pope was forced to take the side of the Archbishop of Rheims and his king, the False Decretals cited by the Bishop of Laon were far too useful for them to be discarded by the Papacy. By the end of the ninth century they had been cited in councils in both East and West Francia, and had been incorporated into an Italian canon law collection. Texts created for a specifically Frankish political problem served the universalist pretensions of the Papacy in the eleventh and twelfth centuries.

An age came to an end with the death of Hincmar in 882. Within a few years had come the deaths of the great political figures of the century: Charles the Bald, Louis the German, Bernard Plantevelue, Baldwin II, Boso of Vienne. Hincmar had already outlived the great intellectual figures of the last phase of the 'Carolingian Renaissance'. With the end of political unity and the intellectual impetus, conciliar activity declined rapidly. In Gaul the last councils were at Fîmes and Ver (881–4) in West Francia, and at Vienne (892) in Burgundy. The kings were little more powerful than their greatest subjects; royal support was no longer useful to the Church in the struggle against the perennial enemy, the aristocracy. Kings were not wholly forgetful of ecclesiastical claims for independence, however. When in 899 the Archbishop of Narbonne came north to protest in person to Charles the Simple that the count and his officers were trying clerics in lay courts, Charles acted promptly to defend the Church. The claims established in the ninth century were remembered. The Pope was accorded a new importance, and papal authority, recognised in 867 when the founder of the monastery of Vézelay gave it in ownership to the See of Rome, underwent further extension with the foundation of Cluny and its dependents. Cluny was particularly important in the later tenth century, in keeping alive the ideal of clerical independence at a time when churches and bishoprics were often falling under lay domination. But French bishops were often free, as German bishops were not, of royal or princely authority, and able to preserve at least some traditions of independent authority and initiative. Those traditions bore fruit at the very end of our period, with the movement of the Peace of God.

The process of political fragmentation and concomitant violence led bishops to join together to intervene, often with the enthusiastic support of the greater aristocrats and of lesser people. The enemy was the lesser aristocrat, the man who in the eleventh century would be called a knight, who supported himself around the year 1000 in looting or organising protection rackets. In the 1040s the Peace Movement could appear to Ralph Glaber as a glorious awakening after the dark days at the end of the first millenium. 'In obedience to divine goodness and mercy the smiling heavens began to clear, to blow favourable winds and to proclaim by their peaceful society the generosity of the Creator. . . . First in the regions of Aquitaine, bishops, abbots and other men dedicated to holy religion began to gather the people in full assembly. To them were carried many bodies of the blessed and cases filled with holy relics.' Assemblies were held to declare peace: 'A voice coming from heaven and speaking to men on the earth could not have accomplished more.' The religious fervour of these occasions was heightened by miracles of healing. 'These miracles excited such enthusiasm that the bishops lifted their crosses towards heaven and all present stretched their hands to God, crying in a single voice: "Peace, peace, peace!" They saw in such miracles the sign of a perpetual agreement and of the obligation which bound them with God.'[13]

The roots of the Peace Movement went right back into the Merovingian period, to the belief in the church's responsibility for the poor and in the inviolability of church property and church sanctuary. In the tenth century there had been earlier attempts to safeguard church property from violation. But the Peace Movement itself began with Bishop Guy of Le Puy, brother to Count Fulk of Anjou and uncle to the Counts of Gévaudan and Brioude. He held the comital rights in his town, but in the rest of the diocese his churches and estates were at the mercy of gangster knights. In 975 he called an assembly of the knights and peasants of the diocese on the meadows of St-Germain outside Le Puy. With the help of his nephews' soldiers he imposed on them an oath to respect the property of the church and of the *pauperes* (that is, the powerless, rather than the poor). In 989/90 the Archbishop of Bordeaux called a council which threatened with excommunication those who attacked the Church, its clergy, or the *pauperes*; in 994 Guy of Le Puy himself held a widely attended council which repeated those warnings. In the first years of the eleventh century such councils were held all over southern France, and the movement began to spread to the north. The movement was not a purely political one; it depended upon and encouraged an outburst of religious fervour among ordinary people such as had not appeared in the written sources since the sixth century, if then. Men looked to the church as a provider of peace, not because of the authority of bishops, but rather because of the power of God, above all as revealed through the relics of the saints. The quest for peace was a religious quest, a re-creation of an earthly Paradise.

The Peace Movement sought to defend the defenceless from the *bellatores*, those whose way of life was war. Knights were, of course, as much a threat to princes as to the church, and the princes thus not only supported the Peace Movement, but also its extension, the Truce of God. This first appeared at the council of Toulouges, in Roussillon, in 1027: the shedding of blood on a Sunday was prohibited. Later councils extended the ban to include Thursday, Friday and Saturday, Advent, Lent and the more important saints' days, leaving only a few weeks in the year available for the pleasures of war. Finally, at Narbonne in 1054, it was declared that 'no Christian should kill another Christian, for whoever kills a Christian undoubtedly sheds the blood of Christ'.[14] As an expression of Christian idealism it was unprecedented in Frankish history. Nor was it entirely irrelevant as a political statement. For example, the Church scored a success in persuading more and more knights that they should undergo penances (such as pilgrimages) after killing fellow-Christians in battle, and later in the century this was, of course, a factor in persuading crusaders to go in search of legitimate slaughter in the Holy Land.

For Ralph Glaber the Peace Movement symbolised the beginning of a new age; historians might well agree with him, although for different reasons. It came at a time when political fragmentation had reached its greatest extent, in the years on either side of 1000; it heralded the resurgence of the power of the princes. Nor was the Truce of God irrelevant to this process, for by putting their weight behind the movement the princes could become its guarantors, and thereby their own forces could, in the name of peace, extend their influence. It also heralded the great age of reform within the Church; in France itself it brought new prestige to the Church, and prepared it for the papally-inspired reforms later in the century. The increased confidence of a reformed episcopate in turn greatly benefited the monarchy; in the twelfth century as in the days of Louis the Pious, bishops tended to favour secular unity. The Peace Movement prepared the French aristocracy for the crusading movement, which it dominated; it lay behind the development of ideas of Christian knighthood and chivalry, which originated among the churchmen and aristocrats of northern France. And, as Glaber noted, simultaneously with the Peace Movement and the growth of lay piety which sustained it, a 'white robe of churches' began to cover the French countryside. The domination which the French were to have over the rest of Latin Christendom in the techniques and aesthetics of church-building was rooted in the late tenth century, and in the same south-west France from which the Peace Movement sprang. It was from there too that a key figure in the history of learning came, the link between the Carolingian Renaissance and that great flourishing of learning in northern France known to historians as the 'twelfth-century Renaissance': Gerbert of Aurillac, an Aquitanian monk, the greatest teacher of his day, the West's leading expert in dialectic, arithmetic and astronomy, who crowned his career by becoming Archbishop of Rheims and, in 999, Bishop of Rome, as Pope Sylvester II. The vitality of the Church, inspired rather than hindered by the subjection of large sectors of it by lay authority, was a major factor in France's emergence in the eleventh and twelfth centuries as the cultural and intellectual centre of the West.

Bibliographies

Abbreviations

A.E.S.C.	*Annales: Économies, Sociétés, Civilisations*
A.H.R.	*American Historical Review*
B.A.R.	British Archaeological Reports
C.C.M.	*Cahiers de Civilisation Médiévale*
C.R.A.I.	*Comptes-Rendus de l'Académie des Inscriptions et Belles-Lettres*
D.A.	*Deutsches Archiv*
E.H.R.	*English Historical Review*
F.S.	*Frühmittelalterliche Studien*
H.Z.	*Historische Zeitschrift*
J.M.H.	*Journal of Medieval History*
K.d.G.	*Karl der Grosse: Lebenswerk und Nachleben (see B3–c)*
M.A.	*Le Moyen Age*
M.G.H., S.S., S.S.R.M.	*Monumenta Germaniae Historica, Scriptores, Scriptores Rerum Merovingicarum*
P.B.A.	*Proceedings of the British Academy*
P.L.	*Patrologia Latina*, ed. J.P. Migne
P.P.	*Past and Present*
R.H.	*Revue Historique*
R.H.E.F.	*Revue de l'Histoire de l'Église de France*
R.N.	*Revue du Nord*
R.S.J.B.	*Recueil de la Société Jean Bodin*
R.V.	*Rheinische Vierteljahrsblätter*
S.C.H.	*Studies in Church History*
Sett.	*Settimane di Studio del Centro Italiano di Studi sull'Alto Medioevo* (Spoleto)
S.F.G.	*Spätantikes und fränkisches Gallien*, by E. Ewig I (Munich, 1976), II (1979)
T.R.H.S.	*Transactions of the Royal Historical Society*
Z.R.G.G.A., K.A.	*Zeitschrift der Savigny-Stiftung für Rechtsgeschichte, Germanistishe Abteilung, Kanonistische Abteilung*

Introductory Note

There are two bibliographies, one for works in English and one for works in other languages. The first I have tried to make fairly comprehensive, as a guide for those who wish to study early medieval Gaul further; the second is inevitably more selective, since the literature in both French and German is vast, and concentrates more particularly on those aspects of the period dealt with in the book. Since the footnotes refer largely to the primary sources, this serves as a guide to most of my own sources. I have divided both sections, A and B, into the following categories:

1. GENERAL WORKS
2. SOURCES

3. GENERAL AND POLITICAL HISTORY
   - *(a)* The late Roman period
   - *(b)* The Merovingian period
   - *(c)* The early Carolingian period
   - *(d)* The late Carolingian period
4. SOCIAL HISTORY
5. ECONOMIC HISTORY
   - *(a)* General
   - *(b)* Trade
   - *(c)* Towns
   - *(d)* The countryside
6. THE CHURCH AND CULTURE
   - *(a)* General
   - *(b)* The Merovingian Church
   - *(c)* The Carolingian Church

Cross-references will be given in the form, e.g., B5–c.

A. BIBLIOGRAPHY OF WORKS IN ENGLISH

1. GENERAL WORKS

There is no general introduction to the history of Gaul or France in English which covers the whole period. R. Latouche, *Caesar to Charlemagne: the Beginnings of France* (London, 1968), is lightweight and consists largely of extracts from the sources. For the later part of the period, see R. McKitterick, forthcoming (see below, A3–c). Good short introductions are to be found in J. M. Wallace-Hadrill, *The Barbarian West, 400–1000* (3rd edn, London, 1967), chs 4 and 5, and in D. Talbot Rice (ed.), *The Dark Ages* (London, 1965), chs 10 and 13. Chapter 10 was revised and reissued as a book: P. Lasko, *The Kingdom of the Franks* (London, 1971). The most detailed narrative is still to be found in vols II and III of the *Cambridge Medieval History* (Cambridge, 1913, 1922). The projected replacement of M. Deanesly, *A History of Early Medieval Europe, 476–911* (London, 1956), by J. L. Nelson and I. N. Wood, will be extremely welcome, as will P. McNulty's volume for the Longman series. J. Hubert *et al., Europe in the Dark Ages* (London, 1969) and *Carolingian Art* (London, 1970), are admirable guides to art and architectural history.

2. SOURCES

(a) The late Roman period

The letters and poems of Sidonius Apollinaris have been translated in the Loeb series by W. B. Anderson (2 vols, London, 1936, 1965); the letters alone by O. M. Dalton (2 vols, Oxford, 1915). *On the Government of God,* by Salvian, is translated by E. M. Sanford (New York, 1930). F. R. Hoare, *The Western Fathers* (London, 1954), contains the lives of Martin of Tours, Honoratus of Arles and Germanus of Auxerre.

(b) The Merovingian period

The major narrative sources have all been translated: Gregory of Tours, *History of the Franks* by L. Thorpe (Harmondsworth, 1974), and by O. M. Dalton, 2 vols (London, 1926); Gregory's continuator Fredegar by J. M. Wallace-Hadrill, *The Fourth Book of the Chronicle of Fredegar* (London, 1960); and the *Liber Historiae Francorum* by B. S. Bachrach

(Lawrence, Kansas, 1973). Extracts of other works of Gregory are to be found in E. Peters, ed., *Monks, Bishops and Pagans* (Philadelphia, 1975); complete translations of the Miracles of St Julian and St Martin, by J. Corbett, are in progress (Toronto, forthcoming).

The only legal material in translation is K. F. Drew, *The Burgundian Code* (Philadelphia, 1949). The sermons of Caesarius of Arles have been translated by Sister M. M. Mueller in the *Fathers of the Church* series (3 vols, New York 1956, Washington 1964 and 1973). The only 'Merovingian' saint's life in translation, and only in part, is Jonas's Life of Columbanus, in E. Peters, *op. cit.* Columbanus' own works have been edited and translated by G. S. M. Walker, *Sancti Columbani Opera* (Dublin, 1970). Various types of Merovingian source material can be found in J. N. Hillgarth, ed., *The Conversion of Western Europe, 350–750* (Englewood Cliffs, New Jersey, 1969).

(c) The Carolingian period

B. S. Scholz, ed., *Carolingian Chronicles* (Ann Arbor, 1970), contains the Royal Frankish Annals and Nithard's Histories. H. R. Loyn and J. Percival, *The Reign of Charlemagne* (London, 1975), contains selections from capitularies, charters etc. Several biographies have been translated *in toto*: Einhard and Notker in *Two Lives of Charlemagne* by L. Thorpe (Harmondsworth, 1969); the Astronomer in *Son of Charlemagne: a Contemporary Life of Louis the Pious* by A. Cabaniss (Syracuse, New York, 1961) and lives of Adalard and Wala in *Charlemagne's Cousins* by A. Cabaniss (Syracuse, New York, 1967). Adalard's own 'Customs of Corbie' have been translated by C. W. Jones in vol III of E. Horn and W. Born, *The Plan of St Gall* (Berkeley, California, 1979).

Four collections of letters have been completely or partially translated: *The Letters of Saint Boniface* by E. Emerton (New York, 1940) (for Willibald's Life of Boniface, see C. H. Talbot, ed., *The Anglo-Saxon Missionaries in Germany* (London, 1954)); the letters of Alcuin in *Alcuin of York* by S. Allott (York, 1974); *The Letters of Lupus of Ferrières* by G. W. Regenos (The Hague, 1966); and *The Letters of Gerbert, with his Papal Privileges as Sylvester II*, by H. P. Lattin (New York, 1961). Very few sources from the late ninth or tenth century have been translated. The only work by Hincmar of Rheims known to me in translation is the *De ordine palatii*, to be found in *The History of Feudalism*, ed. D. Herlihy (London, 1971), together with extracts from Merovingian and Carolingian sources relating to 'feudalism'. Two important tenth-century saints' lives, Odo's Life of Gerald of Aurillac and John of Salerno's Life of Odo, are to be found in G. Sitwell, ed., *St Odo of Cluny* (London, 1958). Some idea of Carolingian learning can be gathered from *Dicuili Liber de Mensura Orbis Terrae*, ed. and trans. J. J. Tierney (Dublin, 1967), and John Scotus Eriugena, *Periphyseon: On the Division of Nature*, trans. M. Uhlfelder (Indianapolis, 1976). (Vol. I is edited and translated by I. P. Sheldon-Williams (Dublin, 1968).) See also, as an example of vision–literature, D. A. Traill, *Walahfrid Strabo's Visio Wettini* (Berne/Frankfurt, 1974).

3. GENERAL AND POLITICAL HISTORY

(a) The late Roman period

The major work is A. H. M. Jones, *The Later Roman Empire, 284–602* (3 vols plus maps, Oxford, 1964). On later Roman Gaul, see sections in J. Matthews, *Western Aristocracies and the Imperial Court* (Oxford, 1975); C. E. Stevens, *Sidonius Apollinaris and His Age* (Oxford, 1933); and N. K. Chadwick, *Poetry and Letters in Early Christian Gaul* (Cambridge, 1955). On the invasions, see above all L. Musset, *The Germanic Invasions* (London, 1975). The settlement of the Visigoths and Burgundians has been discussed by E. A. Thompson, 'The Settlement of the Barbarians in Southern Gaul', *Journal of Roman Studies*, XLVI (1956) pp. 65–75, 'The Barbarian Kingdoms in Gaul and Spain', *Nottingham*

Medieval Studies, VII (1963) pp. 3–33, and 'The Visigoths from Fritigern to Euric', *Historia*, XII (1963) pp. 105–26; by J. M. Wallace-Hadrill, 'Gothia and Romania', in his *The Long-Haired Kings* (London, 1962); and by W. Goffart, *Barbarians and Romans, A.D. 418–584. The Techniques of Accommodation* (Princeton, 1980).

For Frankish settlement, see C. Verlinden, 'Frankish Colonisation: a New Approach', *T. R. H. S., 5th ser.*, IV (1954) pp. 1–17; J. M. Wallace-Hadrill, *The Long-Haired Kings*, pp. 148–63; and E. James, 'Cemeteries and the Problem of Frankish Settlement in Gaul', in P. H. Sawyer, ed., *Names, Words and Graves: Early Medieval Settlement* (Leeds, 1979) pp. 55–89. For the Bretons, see N. K. Chadwick, 'The Colonization of Brittany from Celtic Britain', *P. B. A.*, LI (1965) pp. 235–99; her *Early Brittany* (Cardiff, 1969); and the article of the same title by J. L. Fleuriot and P. Giot, *Antiquity*, LI (1977) pp. 106–16.

(b) The Merovingian period

J. M. Wallace-Hadrill, *The Long-Haired Kings*, provides a study of the kings in his title-essay: there are also important studies on Gregory of Tours and Fredegar. On Gregory see below, A6–*b*, and G. de Nie, 'Roses in January: a Neglected Dimension in Gregory of Tours' *Historiae*, (J. M. H., V (1979) pp. 259–89; on Fredegar, see W. Goffart, 'The Fredegar Problem Reconsidered', *Speculum*, XXXVIII (1963) pp. 206–41. An old-fashioned but entertaining study drawing heavily on Gregory is Sir Samuel Dill's *Roman Society in Gaul in the Merovingian Age* (London, 1926). Other studies of Merovingian rulers include I. N. Wood, 'Kings, Kingdoms and Consent', in P. H. Sawyer and I. N. Wood, eds, *Early Medieval Kingship* (Leeds, 1977) pp. 6–29, and J. L. Nelson, 'Queens as Jezebels: the Careers of Brunhild and Balthild in Merovingian History', in D. Baker, ed., *Medieval Women* (Oxford, 1978) pp. 31–77. Relations between the Merovingian kingdom and the Byzantine Empire are discussed in H. Fischer, 'The belief in the continuity of the Roman Empire among the Franks of the fifth and sixth centuries', *Catholic Historical Review*, IV (1924) pp. 536–55; M. Silber, *The Gallic Royalty of the Merovingians in its Relationship to the 'Orbis Terrarum Romanus'* (Berne, 1971); and W. Goffart, 'Byzantine Policy in the West under Tiberius II and Maurice: the Pretenders Hermenigild and Gundovald (579–585)', *Traditio*, XIII (1957) pp. 73–118.

For Merovingian law and the aristocracy, see below A4. Aspects of the royal government of Gaul are treated by B. S. Bachrach, *Merovingian Military Organisation, 481–751* (Minneapolis, 1972), and A. R. Lewis, 'The Dukes in the Regnum Francorum, A.D. 550-751', *Speculum*, LI (1976) pp. 381–410.

There are only a few regional studies in English. See A. Joris, 'On the Edge of Two Worlds in the Heart of the New Empire: the Romance Regions of Northern Gaul during the Merovingian Period', *Studies in Medieval and Renaissance History*, III (1966) pp. 3–52; portions of E. James, *The Merovingian Archaeology of South-West Gaul* (B. A. R., S25, Oxford, 1977); and *idem*, 'Septimania and its Frontier: an Archaeological Approach', in *idem*, ed., *Visigothic Spain: New Approaches* (Oxford, 1980) pp. 223–41. Also of importance is H. Wolfram, 'The Shaping of the Early Medieval Principality as a Type of Non-Royal Rulership', *Viator*, II (1971) pp. 33–51.

(c) *The Early Carolingian Period*

R. McKitterick, *The Frankish Kingdoms under the Carolingians, 751–987* (London, forthcoming), covers the whole period to 987; L. Halphen, *Charlemagne and the Carolingian Empire* (Amsterdam, 1977), ends around 900. Most books in English have concentrated on Charlemagne almost exclusively. Of the general books, H. Fichtenau, *The Carolingian Empire* (Oxford, 1968), is probably the most stimulating, although D. Bullough, *The Age of Charlemagne* (London, 1965), covers more ground, and contains, like J. Boussard, *The Civilisation of Charlemagne* (London, 1968), some excellent illustrations. P. Riché, *Daily Life in the World of Charlemagne* (Liverpool, 1978), has a broader scope than its title suggests, and contains a wealth of often out-of-the-way detail; more so than

P. Munz, *Life in the Age of Charlemagne* (London, 1969). The mid-1960s saw a great number of books on Charlemagne appear on the Continent: D. A. Bullough, '*Europae Pater*: Charlemagne and his achievement in the light of recent scholarship', *E. H. R.*, LXXXV (1970) pp. 59–105 is a masterly review of these.

Much of the literature has concerned itself with the imperial coronation. On the Roman background, see D. H. Miller, 'The Roman Revolution of the Eighth Century', *Medieval Studies*, XXXVI (1974) pp. 79–133 and 'The Motivation of Pepin's Italian Policy, 754–768', *Studies in Medieval Culture*, IV (1973) pp. 44–54; see also P. Llewellyn, *Rome in the Dark Ages* (London, 1970), chs 8 and 9. The best single introduction to the problem is R. Folz, *The Coronation of Charlemagne* (London, 1974); R. E. Sullivan's book of the same title (Boston, 1959) is a useful collection of readings. Folz has put the problem in a much wider setting in *The Concept of Empire in Western Europe from the Fifth to the Fourteenth Century* (London, 1969). See also P. Munz, *The Origin of the Carolingian Empire* (Leicester 1960), and 'The Imperial Coronation of Charlemagne', in F. L. Ganshof, *The Carolingians and the Frankish Monarchy* (London, 1971).

This collection of articles by Ganshof, containing a number on Charlemagne's reign, also constitutes, when taken together with Ganshof, *Frankish Institutions under Charlemagne* (Providence, Rhode Island, 1968), the best introduction to Charlemagne's government. See also *idem*, 'The Treaties of the Carolingians', *Medieval and Renaissance Studies*, III (1968) pp. 23–52; F. N. Estey, 'The Scabini and the Local Courts', *Speculum* XXVI (1951) pp. 119–29; for the next reign, J. T. Rosenthal, 'The Public Assembly in the Time of Louis the Pious', *Traditio* XX (1964) pp. 25–40. Part of Perroy's book (see B3–*c*) has been translated as 'Carolingian Administration', in S. L. Thrupp, ed., *Early Medieval Society* (New York, 1967) pp. 129–46. There are some stimulating comments on Carolingian administration in J. Campbell, 'The Significance of the Anglo-Norman State in the Administrative History of Western Europe', in Paravicini and Werner (B3–*c*), pp. 117–34.

On Carolingian vassalage and the origins of 'feudalism' see above all F.-L. Ganshof, *Feudalism* (3rd edn, London, 1964). An interesting introduction is provided now by J. Le Goff, 'The Symbolic Ritual of Vassalage', in his collected essays (A5–*d*), pp. 236–87. Three studies by C. Odegaard are very useful for Charlemagne's own reign: 'Carolingian Oaths of Fidelity', *Speculum*, XVI (1941) pp. 284–96; 'The Concept of Royal Power in Carolingian Oaths of Fidelity', *Speculum*, XX (1945) pp. 279–89; and *Vassi and Fideles in the Carolingian Empire* (Cambridge, Mass., 1945). B. S. Bachrach in 'Military Organization in Aquitaine under the Early Carolingians', *Speculum*, XLIX (1974) pp. 1–33, and 'Charles Martel, Mounted Shock Combat, the Stirrup and Feudalism', *Studies in Medieval and Renaissance History*, VII (1970) pp. 47–75, looks at the origins of 'feudalism': the latter is a study of Lynn White jr.'s famous theories, expressed in *Medieval Technology and Social Change* (Oxford, 1962). See also G. Fourquin, *Lordship and Feudalism in the Middle Ages* (London, 1976), and, of course, the classic *Feudal Society* (London, 1962), by Marc Bloch. I have tried to follow the advice of E. A. R. Brown, 'The Tyranny of a Construct: Feudalism and Historians of Medieval Europe', *A. H. R.*, LXXIX (1974) pp. 1063–88, and in the main body of the book have avoided the word 'feudalism' altogether.

On developments of ideas of kingship there has been a considerable literature. See J. M. Wallace-Hadrill, *Early Germanic Kingship in England and on the Continent* (Oxford, 1971) chs 5 and 6; *idem*, 'The *Via Regia* of the Carolingian Age', in his *Early Medieval History* (Oxford, 1975) pp. 181–200; E. Kantorowicz, *The King's Two Bodies* (Princeton, 1957), and *Laudes Regiae* (2nd edn, Princeton, 1958); W. Ullmann, *The Carolingian Renaissance and the Idea of Kingship* (London, 1969); and a number of studies by J. L. Nelson on inauguration rituals – in P. H. Sawyer and I. N. Wood, eds (A3–*b*) and in *S. C. H.*, 7 (1971), 11 (1975) and 13 (1976). R. Sullivan, *Aix-la-Chapelle in the Age of Charlemagne*

(Norman, Oklahoma, 1963), is relevant here, as is the useful discussion of Schramm's important work on symbols of rulership in J. Bak, 'Medieval Symbology of the State: Percy E. Schramm's contribution', *Viator*, IV (1973) pp. 33–63.

Apart from Halphen, McKitterick and Ganshof, *The Carolingians* . . . (above), and the translated sources (above A2–*c*), esp. Scholz and Cabaniss, there is very little on Louis the Pious in English. E. S. Duckett, *Carolingian Portraits* (Ann Arbor, 1962) provides a sympathetic sketch; and there is the equally lightweight T. F. X. Noble, 'The Monastic Ideal as a Model for Empire: the Case of Louis the Pious', *Revue Bénédictine*, LXXXVI (1976) pp. 235–50. There is very little in the way of regional studies either; two stand out – A. R. Lewis, *The Development of Southern French and Catalan Society, 718–1050* (Austin, Texas, 1965), and A. J. Zuckerman, *A Jewish Princedom in Feudal France, 768–900* (New York, 1972) – but the former more for its patchiness and inaccuracy, and the latter for its audacity, in claiming that a number of important Carolingian magnates, including William of Gellone, were Jewish: a claim difficult to refute, for me, in that it rests upon sources in Hebrew.

(d) The Late Carolingian Period

See again Halphen, McKitterick, the *Cambridge Medieval History* and, for the end of the period, *Capetian France 987–1328* by E. M. Hallam (London, 1980).

There is little satisfactory in English on the political events of this period. The only monarch whose reign is well covered is Charles the Bald, thanks largely to the recent *Charles the Bald: Court and Kingdom*, ed. M. Gibson and J. Nelson (B. A. R., S101, Oxford 1981); the projected book on Charles by J. Nelson is eagerly awaited. In the meantime there is considerable reference to his reign in the works on kingship (above, A3–*c*); in addition, see J. L. Nelson, 'Kingship, Law and Liturgy in the Political Thought of Hincmar of Rheims', *E. H. R.*, XCII (1977) pp. 241–79, and M. J. Enright, 'Charles the Bald and Aethelwulf of Mercia: the Alliance of 856 and Strategies of Royal Succession', *J. M. H.*, V (1979) pp. 291–303.

Some discussion of the Vikings in Gaul will be found in standard histories such as T. D. Kendrick, *A History of the Vikings* (London, 1930), but see in particular J. M. Wallace-Hadrill, 'The Vikings in Francia', in his *Early Medieval History* (Oxford, 1975) pp. 217–36. On the Viking settlements see the important studies by D. C. Douglas: 'Rollo of Normandy', *E. H. R.*, LVII (1942) pp. 417–36; 'The Rise of Normandy', *P. B. A.* XXXIII (1947) pp. 101–31; and 'The earliest Norman Counts', *E. H. R.*, LXI (1946) pp. 129–56. See also L. W. Breese, 'The Persistence of Scandinavian Connections in Normandy in the Tenth and Eleventh Centuries', *Viator*, VIII (1977) pp. 47–61.

Little other work on the regions has been published in English apart from that in M. Gibson and J. Nelson, eds (above). There have, however, been some useful studies of the aristocracy. See in particular J. Martindale, 'The French Aristocracy in Early Middle Ages: a Reappraisal', *P. P.*, LXXV (1977) pp. 5–45 (*cf.* K. Leyser, 'The German Aristocracy from the Ninth to the Early Twelth Century', *P. P.*, XLI (1968) pp. 25–53), and, now, C. B. Bouchard, 'The Origins of the French Nobility: a Reassessment', *A. H. R.*, LXXXVI (1981) pp. 501–32. Among the translated extracts in the useful collection edited by F. L. Cheyette, *Lordship and Community in Medieval Europe* (New York, 1968), are L. Génicot, 'The Nobility in Medieval Francia: Continuity, Break or Evolution?' (pp. 128–36), G. Duby, 'The Nobility in Eleventh and Twelfth Century Mâconnais' (pp. 137–55), and J. F. Lemarignier, 'Political and Monastic structures in France at the End of the Tenth and Beginning of the Eleventh Century' (pp. 100–27). American scholars have done more work on these questions than English scholars: see A. R. Lewis (A3–*c*) and 'Count Gerald of Aurillac and Feudalism in South-Central France in the Early Tenth Century', *Traditio*, XX (1964) pp. 41–58; G. T. Beech, 'The Origin of the Viscounts of Thouars', *Etudes de Civilisation Médiévale: Mélanges Labande* (Poitiers, 1975) pp. 25–31; and B. S. Bachrach, 'Towards a Reappraisal of William the Great, Duke of Aquitaine (995–1030)', *J. M. H.*, V (1979) pp. 11–22. Finally, on castle-building, see *idem*, 'Early Medieval Fortifications in the "west" of France: a Revised Technical Vocabularly', *Technology and Culture*, XVI (1975) pp. 531–69; *idem*, 'Fortifications and Military Tactics: Fulk Nerra's Strongholds circa 1000', *Technology and Culture*, XX (1979) pp. 531–49; and C. L. H. Coulson, 'Fortresses and Social Responsibility in Late Carolingian France', *Zeitschrift für Archäologie des Mittelalters*, IV (1976) pp. 29–36.

4. SOCIAL HISTORY

Legislation is a major source of evidence: see, as general introductions, K. F. Drew, 'The Barbarian Kings as Lawgivers and Judges', in R. S. Hoyt, ed., *Life and Thought in the Early Middle Ages* (Minneapolis, 1967) pp. 7–29, and 'Legal Materials as a Source for Early Medieval Social History', *Rice University Studies* LX (Fall, 1974) pp. 33–43. But these would have to be seen in conjunction with P. Wormald, '*Lex Scripta* and *Verbum Regis*: Legislation and Germanic Kingship, from Euric to Cnut', in P. H. Sawyer and I. N. Wood, eds (A3–*b*), by far the best introduction to early medieval law. S. Stein, in *Speculum*, XXII (1947) pp. 113–34 and 395– 418, gives a fascinating account of the problems of editing Lex Salica, but his conclusion that it is a ninth-century forgery has been accepted by no-one: see J. M. Wallace-Hadrill, 'Archbishop Hincmar and the Authorship of Lex Salica', in his *The Long-Haired Kings*, pp. 95–120. On the Roman background, see E. Levy, 'Vulgarization of Roman Law in the Early Middle Ages', *Medievalia et Humanistica*, I (1943) pp. 14–40 and *West Roman Vulgar Law: the Law of Property* (Philadelphia, 1951). The best book in English on Frankish law, despite its title, is J. Goebel, *Felony and Misdemeanor: a Study in the History of English Criminal Procedure* (New York, 1937). Also interesting are S. L. Guterman, *From Personal to Territorial Law* (Metuchan, New Jersey, 1972) and R. V. Colman, 'Reason and Unreason in Early Medieval Law', *Journal of Interdisciplinary History*, IV (1974) 571–91.

Not enough work has yet been done on families and other social groupings (but see D. A. Bullough, 'Early Medieval Social Groupings: the Terminology of Kinship', *P. P.* XLV (1969) pp. 3–18), except of course, for the aristocracy. The best introduction available in English on recent developments in this field is K. F. Werner, 'Important Noble Families in the Kingdom of Charlemagne', in T. Reuter, ed., *The Medieval Nobility* (Amsterdam, 1979) pp. 137–202, a very useful volume which also includes F. Irsigler, 'On the Aristocratic Character of Early Frankish Society', pp. 105–136. See also F. D. Gillard, 'The Senators of Sixth-Century Gaul', *Speculum*, LIV (1979) pp. 685–97. D. H. Green, *The Carolingian Lord* (Cambridge, 1965), is an interesting linguistic study. On the family, see K. F. Drew, 'The Germanic Family of the Lex Burgundionum', *Medievalia et Humanistica* XV (1963) pp. 5–14; J. A. McNamara and S. F. Wemple, 'Marriage and Divorce in the Frankish Kingdom', in S. M. Stuard, ed., *Women in Medieval Society* (Philadelphia, 1976) pp. 95–124; E. R. Coleman, 'Infanticide in the Early Middle Ages', in the same volume, pp. 47–70; and *idem*, 'Medieval marriage Characteristics: a Neglected Factor in the History of Medieval Serfdom', *Journal of Interdisciplinary History*, II (1971–2) pp. 205–19. I have not myself referred to her 1972 dissertation *The Serfs of St-Germain-des-Prés: a Social and Demographic Study*. P. Bonnassie, 'A Family of the Barcelona Countryside and its Economic Activities around the Year 1000', in S. L. Thrupp, ed., *Early Medieval Society* (New York, 1967) pp. 102–23, is of great interest, although outside our geographical scope. The legal implications of family solidarity have been discussed in J. M. Wallace-Hadrill, 'The Bloodfeud of the Franks', in his *The Long-Haired Kings*, pp. 121–47. A broad view of the question is taken by D. Herlihy, in 'Land, Family and Women in Continental Europe, 701–1200', *Traditio*, XVIII (1962) pp. 89–120. On slavery there is almost nothing in English save the collected essays of M. Bloch, *Slavery and Serfdom in the Middle Ages* (Berkeley, California, 1975).

The first important study of the Jews was S. Katz, *The Jews in the Visigothic and Frankish Kingdoms of Spain and Gaul* (Cambridge, Mass., 1937). A less lachrymose view, as he puts it, has recently been provided by B. S. Bachrach, *Early Medieval Jewish Policy in Western Europe* (Minneapolis, 1977), who has also edited a collection of translated sources: *Jews in Barbarian Europe* (Lawrence, Kansas, 1977). See in addition A. J. Zuckerman (A3–*b*) and *idem*, 'The Political Uses of Theology: the Conflict of Bishop Agobard and the Jews of Lyons', *Studies in Medieval Culture* III (1970) pp. 23–51; A. Cabaniss, 'Bodo-Eleazar: a Famous Jewish Convert', *Jewish Quarterly Review*, XLIII (1953) pp. 313–28; and, for the very end of the period, R. Chazan, *Medieval Jewry in Northern France: a Political and Social History* (Baltimore, 1973).

5. ECONOMIC HISTORY

(a) General

The best general introduction is R. Latouche, *The Birth of Western Economy* (2nd edn London, 1967). R. Doehaerd, *The Early Middle Ages in the West – Economy and Society* (Amsterdam, 1978), and G. Duby, *The Early Development of the European Economy* (London, 1974), are also good, in their very different ways, and much can still be learnt from the classic by A. Dopsch, *The Economic and Social Foundations of European Civilisation* (London, 1937). The most important of Marc Bloch's articles on early medieval economic history have been translated in *Land and Work in Medieval Europe* (London, 1966). There are some interesting speculations on the early medieval scene in H. D. Clout, ed., *Themes in the Historical Geography of France* (London, 1977).

(b) Trade

H. Pirenne, *Mohammed and Charlemagne* (London, 1939), still lurks behind every discussion on this topic. See A. F. Havighurst, ed., *The Pirenne Thesis* (Boston, 1958; 3rd edn, Lexington, Mass., 1976), for a reprinting of the more important criticisms, and see P. Brown, 'Mohammed and Charlemagne by Henri Pirenne', *Daedalus* (Winter, 1974) pp. 25–33, for a short appraisal. Probably the most important criticisms have come from P. Grierson, 'Commerce in the Dark Ages: a Critique of the Evidence', *T. R. H. S.*, 5th ser. IX (1959) pp. 123–40. Pirenne concentrates largely on Mediterranean trade; for Atlantic trade, A. R. Lewis, *The Northern Seas: Shipping and Commerce in Northern Europe, AD 300–1000* (Princeton, 1958), can be read with profit only if his references are checked, and P. Grierson's review in *E. H. R.*, LXXVI (1961) pp. 311–15 is read, for it abounds in errors (of which I relish in particular his reference to the discovery in the Sutton Hoo boat-grave of a cenotaph, helmet and shield 'of pure gold', p. 145). See parts of E. James, 'Ireland and Western Gaul in the Merovingian Period', in D. Whitelock, D. Dumville and R. McKitterick, eds, *Ireland in Early Medieval Europe* (Cambridge, forthcoming) pp. 362–86. R. Hodges, *Dark-Age Economics* (forthcoming), promises to be an exciting new look at these problems, from the point of view of a 'new archaeologist'.

Probably the best introduction to Merovingian numismatics is now provided by J. P. C. Kent, 'The Coins and the Date of Burial', in R. L. S. Bruce-Mitford, ed., *The Sutton Hoo Ship Burial*, vol. I (London, 1975) pp. 578–682; see *idem*, 'Problems of Chronology in the Seventh-Century Merovingian Coinage', *Cunobelin*, XIII (1967) pp. 24–30, and 'Gold Standard of the Merovingian Coinage, A.D. 580–700', in E. T. Hall and D. M. Metcalf, eds, *Methods of Chemical and Metallurgical Investigation of Ancient Coinage* (London, 1972) pp. 69–74. Other work on gold content, with important implications for historians, is discussed in D. M. Metcalf, J. M. Merrick and L. K. Hamblin,

Studies in the Composition of Early Medieval Coins (Newcastle upon Tyne, 1968). The study of Carolingian coins has been dominated by P. Grierson: see now his collected papers, *Dark-Age Numismatics* (London, 1979).

(c) Towns

This topic too has been overshadowed by H. Pirenne, *Medieval Cities: their Origins and the Revival of Trade* (Princeton, 1925). D. M. Nicholas, 'Medieval Urban Origins in Northern Continental Europe. State of Research and Some Tentative Conclusions', *Studies in Medieval and Renaissance History*, VI (1969) pp. 53–114, provides a more up-to-date introduction to the area Pirenne knew most about. D. A. Bullough, 'Social and Economic Structure and Topography in the Early Medieval City', *Sett.*, XXI (1974) pp. 351–99, is an excellent introduction to the earlier period. E. Ennen, *The Medieval Town* (Amsterdam, 1979), is a good recent guide. But above all see various chapters in M. W. Barley, *European Towns: Their Archaeology and Early History* (London, 1977), particulary Amand, de Boüard and Fournier, and Böhner in Part One, Wightman, Févríer and Martin in Part Two, Brühl in Part Three, and Brooke in Part Four. The important article by E. Ewig on towns as royal 'capitals' has been partially translated in Thrupp (A4). There are no studies in English on individual Gallic towns.

(d) The Countryside

The books mentioned at A5–*a* above provide the best introductions, but *The Cambridge Economic History of Europe*, I, ed. J. H. Clapham and E. Power, is still of great value. See also the important works by G. Duby, *Rural Economy and Country Life in the Medieval West* (London, 1968), and B. H. Slicher van Bath, *The Agrarian History of Western Europe, A.D. 500–1850* (London, 1963). Aspects of the Gallo-Roman background are discussed in J. Percival, 'Seigneurial Aspects of Late Roman Estate Management', *E. H. R.*, LXXXIV (1969) pp. 449–73, and S. Appelbaum, 'The Late Gallo-Roman Rural Pattern in the Light of the Carolingian Cartularies', *Latomus*, XXIII (1964) pp. 774–87. For the Merovingian period, see J. Le Goff. 'Labor, Techniques and Craftsmen . . .' and 'Peasants and the Rural World . . .' in his *Time, Work and Culture in the Middle Ages* (Chicago, 1980) pp. 71–97; and W. Janssen, 'Some Major Aspects of Frankish and Medieval Settlement in the Rhineland', in P. H. Sawyer, ed., *Medieval Settlement* (London, 1976) pp. 41–60. For the later period, see F.-L. Ganshof, 'Manorial Organisation in the Low Countries in the 7th, 8th and 9th Centuries', *T. R. H. S.*, 4th ser. XXXI. (1949) pp. 29–59; J. W. Thompson, 'The Statistical Sources of Frankish History', *A. H. R.*, XL (1935) pp. 625–45; F. Cheyette, 'The Origin of European Villages and the First European Expansion', *Journal of Econ. Hist.*, XXXVII (1977) pp. 182–206; and D. Herlihy, 'The Agrarian Revolution in Southern France and Italy, 801–1150', *Speculum* , XXXIII (1958) pp. 23–41. The famous *Capitulare de Villis*, *c.* 794–800, is translated in Loyn and Percival (A2–*c*) pp. 64–73.

6. THE CHURCH AND CULTURE

(a) General)

The best introductions are probably provided by the translations of the *Handbuch der Kirchengeschichte*, vols II and III: *History of the Church, Vol. II: The Imperial Church from Constantine to the Early Middle Ages*, by K. Baus, H.-G. Beck, E. Ewig and H. J. Vogt (London, 1980) and *Handbook of Church History Vol. III: The Church in the Age of Feudalism*, by F. Kempf, H.-G. Beck, E. Ewig and J. A. Jungmann (London, 1969). The general editors are H. Jedin and J. Dolan. The Pelican History of the Church dismissed the whole period in six pages, entitled 'The primitive age', or at least the medieval volume does – S. Neill, *A History of Christian Missions* (Harmondsworth, 1964), does devote much more space himself. The projected Oxford History of the Church, a much more ambitious project, will be giving a much more balanced picture, and will be very welcome.

(b) The Merovingian Church

On the work of the church as a whole, see H. G. J. Beck, *The Pastoral Care of Souls in South-East France during the Sixth Century* (Rome, 1950), and W. Ullmann, 'Public Welfare and Social Legislation in the Early Medieval Councils', *S. C. H*, VII (1971) pp. 1–39. On the work of individual bishops see W. M. Daly, 'Caesarius of Arles, a Precursor of Medieval Christendom', *Traditio*, XXVI (1970) pp. 1–29; W. C. McDermott, 'Felix of Nantes: a Merovingian Bishop', *Traditio*, XXXI (1975) pp. 1–24; and P. Fouracre, 'The Work of Audoenus of Rouen and Eligius of Noyon in Extending Episcopal Influence from the Town to the Country in Seventh-Century Neustria', *S. C. H.*, XVI (1979) pp. 77–91. That volume contains two other important studies on the same theme: C. E. Stancliffe, 'From Town to Country: the Christianisation of the Touraine, 370–600', pp. 43–59, and I. N. Wood, 'Early Merovingian Devotion in Town and Country', pp. 61–76. Characteristically brilliant insights are to be found in P. R. L. Brown, *Relics and Social Status in the Age of Gregory of Tours* (Stenton Lecture, 1976) (Reading, 1977); see now also his *The Cult of the Saints* (London/Chicago, 1981), and J. H. Corbett, 'The Saint as Patron in the Work of Gregory of Tours', *J. M. H.*, VII (1981) pp. 1–13.

Surprisingly little has been written in English on the Irish in Merovingian Gaul. As an introduction see James (A5–*b*) and L. Bieler, *Ireland, Harbinger of the Middle Ages* (2nd edn, London, 1966). The sources have been discussed by J. F. Kenney, *The Sources for the Early History of Ireland* (New York, 1929). On Columbanus see the somewhat lightweight *Columbanus in His Own Words* (Dublin, 1974), by Cardinal Tomás Ó Fiaich, and, above all, *Columbanus and Merovingian Monasticism*, ed. H. B. Clarke and M. Brennan (B. A. R. S–113, Oxford, 1981), with chapters by Prinz, Riché, Wood and others.

The influence of the Anglo-Saxons on the late Merovingian/early Carolingian church has been discussed above all by W. Levison, *England and the Continent in the Eighth Century* (Oxford, 1946), but see also J. M. Wallace-Hadrill, 'A Background to St Boniface's Mission', in his *Early Medieval History* (Oxford, 1975) pp. 138–54, and T. Reuter, 'St Boniface and Europe', in *idem*, ed., *The Greatest Englishman* (Exeter, 1980) pp. 71–94.

There is no comprehensive work on Merovingian monasticism in English. F. Prinz, 'Aristocracy and Christianity in Merovingian Gaul', in K. Bosl, ed., *Gesellschaft, Kultur, Literatur: Beiträge L. Wallach gewidmet* (Stuttgart, 1975) pp. 154–65, is a useful short introduction to Prinz's important work. See also Prinz and others in Clarke and Brennan, *op. cit.*, particularly R. McKitterick, for monastic scriptoria. W. Horn, 'The Origins of the Medieval Cloister', *Gesta*, XII (1973) pp. 13–52, offers some comments on monastic architecture in the period; on which see E. James, in Clarke and Brennan, *op. cit.*, pp. 33–55. There is much to interest the monastic historian in P. Riché, *Education and Culture in the Barbarian West, Sixth through Eighth Centuries* (Columbia, S. Carolina, 1976), one of the most important works on early medieval history of the last couple of decades. An interesting footnote is provided by J. Le Goff, 'Clerical Culture and Folklore Traditions in Merovingian Civilization', in Le Goff's collected essays (A5–*d*) pp. 153–8.

(c) The Carolingian Church

Apart from the general books at A3–*c* and *d*, see R. McKitterick, *The Frankish Church and the Carolingian Reforms, 789–895* (London, 1977). There are a number of important studies in F. L. Ganshof, *The Carolingians and the Frankish Monarchy* (London, 1971). Although rather reminiscent of the historical novel, E. S. Duckett's *Carolingian Portraits* does provide handy accounts of Einhard, Amalarius of Metz, Walafrid Strabo, Lupus of Ferrières and Hincmar of Rheims. Other individual bishops are discussed in A. Cabaniss, 'Agobard of Lyons', *Speculum*, XXVI (1951) pp. 50–76, and *Agobard of Lyons: Churchman and Critic* (Syracuse, New York, 1953); and in P. R. McKeon, 'Archbishop Ebbo of Reims (816–835)· A Study in the Carolingian Empire and Church', *Church History*, XLIII (1974) pp. 437–47, and *Hincmar of Laon and Carolingian Politics* (Urbana, Illinois, 1978). See also his 'The Carolingian Councils of Savonnières (859) and Tusey (860) and their Background', *Revue Bénédictine*, LXXXIV (1974) pp. 75–110.

W. Goffart, *The Le Mans Forgeries* (Cambridge, Mass., 1966), contains the best discussions on church property in English. See also D. Herlihy, 'Church Property on the European Continent, 701–1208', *Speculum*, XXXVI (1961) pp. 81–105. There is discussion of the Pseudo-Isidorian material in W. Ullmann, *The Growth of Papal Government in the Middle Ages* (London, 1955), which contains much more about the Carolingian Church than its title suggests; there is also a useful summary by the leading Pseudo-Isidorian scholar of his day, E. Seckel, in *The New Schaff-Herzog Encyclopedia of Religious Knowledge*, vol. IX ed. S. M. Jackson (London and New York, 1911) pp. 343–50. See also G. Constable,' "Nona et decima". An Aspect of Carolingian Economy', *Speculum*, XXXV (1960) pp. 224–50, and *Monastic Tithes* (Cambridge, 1964).

W. Horn and E. Born's lavish three volumes *The Plan of St Gall* (Berkeley, California, 1979) provide a fascinating, if at times eccentric, introduction to Carolingian monasticism. See also now R. McKitterick, 'Town and Monastery in the Carolingian Period', *S. C. H.*, XVI (1979) pp. 103–118 (although on St-Riquier, see T. Evergates, 'Historiography and Sociology in Early Feudal Society: the Case of Hariulf and the 'Milites' of St-Riquier', *Viator*, VI (1975) pp. 35–49), a volume which also contains J. Nelson's useful 'Charles the Bald and the Church in Town and Countryside', pp. 103–118. There is a very interesting look at tenth-century monasticism in D. A. Bullough, 'The Continental Background of the Reform', in D. Parsons, ed., *Tenth-Century Studies* (London and Chichester, 1975) pp. 20–36. See also J. Evans, *Monastic Life at Cluny, 910–1157* (Oxford, 1931); N. Hunt, ed., *Cluniac Monasticism in the Central Middle Ages* (London, 1971); C. B. Bouchard, 'Laymen and Church Reform around the Year 1000: the Case of Otto-William, Count of Burgundy', *J. M. H.*, V (1979) pp. 1–10; and H. E. J. Cowdrey, 'The Peace and Truce of God in the Eleventh Century', *P. P.* XLVI (1970) pp. 42–67.

Finally, the 'Carolingian Renaissance'. Again, see the general books at A3–*c*, including W. Ullmann, *The Carolingian Renaissance and the Idea of Kingship*. As background, M. L. W. Laistner, *The Intellectual Heritage of the Early Middle Ages* (New York, 1957), and *Thought and Letters in Western Europe, 500–900* are very useful. See also J. L. Nelson, 'On the Limits of the Carolingian Renaissance', *S. C. H.*, (1977) pp. 61–69; G. W. Trompf 'The Concept of the Carolingian Renaissance', *Journal of the History of Ideas*, XXXIV (1973) pp. 3–26, D. A. Bullough, 'Roman Books and Carolingian *Renovatio*', *S. C. H.*, XIV (1977) 23–50; and H. Liebeschütz, 'Theodulf of Orleans and the Problem of the Carolingian Renaissance', in D. J. Gordon, ed., *Fritz Saxl, 1890–1948* (London, 1957) pp. 77–92. On Theodulf and the Libri Carolini, see the important articles by A. Freeman in *Speculum*, XXXII (1957) pp. 663–705, and *Speculum* XL (1965) pp. 203–89. On Alcuin there is Allott (A2–*c*) and E. S Duckett, *Alcuin, Friend of Charlemagne* (New York, 1951), as well as the more scholarly (and controversial) L. Wallach, *Alcuin and Charlemagne: Studies in Carolingian History and Literature* (New York, 1959). On Lupus of Ferrières, see C. H. Beeson, *Lupus of Ferrières as Scribe and Text Critic* (Cambridge, Mass., 1930) (which includes the facsimile of a manuscript annotated by Lupus) and R. J. Gariépy, 'Lupus of Ferrières: Carolingian Scribe and Text critic', *Medieval Studies*, XXX (1968) pp. 90–105. For Eriugena, see J. J. O'Meara, *Eriugena* (Cork, 1969), and *idem*, and L. Bieler, ed., *The Mind of Eriugena* (Dublin, 1973). The practical aspects of Carolingian learning are dealt with by R. McKitterick, 'Charles the Bald (823–877) and his Library: the Patronage of Learning', *E. H. R.*, XCV (1980) pp. 28–47, and *idem*, 'The Palace School of Charles the Bald', in Gibson and Nelson (A3–*d*) pp. 385–400 (see also Contreni and Marenbon in that volume), and by J. J. Contreni, *The Cathedral School of Laon from 850–930. Its Manuscripts and Masters* (Munich, 1978). The aftermath of the Renaissance is discussed in M. Gibson, 'The Continuity of Learning, circa 850 – circa 1050', *Viator*, VI (1975) pp. 1–13.

B. Bibliography of Works in Other Languages

1. GENERAL WORKS

F. Lot, *Naissance de la France* (Paris, 1948), is probably the best single introduction to the whole period; the most recent edition (Paris, 1970) has an up-to-date bibliography by J. Boussard. More recent, and more general, is J.-F. Lemarignier, *La France médiévale: institutions et sociétés* (Paris, 1970). For the earlier period see the excellent little *Les Mérovingiens* by G. Fournier (Paris, 1966); for the later, see E. Perroy, *Le Monde carolingien* (Paris, 1974). The *Nouvelle Clio* series always have excellent bibliographies: for this period see, so far, L. Musset, *Les Invasions*, 2 vols (Paris, 1965) (the first translated, see above A3–*a*); R. Doehaerd, *Le Haut moyen âge occidental* (Paris, 1971) (translated, A5–*a*); and J.-P. Poly and E. Bournazel, *La Mutation féodale, Xe–XIIe siècles* (Paris, 1980). Useful narratives and bibliographies are to be found in Gebhardt, ed., *Handbuch der Deutsche Geschichte*, vol. I (9th edn, Stuttgart, 1970), and T. Schieffer, ed., *Handbuch der Europäischen Geschichte*, Band I (Stuttgart, 1976). Interpretative essays by K. Hauck, 'Von einer spätantiken Randkultur zum karolingischen Europa', *F. S.*, I (1967) pp. 3–93, and W. Schlesinger, 'Die Auflösung des Karlsreiches', *K. d. G.*, I pp. 792–857, are useful beginnings. There are general studies of the different peoples of France by E. Zöllner, *Die politische Stellung der Völker im Frankenreich* (Vienna, 1950), and W. Kienast, *Studien über die französischen Volksstämme des Frühmittelalters* (Stuttgart, 1968). On the problem of terminology, see M. Lugge, *Gallia und Frankia im Mittelalter* (Bonn, 1960).

There are a number of useful collections of essays on the period: mention should be made of G. Kurth, *Etudes franques*, 2 vols (Brussels, 1919); W. Levison, *Aus Rheinischer und Fränkischer Frühzeit* (Dusseldorf, 1948); M. Bloch, *Mélanges Historiques*, 2 vols (Paris, 1963); and F. Lot, *Recueil des travaux historiques de Ferdinand Lot*, 3 vols (Geneva, 1968, 1970, 1973).

There are often handy sections on the early medieval period in the several dozen volumes of the *Univers de la France* series published by Privat of Toulouse; e.g. *Histoire de la Bretagne*, ed. J. Delumeau, or *Histoire de Marseilles*, ed. E. Baratier. Some of these have companion volumes of translated documents: e.g. *Documents de l'histoire de l'Aquitaine*, ed. C. Higounet. An excellent short provincial history is L. Boehm, *Geschichte Burgunds* (Stuttgart, 1971).

Finally, there are a number of useful reference works: e.g. F. Cabrol and H. Leclercq, *Dictionnaire d'archéologie chrétienne et de liturgie; Dictionnaire de théologie catholique; Dictionnaire d'histoire et géographie ecclésiastique* (so far up to 'G'); *Dictionnaire de biographie française* (up to 'F'); and *Reallexicon der Germanischen Altertumskunde* (up to 'C').

2. SOURCES

The best guide to the sources is Wattenbach-Levison, *Deutschlands Geschichtsquellen im Mittelalter: Vorzeit und Karolinger*, in 5 fascicules (Weimar, 1952–), with a Beiheft ed. by R. Buchner on legislative material. The old *Les Sources de l'histoire de la France* by A. Molinier is being replaced, but so far only the volumes on Roman Gaul are published. All the important source material is in print, often in one of the great series: *Patrologia*

Latina, ed. J. P. Migne (1844–); *Corpus Christianorum* (e.g. C. de Clercq, ed., *Concilia Galliae, 511–695* (1963)); and above all, *Monumenta Germaniae Historica*. There are various series within the *Monumenta:* for example, *Auctores Antiquissimi* for authors such as Sidonius, Avitus of Vienne or Venantius Fortunatus; *Scriptores Rerum Merovingicarum* for Gregory of Tours, Fredegar and Merovingian saints' lives; *Leges* for the laws; *Scriptores rerum Germanicarum in usum scholarum* for Carolingian annals, etc. Royal diplomas of the West Frankish kings have been published in a series of *Chartes et diplomes relatives à l'histoire de France*, e.g. those of Charles the Bald by G. Tessier (Paris 1943, 1952 and 1965), of Odo by R.-H. Bautier (Paris, 1967), of the kings of Provence by R. Poupardin (Paris, 1920), etc. A useful guide is G. Tessier, *La Diplomatique royale française* (Paris, 1962). Many cartularies and polyptychs have been edited: e.g. A. Bruel, *Recueil des chartes de l'Abbaye de Cluny* (Paris 1876–1903); B. Guérard, *Polyptyque de l'Abbé Irminon. . . de Saint-Germain-des-Prés* (Paris, 1844); F.L. Ganshof, *Le Polyptyque de l'Abbaye de Saint-Bertin* (Paris, 1975). See F. Lot, ed., 'Liste des cartulaires et recueils contenant des pièces antérieures à l'an 1000', *Bulletin du Cange*, XV (1940) pp. 5–24; *Bulletin du Cange*, XIV (1939) pp. 113–230 lists the Gallic saints' lives of the period 500–1000. Inscriptions have still not been fully exploited, nor edited in recent times: scholars still have to rely on E. Le Blant's three volumes (Paris, 1856, 1865 and 1892). For a recent example of their use, see I. Heidrich, 'Südgallische Inschriften des 5.–7. Jahrhunderts als Historische Quellen', *R. V.*, XXXII (1968) pp. 167–83.

Numerous Latin sources have been translated into French or German. Of particular note are the dual language series, such as *Les Classiques de l'histoire de France au moyen âge* (e.g. H. Waquet, ed., *Abbon: Le Siège de Paris par les Normands* (Paris, 1964), or R. Latouche, ed., *Richer: Histoire de France (888–995)* (Paris, 1967), etc.); *Ausgewählte Quellen zur Deutschen Geschichte des Mittelalters* (e.g. Gregory of Tours, ed. R. Buchner (rev. ed. Darmstadt, 1977), or the Annals of St Bertin, St Vaast and Xanten, ed. R. Rau (Darmstadt, 1958), etc.); or *Sources chrétiennes* (e.g. P. Riché, ed., *Dhuoda: Manuel pour mon fils* (Paris, 1975), etc.).

3. GENERAL AND POLITICAL HISTORY

(a) The Late Roman Period

Musset (A3-*a*) provides a useful bibliography. Particularly important are P. Courcelle, *Histoire littéraire des grandes invasions germaniques* (3rd edn Paris, 1964); K. F. Stroheker, *Germanentum und Spätantike* (Zürich and Stuttgart, 1965); R. Wenskus, *Stammesbildung und Verfassung. Das Werden der frühmittelalterlichen Gentes* (Cologne and Graz, 1961). Up-datings of L. Schmidt, *Geschichte der deutschen Stämme bis zum Ausgang der Völkerwanderung*, have appeared for two Germanic peoples: both books end *c.* 550 – E. Zöllner, *Geschichte der Franken* (Munich, 1970), and H. Wolfram, *Geschichte der Goten* (Munich, 1979). On the Franks see also C. Verlinden, *Les Origines de la frontière linguistique en Belgique et le colonisation franque* (Brussels, 1955). There has been much work from linguists and archaeologists on Germanic settlements in Gaul: see in particular F. Irsigler, ed., 'Hauptprobleme der Siedlung, Sprache und Kultur des Frankenreiches', *R.V.*, XXXV (1971) pp. 1–106; F. Petri, ed., *Siedlung, Sprache und Bevölkerungsstruktur im Frankenreich* (Darmstadt, 1973); M. Fleury and P. Périn, eds, *Problèmes de chronologie relative et absolue concernant les cimetières mérovingiens d'entre Loire et Rhin* (Paris, 1978); P. Périn, *La Datation des tombes mérovingiennes* (Geneva, 1980); and the bibliography in James A3-*c*.

(b) The Merovingian period

There are general books on the period by Fournier (B1); G. Tessier, *Le Baptême de Clovis* (Paris, 1964), and C. Lelong, *La Vie quotidienne en Gaule à l'époque mérovingienne* (Paris, 1963). E. Salin, *La Civilisation mérovingienne, d'après les sépultures, les textes et la laboratoire*,

4 vols, (Paris 1950, 1952, 1957, 1959), deals with many aspects of Merovingian culture, from the point of view of the archaeologist.

For Merovingian kingship, see R. Buchner, 'Das merowingische Königtum', in *Das Königtum* (Vorträge und Forschungen III, Sigmaringen 1956) pp. 143–54; R. Doehaerd, 'La Richesse des Mérovingiens', in *Studi in Onore di G. Luzzato* vol. I (Milan, 1949) pp. 30–46; R. Schneider, *Königswahl und Königserhebung im Frühmittelalter* (Stuttgart, 1972); H. Wolfram, *Intitulatio I. Lateinische Königs und Fürstentitel bis zum Ende des 8. Jahrhunderts* (Graz, etc., 1967); C. Courtois, 'L'Avènement de Clovis II et les règles d'accession au trône chez les Mérovingiens', *Mélanges L. Halphen* (Paris, 1951) pp. 155–64; L. Dupraz, *Contribution à l'histoire du Regnum Francorum pendant le troisième quart du septième siècle* (Fribourg, 1948); but above all the various articles by E. Ewig now collected in his *Spätantikes und Fränkisches Gallien*, Band I (Munich, 1976), ed. H. Atsma, esp. 'Die fränkischen Teilungen und Teilreiche (511–613)' pp. 114–71, and 'Die fränkischen Teilreiche im 7. Jahrhundert (613–714)' pp. 172–230. See also his 'Studien zur Merowingischen Dynastie', *F. S.*, VIII (1974) pp. 15–59.

For the Pippinids/early Carolingians, see E. Ewig, 'Noch einmal zum Staatsstreich Grimoalds', in Ewig *S. F. G.*, I, pp. 573–7; H. Thomas, 'Die Namenliste des Diptychon Barberini und der Sturz des Hausmeiers Grimoald', *D. A.*, XXV (1969) pp. 17–63; I. Heidrich, 'Titulatur und Urkunden der Arnulfingischen Hausmeier', *Archiv f. Diplomatik*, XI/XII (1965–6) pp. 71–279; J. Semmler, 'Zur pippinidisch-karolingischen Sukzessionskrise, 714–723', *D. A.*, XXXIII (1977) pp. 1–36; and U. Nonn, 'Das Bild Karl Martells in den lateinischen Quellen vornehmlich des 8. und 9. Jahrhunderts', F. S., IV (1970) pp. 70–137 and 'Vom Maior Domus zum Rex. Die Auffassung von Karl Martells Stellung im Spiegel der Titulatur', *R. V.*, XXXVII (1973) pp. 107–16. On the supposed blood-relationship between the two royal dynasties, see K.-U. Jäschke, 'Die Karolingergenealogien aus Metz und Paulus Diaconus', *R. V.*, XXXIV (1970) pp. 190–218; K. A. Eckhardt, *Merowingerblut* (Witzenhausen, 1965) and *Studia Merovingica* (Aalen, 1975); and E. Hlawitschka, 'Studien zur Genealogie und Geschichte der Merowinger und der frühen Karolinger', *R. V.*, XLIII (1979) pp. 1–99.

On the survival of Roman institutions in Gaul, see E. Ewig, in *S. F. G.*, I pp. 409–34; P. Classen, 'Kaiserreskript and Königsurkunde', *Archiv f. Diplomatik*, I (1955) p. 1–87 and II (1956) pp. 1–115, now reprinted as a book (Thessaloniki, 1977); and below B4. Some of the institutions of government have been discussed in R. Sprandel, 'Dux und Comes in der Merowingerzeit', *Z. R. G. G. A.*, LXXIV (1957) pp. 41–84; D. Claude, 'Untersuchungen zum frühfränkischen Comitat', *Z. R. G. G. A.*, LXXXI (1964) pp. 1–79; F. L Ganshof, 'L'Immunité dans la monarchie franque', *R. S. J. B.*, I (1958) pp. 171–216; *idem*, 'A propos du tonlieu sous les Mérovingiens', *Studi A. Fanfani*, I (Milan, 1962) pp. 293–315; R. Kaiser, 'Steuer und Zoll in der Merowingerzeit', *Francia*, VII (1979) pp. 1–18; and *idem*, '*Teloneum episcopi*. Du Tonlieu royal au tonlieu episcopal dans les civitates de la Gaule', in W. Paravicini and K. F. Werner, *Histoire comparée de l'administration* (Beiheft der Francia, 9) (Munich, 1980) pp. 469–85.

The best introductions to the regional history of Merovingian Gaul are E. Ewig, 'Volkstum und Volksbewusstsein im Frankenreich des 7. Jahrhunderts', *Sett.*, V (1958) pp. 587–648 and *S. F. G.*, I, pp. 231–73; and K. F. Werner, 'Les Principautés périphériques dans le monde franc du VIIIe siècle', *Sett.*, XX (1974) pp. 483–514, and in his *Structures politiques du monde franc (VIe–XIIe s.)* (London, 1979). There are also a number of regional studies: M. Chaume, *Les Origines du duché de Bourgogne* (Dijon, 1925): R. Buchner, *Die Provence in Merovingische Zeit* (Stuttgart, 1933); G. Fournier, *Le Peuplement rural en Basse-Auvergne durant le haut moyen âge* (Paris, 1962); M. Martin, *Die Schweiz im Frühmittelalter* (Berne, 1975); E. Ewig, 'Die Stellung Ribuariens in der Verfassungsgeschichte des Merowingerreichs', *S. F. G.*, I, pp. 450–71; G. Faider-Feytmans, *La Belgique à l'époque mérovingienne* (Brussels, 1964); M. Roblin, *Le Terroir de Paris aux époques gallo-romaine et franque* (Paris, 1951) and *Le Terroir de l'Oise aux époques Gallo-Romaine et Franque* (Paris, 1978); J. Boussard, 'L'Ouest du royaume franque aux VIIe et VIIIe siècles', *Journal des Savants* (1973) pp. 3–27; R. Kaiser, *Untersuchungen zur Geschichte der Civitas und Diözese Soissons in römischer und merowingischer Zeit* (Bonn, 1973); and, above all, M. Rouche, *L'Aquitaine des Wisigoths aux Arabes, 418–781: Naissance d'une région* (Paris, 1979). I have not seen J. L. Fleuriot, *Les Origines de la Bretagne* (Paris, 1980).

(c) The early Carolingian period

Still important reference works are those in the series of *Jahrbücher des fränkischen Reichs*, ed. by B. von Simson, S. Abel, *et al.* On Pippin, see H. Büttner, 'An den Anfängen des abendländischen Staatsgedankens: die Königserhebung Pippins', in *Das Königtum* (Vorträge und Forschungen III, Sigmaringen 1956) pp. 155–67; and W. Affeldt, 'Untersuchungen zur Königserhebung Pippins', *F. S.*, XIV (1980) pp. 95–187. See also *idem*, 'Das Problem der Mitwirkung des Adels an politischen Entscheidungsprozessen in Frankenreich des 8. Jahrhunderts', *Festschrift f. H. Herzfeld* (Berlin, 1972) pp. 404–23.

There is naturally a huge bibliography on Charlemagne. See above all the four volumes of *Karl der Grosse: Lebenswerk und Nachleben*, vol. 1 (*Persönlichkeit und Geschichte*), ed. H. Beumann (Düsseldorf, 1965), vol. 2 (*Das geistige Leben*), ed. B. Bischoff (1965), vol. 3 (*Karolingische Kunst*), ed. W. Braunfels and H. Schnitzler (1965), and vol. 4 (*Das Nachleben*), ed. W. Braunfels and P. E. Schramm (1967). These, above all vol. 1, provide excellent studies on most aspects of Charlemagne's reign. The catalogue of the 1965 Aachen exhibition, *Charlemagne: oeuvre, rayonnement et survivances* treats some of the themes in abbreviated form.

The literature of Carolingian kingship and the Empire is also large. The work of P. E. Schramm has been important (see A3–*c*); in particular *Herrschaftszeichen und Staatssymbolik*, 3 vols (1954) and *Kaiser, Könige und Päpste* (Stuttgart, 1968). See also H. H. Anton, *Fürstenspiegel und Herrscherethos in der Karolingerzeit* (Bonn, 1978); C. Brühl, 'Fränkische Krönungsbrauch und das Problem der Festkrönung', *H. J.*, CXCIV (1962) pp. 265–326; W. Schlesinger, 'Karlingische Königswahlen', in his *Beiträge zur deutsche Verfassungsgeschichte*, I (Göttingen, 1963) pp. 88–138. On the Empire, see P. Classen, 'Romanum gubernans imperium: zur Vorgeschichte der Kaisertitulatur Karls des Grossen', *D. A.*, IX (1951) pp. 103–21; H. Beumann, 'Nomen imperatoris. Studien zur Kaiseridee Karls des Grossen', *H. Z.*, CLXXXV (1958) pp. 515–49; W. Mohr, *Die Karolingische Reichsidee* (Münster, 1962); and K. F. Werner, 'L'Empire carolingien et le saint empire', in M. Duverger, ed., *Le Concept d'empire* (Paris, 1980) pp. 151–202. On the succession and partitions, see W. Schlesinger, 'Kaisertum und Reichsteilung – Zur Divisio regnorum von 806', in *idem, op. cit.* pp. 193–232; P. Classen, 'Karl der Grosse und die Thronfolge im Frankenreich', *Festschrift f. H. Heimpel*, III (Göttingen, 1972) pp. 109–34; T. Mayer, ed., *Der Vertrag von Verdun* (Leipzig, 1943); and P. Classen, 'Die Verträge von Verdun und Coulaines 843 als politischen Grundlagen des westfränkischen Reiches', *H. Z.*, CXCVI (1968) pp. 1–35. See also F. L. Ganshof, 'A propos de la politique de Louis le Pieux avant la crise de 830', *Rev. belge d'archéologie et d'histoire d'art*, XXXVII (1968) pp. 37–48.

Much of Ganshof's fundamental work on Carolingian institutions has been translated (A3–*c*). But see *idem*, *Recherches sur les capitulaires* (Paris, 1958), reprinted from *Rev. hist. de droit français et étranger*, XXXIV (1958) pp. 33–87 and 196–246. See on this R. Schneider, 'Zur rechtliche Bedeutung der Kapitularientexte', *D. A.*, XXIII (1967) pp. 273–94. Other important works on Carolingian institutions include K. F. Werner, 'Missus – marchio – comes. Entre l'administration centrale et l'administration locale de l'empire carolingien', in Paravicini and Werner, *op. cit.* (B3–*b*) pp. 191–239; C. Brühl, *Fodrum, Gistum, Servitium Regis. Studien zu den wirtschaftlichen Grundlagen des Königtums im Frankenreich*, 2 vols (Cologne, 1968); H. Dannenbauer, 'Die Freien in karolingischen Heer', in *Festschrift T. Mayer*, I (Lindau-Konstanz, 1954) pp. 49–64; F. L. Ganshof, 'Les Liens de vassalité dans la monarchie franque', *R. S. J. B.*, I (1958) pp. 153–69; E. Magnou-Nortier, *Foi et fidelité: recherches sur l'évolution des liens personnels chez les Francs du VIIe au IXe siècles* (Toulouse, 1976), and *idem*, 'Nouveaux propos sur "Foi et Fidelité"', *Francia*, VII (1979) pp. 537–50.

On the Vikings, see W. Vogel, *Die Normannen und das fränkische Reich bis zur Gründung der Normandie, 799–911* (Heidelberg, 1906); A. d'Haenens, *Les Invasions normandes en Belgique au IXe siècle* (Louvain, 1967); *idem*, 'Les Invasions normandes dans l'empire franc au IXe siècle. Pour une rénovation de la problématique', *Sett.* XVI (1969) pp. 233–98; and H. Zettel, *Das Bild der Normannen und die Normaneneinfälle in westfränkischen . . . Quellen* (Munich, 1977).

As an introduction to the regional history of Carolingian Gaul, see E. Ewig, 'Beobachtungen zur politisch-geographischen Terminologie des fränkischen Grossreiches und der Teilreiche des 9. Jahrhunderts', in *S. F. G.*, I, pp. 323–61; *idem*, 'Descriptio Franciae', *K. d. G.*, I, pp. 143–77 and *S. F. G.*, I, pp. 274–322; B. Bligny, 'Le Royaume de Bourgogne', *K. d. G.*, I, pp. 247–68; and P. Wolff, 'L'Aquitaine et ses marges', *K. d. G.*, I, pp. 269–306. See also F. L. Ganshof, *La Belgique carolingienne* (Brussels, 1958); L. Auzias, *L'Aquitaine carolingienne (778–987)* (Toulouse–Paris, 1937); E. Magnou-Nortier, *La Société laïque et l'eglise dans la province ecclésiastique de Narbonne, zone cispyrénéenne, de la fin du VIIIe à la fin du XIe siècle* (Toulouse, 1974); J. Boussard, 'Les Destinées de la Neustrie du IXe au XIe siècle', *C. C. M.*, XI (1968) pp. 15–28.

(d) The late Carolingian period

See in particular Poly and Bournazel (B1), particularly for the bibliography. The narrative history of the West Frankish reigns has been studied in a series of books: the first half of Charles the Bald's reign by F. Lot and L. Halphen (Paris, 1909); Odo [Eudes] by E. Favre (1893); Charles the Simple by A. Eckel (1899); Robert I and Ralph [Raoul] by P. Lauer (1910); Louis IV by P. Lauer (1900); Lothar, Louis V and Charles of Lorraine by F. Lot (1891); and Robert II by C. Pfister (1885). Other miscellaneous works on the period are U. Penndorf, *Das Problem der 'Reichseinheitsidee' nach der Teilung von Verdun (843)* (Munich, 1974); J. Calmette, 'Les Comtes Bernard sous Charles le Chauve. Etat actuel d'une énigme historique', *Mélanges L. Halphen* (Paris, 1951) pp. 103–110; K. F. Werner, 'Gauzlin von Saint-Denis und die westfränkische Reichsteilung von Amiens (März 880). Ein Beitrag zur Vorgeschichte von Odos Königtum', *D. A.*, XXXV (1979) pp. 395–462; R. H. Bautier, 'Le Règne d'Eudes à la lumière des diplômes expédiés par sa chancellerie', *C. R. A. I.*, (1961) pp. 140–157; L. Boehm, 'Rechtsformen und Rechtstitel der burgundischer Königserhebungen im 9. Jahrhundert. Zur Krise der karolingischer Dynastie', *Hist. Jahrbuch*, LXXX (1961) pp. 1–59; R. H. Bautier, 'Aux Origines du royaume de Provence. De la sédition avortée de Boson à la royauté légitime de Louis', *Provence Historique*, XXIII (1973) pp. 41–68; B. Schneidmüller, *Karolingische Tradition und frühes französisches Königtum. Untersuchungen zur Herrschaftslegitimation der westfränkisch-französischen Monarchie im 10. Jahrhundert* (Wiesbaden, 1979); J. Ehlers, 'Karolingische Tradition und frühes Nationalbewusstsein in Frankenreich', *Francia*, IV (1976) pp. 213–35. Much important work has been done on the monarchy by J.-F. Lemarignier: see *Recherches sur l'hommage en marche et les frontières féodales* Lille, 1945); 'La Dislocation du *pagus* et le problème des *consuetudines* (Xe–XIe siècles)', *Mélanges L. Halphen* (Paris, 1951) pp. 401–10; 'Les fidèles du Roi de France (936–987)', *Recueil Clovis Brunel*, II (Paris, 1955) pp. 138–62; *Le Gouvernement royal aux premiers temps capétiens 987–1108*) (Paris, 1965); and, most recently, 'Autour des premiers capétiens (987–1108). D'un réseau d'encadrement à un embryo d'administration locale', in Paravicini and Werner, (B3–*b*) pp. 240–5.

On the principalities, see above all J. Dhondt, *Etudes sur la naissance des principautés territoriales en France (IXe–Xe siècles)* (Bruges, 1948). See also K. F. Werner, 'Untersuchungen zur Frühzeit des französischen Fürstentums', *Die Welt als Geschichte*, XVIII (1958) pp. 256–89, XIX (1959) pp. 146–93 and XX (1960) pp. 87–119; on which see J. Boussard, *C. C. M.*, V (1962) pp. 303–22 and 364–62; W. Kienast, *Der Herzogstitel in Frankreich und Deutschland (9.–12. Jahrhunderts)* (Munich, 1968); K. Brunner, 'Der fränkische Fürstentitel im neunten und zehnten Jahrhundert', in H. Wolfram, ed., *Intitulatio*, II (Vienna, 1973) pp. 179–340; and *Les Principautés au moyen age: communications du Congrès de Bordeaux en 1973* (Bordeaux, 1979).

Finally, regional histories: R. Poupardin, *Le Royaume de Provence sous les Carolingiens (855–933)* (Paris, 1901); J.-P. Poly, *La Provence et la société féodale (879–1166)* (Paris, 1976); R. Poupardin, *Le Royaume de Bourgogne, 888–1038. Etude sur les origines du royaume d'Arles* (Paris, 1907); E. Hlawitschka, 'Die Königsherrschaft der Burgundischen Rudolfinger', *Hist. Jahrbuch*, C (1980) pp. 444–56; G. Duby, *La Société aux XIe et XIIe siècles dans la région mâconnaise* (Paris, 1953; 2nd edn 1971); R. Parisot, *Le Royaume de Lorraine sous les Carolingiens, 843–923* (Paris, 1899); *idem, Les Origines de la Haute-Lorraine et sa première maison ducale* (Paris, 1909); E. Hlawitschka, *Lotharingien und das Reich an der Schwelle der deutschen Geschichte* (Stuttgart, 1968); B. Schneidmüller, 'Französische Lothringenpolitik im 10. Jahrhundert', *Jahrbuch f. westdeutsche Landesgeschichte*, V (1979) pp. 1–31; F.-L. Ganshof, *La Flandre sous les premiers comtes* (2nd edn, Brussels, 1944); P. Grierson, 'La Maison d'Evrard de Frioul et les origines du comté de Flandre', *R. N.*, XXIV (1938) pp. 241–66; A. d'Haenens, 'Les Incursions hongroises dans l'espace belge', *C. C. M.*, IV (1961) pp. 423–40; R. Fossier, *La Terre et les hommes en Picardie jusqu'à la fin du 13e siècle* (Paris, 1968); M. Bur, *La Formation du comté de Champagne, 950–1150* (Nancy, 1977); A. Chédeville, *Chartres et ses campagnes (XIe–XIIIe siècle)* (Paris, 1973); H. Prentout, *Essai sur les origines et la fondation du duché de Normandie* (Caen, 1911); numerous articles by L. Musset, the most recent of which include 'Les Apports scandinaves dans le plus ancien droit normand', in *Droit privé et institutions régionales: Etudes off. à J. Yver* (Paris, 1976) pp. 559–75; *idem*, 'L'Aristocratie normande au XIe siècle', in P. Contamine, ed., *La Noblesse au moyen âge* (Paris, 1976) pp. 71–96; and *idem*, 'Origines et nature du pouvoir ducal en Normandie jusqu'au milieu du XIe siècle', in *Les Principautés..., op. cit.*, pp. 47–59; J. Yver, 'Les Premières institutions du duché de Normandie', *Sett.*, XVI (1969) pp. 299–366; L. Boehm, 'Nomen Gentis Normannorum. Der Aufsteig der Normannen im Spiegel der normannischen Historiographie', *ibid*, pp. 623–704; R. Latouche, *Histoire du comté du Maine pendant le Xe et le XIe siècle* (Paris, 1910); O. Guillot, *Le Comte d'Anjou et son entourage au XIe siècle* (Paris, 1972); G. Devailly, *Le Berry du Xe au milieu du XIIIe siècle* (Paris, 1973); R. Sanfaçon, *Défrichements, peuplement et institutions seigneuriales en Haut-Poitou du Xe au XIIIe siècle* (Quebec, 1977); M. Garaud, *Les Châtelaines de Poitou et l'avènement du régime féodal, XIe et XIIe siècles* (Poitiers, 1967); C. Higounet, *Le Comté de Comminges* (Toulouse–Paris, 1949); O. Engels, *Schutzgedanke und Landherrschaft im östlichen Pyrenäenraum (9.–13 Jahrhundert)* (Münster, 1970).

4. SOCIAL HISTORY

On general demographic questions, see P. Riché, 'Problèmes de démographie historique du haut moyen âge', *Annales de démogr. hist.*, II (1966) pp. 37–55 and J.-N. Biraben and J. Le Goff, 'La Peste dans le haut moyen âge', *A. E. S. C.*, XXIV (1969) 1484–1510. For the contributions of a linguist to social history, see C. Battisti, 'Latini e Germani nella Gallia del Nord nei Secoli VII e VIII', *Sett.*, V (1958) pp. 445–84.

There is a vast literature on the early medieval aristocracy. See as introduction, G. Duby, *R. H.*, CCVI (1961) pp. 1–22; L. Génicot, *A. E. S. C.*, XVII (1962) pp. 1–22; M. Heinzelmann, *M. A.*, LXXXIII (1977) pp. 133–44.

For the Merovingian aristocracy there are now two useful reference works: K. Selle-Hosbach, *Prosopographie merowingischer Amtsträger in der Zeit von 511–613* (Diss. Bonn,

1974), and H. Ebling, *Prosopographie der Amtsträger des Merowingerreiches von Chlothar II (613) bis Karl Martell (741)* (Munich, 1974). K. F. Stroheker's classic *Der senatorische Adel im spätantiken Gallien* (Tübingen, 1948) includes a prosopography of Roman members of the Merovingian aristocracy. Full bibliographies will be found in F. Irsigler, *Untersuchungen zur Geschichte des frühfränkischen Adels* (Bonn, 1969), and H. Grahn-Hoek, *Die fränkische Oberschicht im 6. Jahrhundert. Studien zu ihre rechtlichen und politischen Stellung* (Sigmaringen, 1976), which have not entirely replaced such works as A. Bergengruen, *Adel und Grundherrschaft im Merowingerreich* (Wiesbaden, 1958), and R. Sprandel, 'Struktur und Geschichte des merowingischen Adels', *Hist. Zeitschrift*, CXCIII (1961) pp. 33–71. See also J. P. Bodmer, *Der Krieger der Merowingerzeit und seine Welt* (Zurich, 1957), and U. Nonn, 'Eine fränkische Adelssippe um 600. Zur Familie des Bischofs Berthram von Le Mans', *F. S.*, IX (1975) pp. 186–201.

Many works on the Carolingian aristocracy have been mentioned above, B3–*c*. See also R. Poupardin, 'Les Grandes Familles comtales à l'époque carolingienne', *R. H.*, LXXII (1900) pp. 72–96; J. Wollasch, 'Eine adlige Familie des frühen Mittelalters. Ihr Selbstverständnis und ihr Wirklichkeit', *Archiv f. Kulturgeschichte*, XXXIX (1957) pp. 150–88; P. Riché, 'Les Bibliothèques de trois aristocrates laïcs carolingiens' *M. A.*, LXIX (1963) pp. 87–104, and *idem*, 'Trésors et collections d'aristocrates laïques carolingiens', *Cahiers archéol.*, XXII (1972) pp. 39–46; J. Schneider, 'Aspects de la société dans l'Aquitaine carolingienne d'après la 'Vita Geraldi Aureliacensis'', *C. R. A. I.* (1973) pp. 8–19; and *Les Structures sociales de l'Aquitaine, du Languedoc et de l'Espagne au premier age féodal. Colloques . . .* (Toulouse–Paris, 1969).

On the family and women, see L. Theis, 'Saints sans famille? Quelques remarques sur la famille dans le monde franc à travers les sources hagiographiques', *R. H.*, CCLV (1976) pp. 3–20; M. Sot, 'Historiographie episcopale et modèle familiale en occident au IXe siècle', *A. E. S. C.*, XXXIII (1978) pp. 433–49; F.-L. Ganshof, 'Le Statut de la femme dans la monarchie franque', *R. S. J. B.*, XII (1962) pp. 5–58; S. Konecny-Scheibein, *Die Frauen des karolingischen Königshauses* (Diss. Vienna, 1974); J. Verson, 'Les Femmes et la politique en France au Xe siècle', *Mélanges E. Perroy* (Paris, 1973) pp. 108–19; *Sett.* XXIV (1977) was devoted to marriage in the early medieval period. See also *Famille et parenté dans l'occident médiéval (Colloque de Rome 1974)* (Rome, 1977).

There have been many fewer studies of the non-aristocratic elements of society, largely because of the inadequacy of the sources. But see K. Bosl, 'Potens et Pauper', *Festschrift O. Brunner* (Göttingen, 1963) pp. 60–87; *idem*, 'Die älteste sogenannten germanischen Volksrechte und die Gesellschaftsstruktur der Unterschichten', in *idem*, ed., *Gesellschaft. Kultur. Literatur: Beiträge L. Wallach gewidmet* (Stuttgart, 1975) pp. 129–52; M. Rouche, 'La Matricule des pauvres', in M. Mollat, ed., *Études sur l'histoire de la pauvreté* (Paris, 1974) pp. 83–110; C. Verlinden, *L'Esclavage dans l'Europe médiévale*, vol. I (Bruges, 1955); and H. Nehlsen, *Sklavenrecht zwischen Antike und Mittelalter* (Göttingen, 1972).

As a general introduction and reference work, H. Brunner, *Deutsche Rechtsgeschichte, II: Die Fränkische Zeit* (2nd ed. Munich, 1928) has not been replaced by such works as K. von Amira, ed. K. A. Eckhardt, *Germanisches Recht* (Berlin, 1960 and 1967). K. A. Eckhardt, who in his series *Germanenrechte* has produced editions and German translations of most Germanic law-codes, has done the fundamental work on Lex Salica. See in particular his 'Zur Entstehungszeit der Lex Salica', *Festchrift z. Feier des 200-jahrigen Bestehens der Akad. d. Wiss. in Göttingen, Phil.-Hist. Kl.*, II (1951) pp. 1–31. Much important work has been done also by F. Beyerle (e.g. 'Zum Kleinreich Sigiberts III und zur Datierung der Lex Ribvaria', *R. V.*, XXI (1956) pp. 357–61) and R. Schmidt-Wiegand (e.g. 'Gens Francorum Inclita. Zu Gestalt und Inhalt des längeren Prologes der Lex Salica', *Festschrift A. Hofmeister* (Halle, 1955) pp. 233–50). See now C. Schott, 'Der Stand der Leges-Forschung', *F. S.*, XIII (1979) pp. 29–55.

A number of relevant fascicules of the series *Ius Romanum Medii Aevi* (*I. R. M. A.*) have appeared: particularly interesting is P. Riché, Enseignement du droit en Gaule du VIe au XIIe siècle', *I. R. M. A.* 5b bb (Milan, 1965). On the survival of Roman law in Gaul, see J. Gaudemet, 'Survivances romaines dans le droit de la monarchie franque du Ve au Xe siècle', *Tijdschrift voor Rechtsgeschiedenis*, XXIII (1955) pp. 149–206; J.-F. Lemarignier, 'Les Actes de droit privé de l'Abbaye de Saint-Bertin au haut moyen âge', *Rev. intern. des droits de l'antiquité*, V (1950) pp. 35–72; and U. Nonn, 'Merowingische Testamente', *Archiv f. Diplomatik*, XVIII (1972) pp. 1–129. For legal practice, see F.-L. Ganshof, 'La Preuve dans le droit franc' *R. S. J. B.*, XVII (1965) pp. 71–98.

On the Jews, see above all two books by B. Blumenkranz: *Juifs et Chrétiens dans le monde occidental, 430–1096* (Paris, 1960) and *Les Auteurs chrétiens latins du moyen âge sur les Juifs et le judaïsme* (Paris, 1963).

5. ECONOMIC HISTORY

(a) General

See Doehaerd (B1) and her bibliography. The major works have all been translated: see A5.

(b) Trade

A. Verhulst, 'Der Handel in Merowingerreich', *Early Medieval Studies*, II (Stockholm, 1970) pp. 2–54, is a useful assemblage of sources. There is nothing comparable for the Carolingian period. Much work on the coinage has been done by J. Lafaurie: see my bibliography in *Merovingian Archaeology* . . . (A3–*b*) pp. 524 ff., and 'Numismatique des Carolingiens aux Capétiens', *C. C. M.*, XIII (1970) pp. 117–37; 'Numismatique des Mérovingiens aux Carolingiens', *Francia*, II (1974) pp. 26–47; and 'La Surveillance des ateliers monétaires au IXe siècle', in Paravicini and Werner (B3–*b*) pp. 486–96. *Sett.* VIII (1961) was devoted to early medieval numismatics.

(c) Towns

Sett. VI (1959) and XXI (1974) were devoted to early medieval towns. Other useful collections include *Studien zu den Anfängen des europäischen Städtewesens* (Vorträge und Forschungen IV; Lindau/Konstanz, 1958) and H. Jankuhn et al., ed., *Vor- und Frühformen der europäischen Stadt*, 2 vols (Göttingen, 1973, 1974). Other general works include J. Lestocquoy, 'Le Paysage urbain en Gaule du Ve au IXe siècle', *A. E. S. C.*, VIII (1953) pp. 159–72, reprinted in his *Etudes d'histoire urbaine* (Arras, 1966); A. Dupont, *Les Cités de la Narbonnaise première depuis les invasions germaniques jusqu'à l'apparition du consulat* (Nîmes, 1942); F.-L. Ganshof, *Etude sur le développement des villes entre Loire et Rhin au moyen âge* (Brussels, 1943); F. Vercauteren, *Etude sur les civitates de la Belgique seconde* (Brussels, 1934); J. Dhondt, 'L'Essor urbain entre la Meuse et la Mer du Nord à l'époque mérovingienne', *Studi in Onore di A. Sapori* (Rome, 1957) pp. 55–78; and individual contributions to the general collections cited above. But see now the first two volumes in G. Duby, gen. ed., *Histoire de la France urbaine*: P. A. Février, ed., *La Ville antique* (Paris, 1980), and A. Chédeville, ed., *La Ville médiévale* (Paris, 1980).

On the town as a centre of government, see E. Ewig, 'Résidence et capitale pendant le haut moyen âge', *R. H.*, CCXXX (1963) pp. 25–72; comments on Ewig by C. Brühl, in *Journal des savants*, XXXV (1967) pp. 193–215; *idem*, *Palatium und Civitas, I. Gallien* (Vienna, 1975); and R. Kaiser, 'Aachen und Compiègne. Zwei Pfalzstädte im frühen und hohen Mittelalter', *R. V.*, XLIII (1979) pp. 100–19.

For individual towns, see H. Gerner, *Lyon im Frühmittelalter* (Cologne, 1968); E. Ewig, *Trier im Merowingerreich* (Trier, 1954); L. Musset, 'La Renaissance urbaine des Xème et XIème siècles dans le Ouest de la France', *Mélanges E. Labande* (Poitiers, 1974) pp. 563–75; D. Claude, *Topographie und Verfassung der Städte Bourges und Poitiers bis in das 11. Jahrhundert* (Lübeck-Hamburg, 1960); H. Galinié, et al., *Les Archives du sol à Tours: survie et avenir de l'archéologie de la ville* (Tours, 1979); *idem*, 'Archéologie et topographie historique de Tours – IVème–XIème siècle', *Zeitschrift f. Archäologie des Mittelalters*, VI (1978) pp. 33–56; C. Higounet, *Bordeaux pendant le haut moyen âge* (Bordeaux, 1963).

(d) The Countryside

Sett. XIII (1966) is devoted to the rural economy. See also the general works mentioned above at B3 and B5. In addition, see C.-E. Perrin, "Une Etape de la seigneurie: l'exploitation de la réserve à Prüm au IXe siècle', *Annales d'Hist. Econ. et Soc.*, *VI (1934) pp. 450–66;* L. Kuchenbuch, *Bauerliche Gesellschaft und Klosterherrschaft im 9. Jahrhundert. Studien zur Sozialstruktur der Familia der Abtei Prüm* (Wiesbaden, 1978); and, above all, G. Duby, ed., *Histoire de la France rurale*, I (Paris, 1975).

6. THE CHURCH AND CULTURE

(a) General

The relevant volumes of A. Fliche and V. Martin, ed., *Histoire de l'eglise (IV–VII)* are showing their age. Much better is the *Handbuch der Kirchengeschichte* (A6–*a*). There have been a number of volumes in the *Sett.* series devoted to the Church and culture: see IV (1957) on monasticism; VII (1960) on the Church; XI (1964) on culture; XIV (1967) on conversion; XVII (1970) on historiography; XIX (1972) on schools; and XXII (1975) on Latin culture. See two contributions in particular: G. Le Bras, 'Sociologie de l'eglise dans le haut moyen âge', *Sett.*, VII (1960) pp. 595–612, and J.-F. Lemarignier, 'Quelques Remarques sur l'organisation ecclésiastique de la Gaule . . .', *Sett.*, XIII (1966) pp. 487–530. Other general works include J. Gaudemet, *Les Elections dans l'eglise latine, des origines au XVIe siècle* (Paris, 1979); C. de Clercq, *La Legislation religieuse franque*, I (Paris/Louvain, 1936) and II (Antwerp, 1958); F. Prinz, *Klerus und Krieg in frühen Mittelalter* (Stuttgart, 1971); and E. Lesne, *Histoire de la propriété ecclésiastique en France*, 4 vols (Lille, Paris, 1910–40), a mine of information on all aspects of Frankish life. On culture and education, see above all P. Riché (A6–*b*); for literary history, see now F. Brunhölzl, *Geschichte des lateinischen Literatur des Mittelalters*, I (Munich, 1975); for a particular type of literature, see M. Aubrun, 'Caractères et portée religieuse et sociale des *Visiones* en occident du VIe au XIe siècle', *C. C.M.*, XXIII (1980) pp. 109–30.

(b) The Merovingian Church

On bishops and their cities, see E. Ewig, 'Kirche und Civitas in der Merowingerzeit', *Sett.*, VII (1960) pp. 45–71; D. Claude, 'Die Bestellung der Bischöfe im merowingische Reiche', *Z. R. G. K. A.*, XLIX (1963) pp. 1–75; F. Prinz, 'Die bischöfliche Stadtherrschaft im Frankenreich vom 5. bis zum 7. Jahrhundert', *H. Z.*, CCXVII (1973) pp. 1–35; M. Heinzelmann, *Bischofsherrschaft in Gallien* (Munich, 1976); and J. Durliat, 'Les Attributions civiles des évêques mérovingiens: L'exemple de Didier, évêque de Cahors (630–655)', *Annales du Midi*, XCI (1979) pp. 237–54. See also H. Wieruszowski, 'Die Zusammensetzung des gallischen und fränkischen Episkopats bis zum Vertrag von Verdun (843)', *Bonner Jahrbücher*, CXXVII (1922) pp. 1–83; J. Champagne and R. Szramkiewicz, 'Recherches sur les conciles des temps mérovingiens', *Rev. hist. de droit français et etranger*, XLIX (1971) pp. 5–49; C. Servatius, '"Per Ordinationem Principis Ordinetur". Zum Modus der Bischofsernennung im Edikt Chlothars II vom Jahre 614', *Zeitschrift f. Kirchengeschichte*, LXXXIV (1973) pp. 1–29. There are a number of important articles on the Church in northern Gaul (by Fontaine, Heinzelmann, Werner, etc) in *R. H. E. F.*, LXII (1976). L. Van der Essen, *Le Siècle des saints (625–739)* (Brussels, 1948) deals with Belgium.

On the cult of the saints, see above all F. X. Graus, *Volk, Herrscher und Heiliger im*

Reich der Merowinger (Prague, 1965); also F. Prinz, 'Heiligenkult und Adelherrschaft im Spiegel merowingischer Hagiographie', *H. Z.*, CCIV (1967) pp. 529–44; and on Gregory, *Gregorio di Tours, 10–13 Ottobre 1971* (Convegni del Centro di Studi sulla Spiritualità Medievale, XII) (Todi, 1977).

For Merovingian monasticism, see above all F. Prinz, *Frühes Mönchtum im Frankenreich* (Munich/Vienna, 1965). There are interesting articles by H. Atsma in *Francia*, IV (1976), 1–57, on inscriptions as a source for monastic historians, and in *R. H. E. F.*, LXII (1976) pp. 163–87, on urban monasticism. E. Ewig has written a number of studies on monastic privileges in *S. F. G.*, II. On the Poitiers nunnery and its revolt, see now G. Scheibelreiter, *Mitteilungen des Inst. f. Oesterreichische Geschichte*, LXXXVII (1979) pp. 1–37.

(c) The Carolingian Church

On the early Carolingian church, see E. Ewig, 'Milo et eiusmodi similes', *S. F. G.*, II, pp. 189–219; T. Schieffer, *Winfrid-Bonifatius und die christliche Grundlegen Europas* (Freiburg, 1954); H. Mordek, *Kirchenrecht und Reform in Frankreich. Die 'Collectio Vetus Gallica'* (Berlin, 1974); E. Ewig, 'St Chrodegang et la réforme de l'église franque', *S. F. G.*, II, pp. 232–59; J. Chélini, 'La Pratique dominicale des laïcs dans l'église franque sous la règne de Pépin', *R. H. E. F.*, XLII (1956) pp. 161–74.

For Charlemagne's church, see above all *K. d. G.*, II; also H. Büttner in *K. d. G.*, I, pp. 454–87. There are good bibliographies in *Handbook of Church History*, III (A6–*a*). See also A. Angenendt, 'Das geistliche Bündnis der Päpste mit den Karolingern (754–96)', *Hist. Jahrbuch*, C (1980) pp. 1–94; P. Brommer, 'Die bischöfliche Gesetzgebung Theodulfs von Orléans', *Z. R. G. K. A.*, XCI (1974) pp. 1–20.

The works of J. Semmler are essential for the reforms of Louis's reign: see 'Karl der Grosse und das fränkische Monchtum', *K. d. G.*, II, pp. 255–89; 'Traditio und Königsschutz. Studien zur Geschichte der königlichen Monasteria', *Z. R. G. K. A.*, LXXVI (1959) pp. 1–33; 'Zum Uberlieferung der monastischer Gesetzgebung Ludwigs des Frommen', *D. A.*, XVI (1960) pp. 309–88; 'Reichsidee und kirchliche Gesetzgebung', *Zeitschr. f. Kirchengeschichte*, LXXI (1960) pp. 37–65; 'Die Beschlüsse des Aachener Konzils im Jahre 816', *ibid.*, LXXIV (1963) pp. 15–82; and 'Episcopi Potestas und karolingische Klosterpolitik', in A. Borst, ed., *Mönchtum, Episkopat und Adel zur Gründungszeit des Klosters Reichenau* (Vorträge und Forschungen, XX, Sigmaringen 1974), pp. 305–96. In this volume there is a useful article by F. Felten, 'Laienäbte in der Karolingerzeit. Ein Beitrag zum Problem der Adelsherrschaft über die Kirche', pp. 397–431: see now his book on lay-abbots.

A number of studies have been made on individual churchmen; e.g. E. Boshof, *Erzbischof Agobard von Lyon* (Cologne, 1969); G. Schneider, *Erzbischof Fulco von Reims (883–900) und das Frankreich* (Munich, 1973); but above all J. Devisse, *Hincmar, archévêque de Reims, 845–882*, 3 vols (Geneva, 1975–6), an essential work which illuminates nearly every corner of the ninth-century Church.

On Pseudo-Isidore, see H. Fuhrmann, *Einfluss und Verbreitung der pseudo-isidorischen Fälschungen*, 3 vols (Stuttgart, 1972, 1973, 1974).

For 10th-century developments, see a number of the regional histories cited at B3–*d*, and also Magnou-Nortier (B3–*c*, end). In addition, see J. Wollasch, 'Königtum, Adel und Kloster im Berry während des 10. Jahrhunderts', in G. Tellenbach, ed., *Neuer Forschungen über Cluny* (Fribourg, 1959) pp. 19–165; K. Hallinger, *Gorze-Cluny*, 2 vols (Rome, 1950–1); J. Caille, 'Origine et développement de la seigneurie temporelle de l'archévêque dans la ville et le terroir de Narbonne (IXe–XIIe siècles)', *Narbonne, archéologie et histoire: 45e Congrès de la féd. hist. Languedoc medit, Narbonne 1972* (Narbonne, 1973) vol. 2, pp. 9–36; P. Desportes, 'Les Archévêques de Reims et les droits comtaux', *Mélanges E. Perroy*, (Paris, 1973) pp. 79–89; J. Boussard, 'Les Evêques en Neustrie avant la réforme grégorienne', *Journal des savants* (1970) pp. 161–96; and H. Hoffmann, *Gottesfriede und Treuga Dei* (Stuttgart, 1964).

P. Riché, *Education and Culture . . . (A6–b)* is excellent background for the Carolingian Renaissance; unfortunately he has not yet continued into the ninth century in the same detail. However, see his two articles cited at B4; *Les Ecoles et l'enseignement dans l'occident chrétien de la fin du Ve siècle au milieu du XIe siècle* (Paris, 1979); 'Les Hagiographes bretons et la renaissance carolingienne', *Bulletin de Philologie Hist.* (1966) pp. 651–9; 'Conséquences des invasions normandes sur la culture monastique dans l'occident franc', *Sett.*, XVI (1969) pp. 705–22; and 'La "Renaissance" intellectuel du Xe siècle en occident', *Cahiers d'histoire*, XXI (1976) pp. 27–42. On the origins of the Renaissance, see *idem*, 'Le Renouveau culturel à la cour de Pépin III' and J. Hubert, 'Les Prémisses de la renaissance carolingienne au temps de Pépin III', in *Francia*, II (1974) pp. 59–70 and 49–58. For Charlemagne's reign, see *K. d. G.*, II and III. For further bibliography, see *Handbook of Church History*, III (A6–*a*). Of particular interest are studies on writers of history: see *Sett.* XVII (1970); H. Löwe, 'Regino von Prüm und das historische Weltbild der Karolingerzeit', *R. V.*, XVII (1952) pp. 151–79; *idem*, 'Geschichtsschreibung der ausgehenden Karolingerzeit', *D. A.*, XXIII (1967) pp. 1–30; and P. C. Jacobsen, *Flodoard von Reims* (Leiden/Cologne, 1978).

References

Full references to the sources in translation will be found in Bibliography A2.

INTRODUCTION

1. Quoted by T. Zeldin, *France 1848–1945*, vol. II (Oxford, 1977) p. 36.
2. See E. Weber, *Peasants into Frenchmen: the Modernization of Rural France 1870–1914* (London, 1977) p. 67.
3. *Idem*, p. 110.
4. F. Lot, *Naissance de la France* (Paris, 1970) p. 483.
5. L. White, jr., *Medieval Technology and Social Change* (Oxford, 1962) p.2.

1. THE PEOPLES OF GAUL

1. Sulpicius Severus, *Dialogues*, I. 8 and 27, trs Hoare, pp. 77 and 100; Gregory of Tours, *Historiae*, VI. 9, trs Thorpe, p. 340 [Thorpe's translations sometimes adapted by author].
2. A phrase found in some versions of Gennadius, *De viris illustribus*, *c*. 92.
3. Sidonius Apollinaris, *Epist*. V. 17, trs Anderson, II p. 231.
4. *Idem*, *Epist*. I. 7, trs Anderson, I p. 371.
5. Salvian, *On the Government of God*, V. 8, trs Sanford, p. 148.
6. Sidonius, *Epist*. VIII. 9, trs Anderson, II p. 44.
7. Astronomer, *Life of Louis the Pious*, 4. 2, trs Cabaniss, p. 36.
8. Quoted by Kienast, *Herzogstitel* (B3–*d*) p. 271.
9. Sidonius, *Epist*. V. 5, trs Anderson, p. 83.
10. *Passio S. Sigismundi*, *M. G. H.*, *S. S. R. M.*, II p. 333.
11. See Kienast, *Studien über die französischen Volksstämme* (B1) p. 39.
12. Procopius, *Wars* V. 12, trs H. B. Dewing, *Procopius*, vol. III (London, 1919) p. 121.
13. Sidonius, *Epist*. IV 17, trs Dalton, II p. 31.
14. Remigius, trs in Hillgarth, *Conversion* (A2–*b*) pp. 74–5.
15. Avitus, trs Hillgarth, p. 76.
16. Gregory of Tours, *Hist*. II. 31, trs Thorpe, p. 144.
17. Remigius, tr. Hillgarth, p. 77–8.
18. Gregory of Tours, *Hist*. II. 42: tr. Thorpe, p. 158.
19. *Vita Maximini Treverensis*, 10: *Acta Sanctorum* May VII, 23.
20. *M. G. H.*, *S. S. R. M.* VII p. 773.
21. 'Hutz! Hutz!': Astronomer, *Life of Louis the Pious*, 64. 2: tr. Cabaniss, p. 125.
22. From *Otfrids Evangelienbuch*, ed. O. Erdemann and E. Schröder (2nd edn Halle, 1934) pp. 12–14.
23. K. A. Eckhardt, *Lex Salica. 100-Titel Text* (Weimar, 1953) pp. 83–91.
24. Zosimus, *Historia Nova* VI. 5: tr. J. Buchanan and H. T. Davis (San Antonio, Texas, 1967) p. 253.
25. Sidonius, *Epist*. III. 9: tr. Anderson, II p. 37.
26. Gregory of Tours, *Hist*. IV. 4: tr. Thorpe, p. 199.
27. Sidonius, *Carmen* VII. 375: tr. Anderson, I p. 151.
28. Gregory of Tours, *Hist*. X. 19.
29. *M. G. H., Leges Nationum Germanicarum III:* ed. Beyerle and Buchner, p. 87.
30. Adrevald, *De Mirac. S. Benedicti*, 25: *M. G. H.*, *S. S.* XV (i) pp. 489–90.
31. *M. G. H.*, *Epist. Karol.* III p. 159.
32. *Ibid.*, p. 164.

2. CITIES AND TOWNS

1. *Expositio Totius Mundi et Gentium*, *c.* 58: ed. J. Rougé (Sources Chrétiennes 124) (Paris, 1966) p. 198.
2. Isidore, *Etymologies* XV. ii. 1: quoted by D. A. Bullough (A5–c) p. 351.
3. Ausonius, *M. G. H.*, *A. A.* V (ii), Carmen XVIIII. 166–7, p. 103.
4. Sidonius, *Epist.* IV. 21 and elsewhere.
5. Gregory of Tours, *Hist.* VI. 46: tr. Thorpe, p. 380.
6. Gregory, *Hist.* IV. 15: tr. Thorpe, p. 210.
7. Gregory, *Hist.* X. 31: tr. Thorpe, p. 600.
8. Gregory, *Hist.* V. 49: tr. Thorpe, p. 321.
9. Sidonius, *Epist.* IV. 25: tr. Dalton, II p. 46.
10. Sidonius, *Epist.* VII. 9: tr. Dalton, II p. 114.
11. Gregory of Tours, *Vitae Patrum* XVII. 1.
12 See Beck (A6–*b*) p. 266.
13. C. E. Stancliffe (A6–*b*) p. 59.
14. Quoted by Beck, *op. cit.*, p. 5
15. Gregory of Tours, *Vitae Patrum* VIII. 5.
16 Figures cited in H. F. Muller, *L'Epoque Mérovingienne* (New York, 1945) p. 83.
17. See L. Piétri, in *Gregorio di Tours* (1977) (B6–*b*) pp. 107 ff: his figures and conclusions differ slightly from those of Lelong (1963) (B3–*b*) pp. 12 and 57.
18. Gregory of Tours, *Vitae Patrum* XIII.
19. Gregory, *Hist.* VIII. 15: tr. Thorpe, p. 447.
20. *M. G. H.*, *Capitularia* I p. 23.
21. Boniface, *Epist.* 50 (ed. Tangl): tr. Emerton, pp. 79–80.
22. Marculf I. 4: A. Uddholm, *Marculfi Formularum Libri Duo* (Uppsala, 1962) pp. 38–9.
23. Gregory of Tours, *Hist.* III. 19.
24. See L. Halphen, *Le Comté d'Anjou au XIe siècle* (Paris, 1902) pp. 351–2.

3. FAMILY, KIN AND LAW

1. On this, see J. Le Goff, 'Peasants and the Rural World . . .' (A5–*d*). There are interesting parallels with nineteenth-century attitudes among the literate: see 'A Country of Savages', chapter 1 of E. Weber, *Peasants into Frenchmen* (London, 1977).
2. *Vita S. Wandregiseli*, 5: *M. G. H.*, *S. S. R. M.* V p. 15.
3. *Vita S. Arnulfi*, 11: *M. G. H.*, *S. S. R. M.* III p. 436. Quoted by K. F. Werner in *R. H. E. F.* LXII (1976) p. 62.
4. Quoted in P. N. Ure, *Justinian and his Age* (Harmondsworth, 1951) p. 162.
5. Gregory of Tours, *Hist.* VII. 45: tr. Thorpe, p. 427.
6. Cartae Senonicae 4: *M. G. H.*, *Formulae Merow. et Karol. Aevi* p. 187.
7. J. M. Wallace-Hadrill has drawn an equally gloomy picture from the archaeological evidence of the excavations of the Merovingian village of Brebières in his *Early Medieval History* (Oxford, 1975) p. 2: for my reservations see James, in Sawyer, ed. (A3–*a*) p. 57.
8. A. Longnon, ed., *Polyptyque de Saint-Germain-des-Prés* II (Paris, 1886) p. 36.
9. See Coleman, in Stuard (A4), a translation of an article originally published in *A. E. S. C.* XXIX (1974) pp. 315–35.
10. See K. F. Werner, 'Problematik und erste Ergebnisse des Forschungsvorhabens PROL zur Geschichte der west- und mitteleuropäischen Oberschichte bis zum 12. Jahrhundert', *Quellen und Forschungen* LVII (1977) pp. 69–87.
11. Werner (A4) and Bullough, *E. H. R.* LXXXV (1970) pp. 74 ff.

12. Boniface, *Epist.* 26 (ed. Tangl): tr. Emerton, p. 53.
13. Boniface, *Epist.* 33: tr. Emerton, p. 63.
14. F.-L. Ganshof, *The Carolingians . . .* (A3–*c*) p. 245.
15. Astronomer, *Life of Louis the Pious* 23.1: tr. Cabaniss, p. 56.
16. J. Devisse, *Hincmar* (B6–*c*) p. 376.
17. *M. G. H., Leges Nat. Germ.* IV (i), *Pactus Legis Salicae*, ed. Eckhardt, pp. 2–3.
18. *Ibid.*, X, p. 51.
19. *M. G. H., Leges* III, *Lex Ribvaria* 61: ed. Beyerle and Buchner, pp. 108–9.
20. Marculf II. 12: Uddholm, *op. cit.*, pp. 218–9.
21. Gregory of Tours, *De Gloria Martyrum* LXXXI.
22. The Burgundian Code, 45: tr. Drew, p. 52.
23. Liutprand 118: tr. K. F. Drew, *The Lombard Laws* (Philadelphia, 1973) p. 196.
24. *M. G. H., Capitularia* I, p. 150.
25. *Lex Ribvaria* XL. 11: *M. G. H., Leges Nat. Germ.* III (2) p. 94.
26. Gregory of Tours, *Hist,* IX. 19: tr. Thorpe, p. 50.
27. Tacitus, *Germania* XXI.

4. THE CHRISTIAN COMMUNITY

1. Council of Auxerre, 561–605: tr. Hillgarth p. 97.
2. Gregory of Tours, *Vitae Patrum* XVII, 5.
3. *Vita S. Eligii* II, 20: quoted by P. Fouracre (A6–*b*) p. 82.
4. Gregory, *Hist.* V. 43.
5. Quoted by G. Jones, *A History of the Vikings* (Oxford, 1968) p. 277.
6. Martin of Braga, *On the Castigation of Rustics*, 16: tr. Hillgarth, pp. 60–1.
7. See Cabrol and Leclercq (B1), I (ii), 'Anges'.
8. *Vita Amandi I*, 15: *M. G. H., S. S. R. M.*V, p. 439; *Vita Martini* XII. 9.
9. Quoted by M. Richter in 'A Socio-Linguistic Approach to the Latin Middle Ages', in *S. C. H.* XI (1974) p. 77.
10. *Theodosian Code* XVI. 8. 1: tr. Bachrach, *Jews* (A4) p. 17.
11. *M. G. H., S. S. R. M.* V p. 504.
12. See Katz (A4) pp. 148 ff.
13. *M. G. H., Capitularia* I *no* 131: tr. Bachrach, *Jews*, p. 41.
14. Agobard, *Epist.* 7: tr. Bachrach, p. 63–4.
15. *Ibid.*: tr. Bachrach, pp. 71–2.
16. Tr. J. F. Benton, in *Self and Society in Medieval France* (New York, 1970) pp. 134–5.
17. *Vitae Patrum Iurensium*, 26: ed. J. Martène (Sources Chrétiennes 142, Paris 1968) pp. 266–9.
18. The councils of Agde (506), c. 27, and Arles (554) c. 2.
19. Gregory of Tours, *Hist.* IX, 39: tr. Thorpe, p. 526.
20. Gregory, *Hist.* X, 16: tr. Thorpe, p. 571.
21. Gregory, *Hist.* X, 15: tr. Thorpe, p. 570.
22. Venantius Fortunatus, IX. 6: *M. G. H., A. A.* IV (i) p. 261.
23. Greogory, *Hist.* XI 40: tr. Thorpe, p. 530.
24. Quoted from Landeric's privilege in J. L. Nelson's splendid 'Queens as Jezebels . . .' (A3–*b*) p. 67.
25. C. Heitz, in his 'Architecture et Liturgie Processionelle à l'Epoque Préromane', *Revue de L'Art* XXIV (1974) pp. 30–47.
26. Letter to the monks of St-Germain, *no* 115: *Loup de Ferrières: Correspondance*, ed. L. Levillain, vol. II pp. 164–5.
27. See B. H. Rosenwein, 'Feudal War and Monastic Peace: Cluniac Liturgy as Ritual Aggression', *Viator* II (1971) pp. 129–57.

5. THE MEROVINGIAN SUPREMACY

1. Sidonius Apollinaris, *Epist.* VIII. 2: tr. Dalton, II p. 139.
2. By M. Roger, *L'Enseignement des Lettres Classiques d'Ausone à Alcuin* (Paris, 1905) p. 102, quoted by P. Riché, *Education and Culture* (A6–*b*) p. 222.
3. See J. Werner, 'Frankish Royal Tombs in the Cathedrals of Cologne and Saint-Denis', *Antiquity* XXXVIII (1964) pp. 201–16.
4. See R. Pirling, *Das römisch-fränkische Gräberfeld von Krefeld-Gellep* II (Berlin, 1974).
5. See P. Périn, 'Trois Tombes de "Chefs" du début de la période Mérovingienne', *Bull. de la Soc. Champenoise* LXIII (1972) pp. 3–70. On all this see James (A3–*a*).
6. Gregory of Tours, *Hist.* VIII. 21.
7. Gregory, *Hist.* IX. 9: tr. Thorpe, pp. 490–1.
8. Gregory, *Hist.* VI. 45: tr. Thorpe, p. 378.
9. Gregory, *Hist.* III. 11: tr. Thorpe, p. 171.
10. *M. G. H.*, *Epist. Merov. et Karol.* I p. 133.
11. Gregory, *Hist.* VI. 4: tr. Thorpe, p. 329.
12. Gregory, *Hist.* IX. 10: tr. Thorpe, p. 493.
13. Gregory, *Hist.* VI. 31: tr. Thorpe, p. 361.
14. Gregory, *Hist.* VII. 8: tr. Thorpe, p. 393.
15. See now J. Fontaine, 'King Sisebut's *Vita Desiderii* and the Political Function of Visigothic Hagiography', in E. James, *Visigothic Spain: New Approaches* (Oxford, 1980) pp. 93–129.
16. Fredegar IV. 42: tr. Wallace-Hadrill, p. 35.
17. Fredegar IV. 27: tr. Wallace-Hadrill, p. 18.
18. Fredegar IV. 58: tr. Wallace-Hadrill, p. 48.
19. Fredegar IV. 60: tr. Wallace-Hadrill, p. 50.
20. H. Mitteis, *The State in the Middle Ages* (Amsterdam, 1975) p. 50.
21. *Edictum c.* 19: *M. G. H.*, *Capitularia* I, p. 23.
22. See above p. 95.

6. MAYORS AND PRINCES

1. Fredegar IV. 84: tr. Wallace-Hadrill, p. 71.
2. Fredegar IV. 85: tr. Wallace-Hadrill, p. 72.
3. Fredegar IV. 86: tr. Wallace-Hadrill, p. 72.
4. See F. Oexle, 'Die Karolinger und die Stadt des heiligen Arnulfs', *F. S.* I (1967) pp. 250–364.
5. J. L. Nelson, 'Queens as Jezebels' (A3–*b*) pp. 69–70.
6. *Lib. Hist. Franc.* 43: tr. Bachrach, p. 101.
7. *Lib. Hist. Franc.* 45: tr. Bachrach, p. 103.
8. *Lib. Hist. Franc.* 45: tr. Bachrach, p. 104.
9. Eddius, Life of Wilfrid, 33: ed. B. Colgrave (Cambridge, 1927) pp. 68–9.
10. *Miracula Martialis*, 3: *M. G. H.*, *S. S.* XV p. 280.
11. *M. G. H.*, *S. S. R. M.* V p. 523.
12. C. de Clercq, *Concilia Galliae, A. 511–A. 695* (Turnholt, 1963) pp. 312–3.
13. See Rouche, *L'Aquitaine* (B3–*b*) p. 106.
14. *Lib. Hist. Franc.* 52: tr. Bachrach, p. 112.
15. *Visio Wettini*, 461–4: tr. Traill, p. 56.
16. On all this, see U. Nonn (B3–*b*).
17. See Rouche, *L'Aquitaine* (B3–*b*) p. 379.
18. *M. G. H.*, *Concilia Aevi Karolini* I p. 2.
19. Annales Regni Francorum, 749: *M. G. H.*, *S. S., Rer. Germ. in usum scholarum*, p. 8.

20. *Ibid.*, 750 (751): pp. 8–10.

7. THE CAROLINGIAN EXPERIMENT

1. Nithard, *Histories* IV : tr. Scholz, p. 165.
2. Fredegar, Continuation 33: Wallace-Hadrill, p. 102.
3. Einhard, *Life of Charlemagne*, 6: tr. Thorpe, p. 60.
4. *R. H.*, LXXII (1900) p. 81 (B4).
5. Nithard, *Histories* IV. 6: tr. Scholz, p. 173.
6. Einhard, *Life of Charlemagne*, 22: tr. Thorpe, p. 77.
7. Fredegar, Continuation 20: tr. Wallace-Hadrill, p. 93.
8. See P. Wolff, 'L'Aquitaine . . .' (B3–*c*) p. 271.
9. Astronomer, *Life of Louis the Pious*, 3.
10. Royal Frankish Annals, 816: tr. Scholz, p. 101.
11. Notker, *De Carolo Magno*, II. 12: tr. Thorpe, p. 156.
12. Royal Frankish Annals, 757: tr. Loyn and Percival, p. 38.
13. Ganshof, *Feudalism* (A3–*c*) p. 111.
14. *Ibid.*, p. 37.
15. Astronomer, *Life of Louis the Pious*, 6: tr. Cabaniss, p. 38.
16. *M. G. H.*, *Capitularia*, I p. 63.
17. Tr. Loyn and Percival, *The Reign of Charlemagne*, p. 74–5.
18. Translated in B. Pullan, *Sources for the History of Medieval Europe* (Oxford, 1966) pp. 38–42.
19. E. Magnou-Nortier, *Foi et Fidelité* (B3–*c*) p. 60.

8. THE FRAGMENTATION OF GAUL

1. K. F. Werner (A4), pointing out the importance of Dhondt's work in this area (B3–*d*).
2. P. Riché, ed., *Dhuoda: Manuel pour mon Fils* (Paris, 1975) XI. 2 pp. 368–71.
3. J. M. Wallace–Hadrill, *The Long-Haired Kings* (A3–*b*) p. 11.
4. Riché, *op. cit.*, III. 2, p. 141.
5. *Ibid.*, p. 27.
6. Nithard, *Histories* III. 2 : tr. Scholz, p. 156.
7. Magnou-Nortier, *Foi et Fidelité*, pp. 98–108, at 100.
8. Ibid, pp. 98.
9. *P. L.*, CXXV. 1085, quoted in Dhondt, *Etudes* (B3–*d*) p. 44.
10. *M. G. H.*, *Ann. Vedast.*, p. 55.
11. See R. Poupardin, *Recueil des Actes des Rois de Provence (855–928)* (Paris, 1920) *no.*XVI pp. 31–3.
12. Translated in Poupardin's chapter to *Cambridge Medieval History*, vol. III (Cambridge, 1922) pp. 62–3.
13. R. Rau, ed., *Quellen zur karolingischen Reichsgeschichte* III (Berlin, 1960) p. 146.
14. Dhondt, *Etudes* (B3–*d*) p. 58.
15. A. Eckel, *Charles le Simple* (Paris, 1899) p. 131.
16. See Kienast, *Herzogstitel* (B3–*d*) p. 14.
17. Richer, *Hist.* III. 71: ed. Latouche (B2), II p. 88.
18. Richer, *Hist.* IV. 12: ed. Latouche, II p. 162.
19. Translated in Halphen's chapter in *Cambridge Medieval History* vol. III, p. 117, slightly altered.
20. See Poly and Bournazel (B3–*d*) p. 152, with references.
21. Thietmar, *Chron.* VII. 30 (*M. G. H.*, *S. S.*, Nova Series IX p. 434) quoted in

Poupardin, *Le Royaume de Bourgogne* (B3–*d*), p. 177.

22. See Kienast, *Herzogstitel* (B3–*d*) pp. 203 ff.
23. *Adémar de Chabannes: Chronique*, III. 41: ed. J. Chavanon (Paris, 1897) p. 163.
24. R. W. Southern, *The Making of the Middle Ages* (London, 1953) pp. 82–6.
25. Kienast, op. cit., pp. 90 ff.
26. See last paragraph of B3–*d*.
27. Duby, *La Société . . . dans la Région Mâconnaise* (1971) (B3–*d*) p. 73.

9. BISHOPS AND COUNCILS

1. Gregory of Tours, *Hist.* IV. 26: tr. Thorpe, p. 220.
2. Ullman, 'Public Welfare . . .' (A6–*b*) p. 5.
3. Tr. Lyon and Percival, p. 74.
4. McKitterick, *Frankish Church* (A6–*c*) pp. 12 ff.
5. Ullmann, *Papal Government* (A6–*b*) p. 134.
6. Tr. in Ullmann, *Carolingian Renaissance* (A3–*c*) p. 69; there is a detailed discussion of events of 833, pp. 64–70.
7. *Ibid.*, p. 66.
8. *Ibid.*, pp. 85–6.
9. Goffart, *The Le Mans Forgeries* (A3–*c*) p. 239.
10. McKitterick, *op. cit.*, p. 21.
11. Seckel (A3–*c*) p. 346.
12. Ullmann, *Papal Government*, p. 188.
13. Tr. Herlihy, p. 28–9.
14. Cowdrey, 'The Peace and Truce of God' (A6–*c*) p. 53.

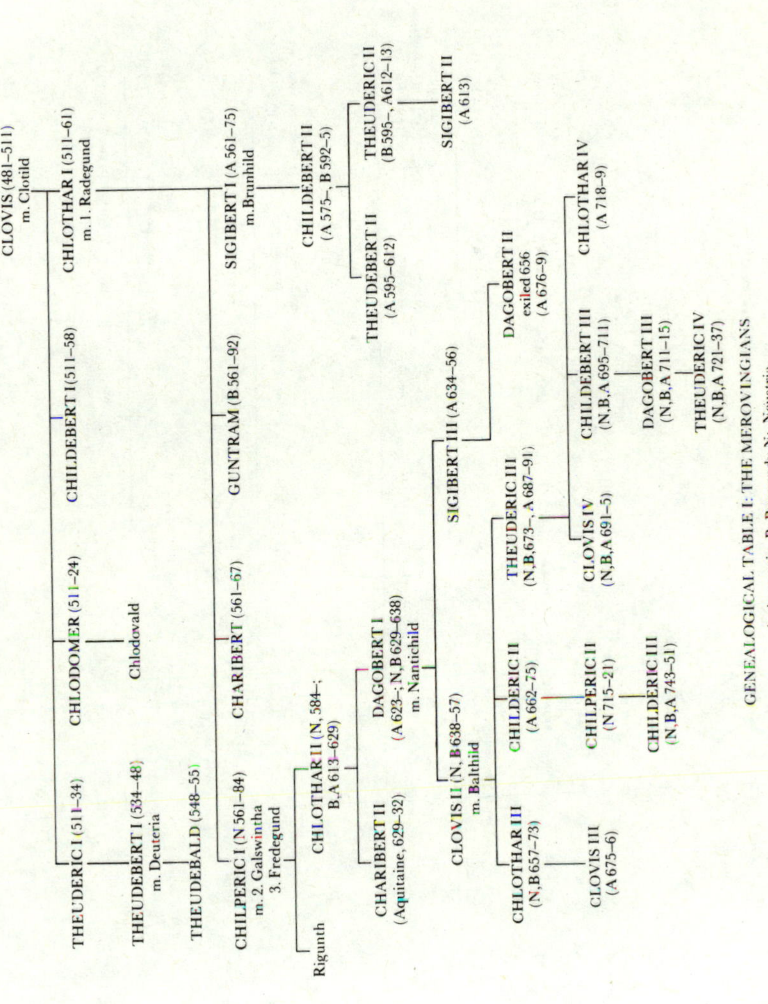
CHILDERIC (d. 481)
CLOVIS (481–511)
m. Clotild
THEUDERIC I (511–34)
CHLODOMER (511–24)
CHILDEBERT I (511–58)
CHLOTHAR I (511–61)
m. 1. Radegund
THEUDEBERT I (534–48)
m. Deuteria
Chlodovald
THEUDEBALD (548–55)
CHILPERIC I (N 561–84)
m. 2. Galswintha
3. Fredegund
CHARIBERT (561–67)
GUNTRAM (B 561–92)
SIGIBERT I (A 561–75)
m. Brunhild
Rigunth
CHLOTHAR II (N, 584–; B, A 613–629)
CHILDEBERT II
(A 575–, B 592–5)
THEUDEBERT II
(A 595–612)
THEUDERIC II
(B 595–, A 612–13)
SIGIBERT II
(A 613)
CHARIBERT II
(Aquitaine, 629–32)
DAGOBERT I
(A 623–; N, B 629–638)
m. Nantichild
CLOVIS II (N, B 638–57)
m. Balthild
SIGIBERT III (A 634–56)
DAGOBERT II
exiled 656
(A 676–9)
CHLOTHAR III
(N, B 657–73)
CHILDERIC II
(A 662–75)
THEUDERIC III
(N, B, 673–, A 687–91)
CLOVIS III
(A 675–6)
CHILPERIC II
(N 715–21)
CLOVIS IV
(N, B, A 691–5)
CHILDEBERT III
(N, B, A 695–711)
CHLOTHAR IV
(A 718–9)
CHILDERIC III
(N, B, A 743–51)
DAGOBERT III
(N, B, A 711–15)
THEUDERIC IV
(N, B, A 721–37)

GENEALOGICAL TABLE I: THE MEROVINGIANS

A: Austrasia. B: Burgundy. N: Neustria

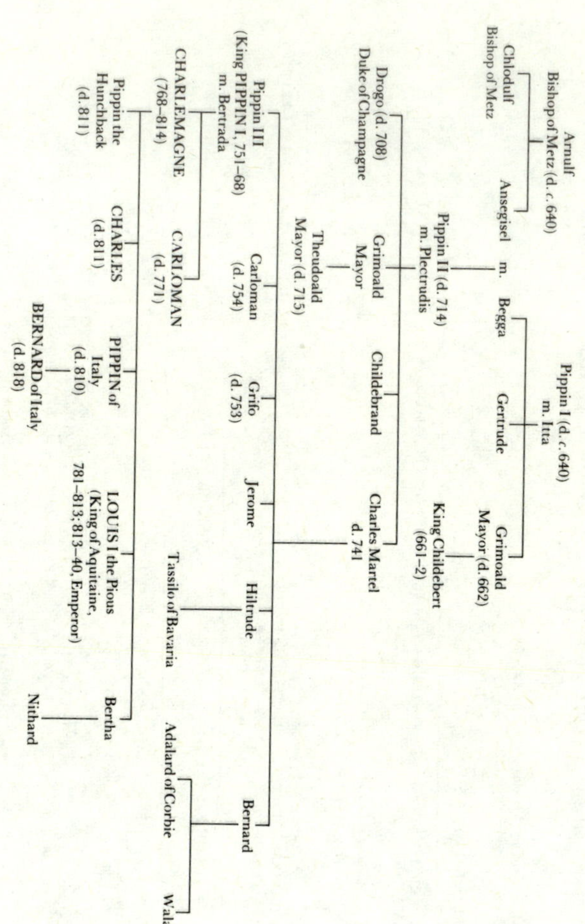

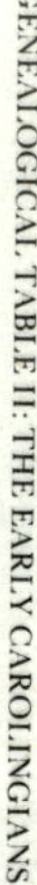
GENEALOGICAL TABLE II: THE EARLY CAROLINGIANS

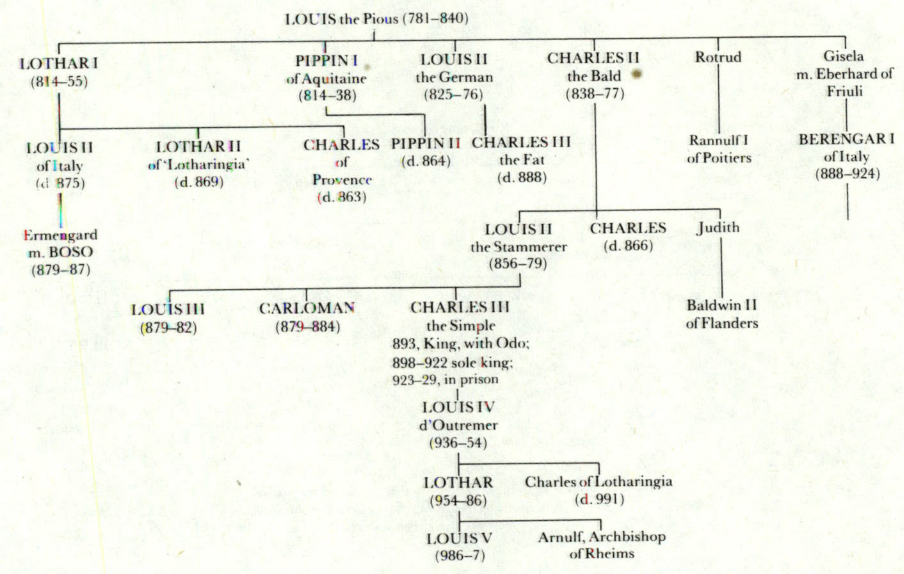

LOUIS the Pious (781–840)
LOTHAR I (814–55)
PIPPIN I of Aquitaine (814–38)
LOUIS II the German (825–76)
CHARLES II the Bald (838–77)
Rotrud
Gisela m. Eberhard of Friuli
LOUIS II of Italy (d. 875)
LOTHAR II of 'Lotharingia' (d. 869)
CHARLES of Provence (d. 863)
PIPPIN II (d. 864)
CHARLES III the Fat (d. 888)
Rannulf I of Poitiers
BERENGAR I of Italy (888–924)
Ermengard m. BOSO (879–87)
LOUIS II the Stammerer (856–79)
CHARLES (d. 866)
Judith
LOUIS III (879–82)
CARLOMAN (879–884)
CHARLES III the Simple 893, King, with Odo; 898–922 sole king; 923–29, in prison
Baldwin II of Flanders
LOUIS IV d'Outremer (936–54)
LOTHAR (954–86)
Charles of Lotharingia (d. 991)
LOUIS V (986–7)
Arnulf, Archbishop of Rheims

GENEALOGICAL TABLE III: THE LATER CAROLINGIANS

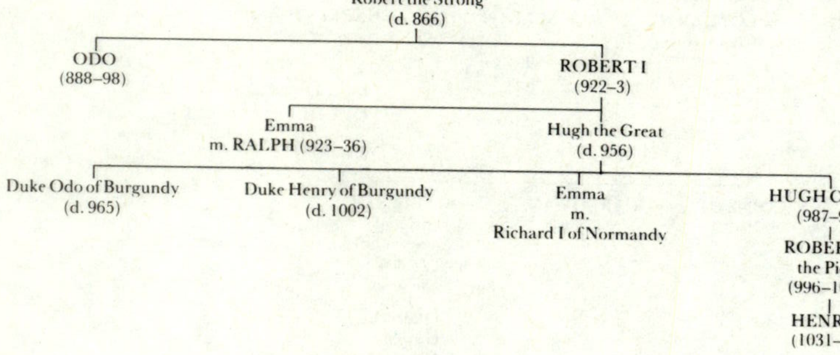

NOTE: In these tables kings are distinguished by capital letters: the dates in brackets after their names are their regnal years.

GENEALOGICAL TABLE IV: THE ROBERTIANS/CAPETIANS

Index

Abbreviations: a: abbot, abbess; abp: archbishop; bp: bishop; c: count; d: duke; k: king